THE ARCHITECTURE OF POLAND

THE ARCHITECTURE OF POLAND

BRIAN KNOX

BARRIE & JENKINS
LONDON

© 1971 by Brian Knox.
First published 1971 by
Barrie & Jenkins Ltd
2 Clement's Inn, London WC2.
Type set in Monotype Baskerville
by Yendall & Co Ltd, London.
Printed in the Netherlands by
N.V. Grafische Industrie, Haarlem.
Bound in Great Britain by
James Burn & Co Ltd, Esher.
ISBN 0.214.65211.4

CONTENTS

ILLUSTRATIONS

Photographs

(All of which appear at the end of the book and are referred to by a number in the text margins)

CRACOW AND LITTLE POLAND

Plans and
Diagrams

Prologue

Out on the embankment the Rover fried in the sun. The East German frontier post was disobliging. Some of my travelling library did not correspond accurately enough to the political situation of May 1962. The customs man tonelessly recited paragraphs of early mediaeval history. The policeman was sardonic: '*Es gibt kein "Schlesien" mehr. Das hat uns Hitler verschmissen.*'

And when I moved on, mercifully still with my books, the character of Poland was indeed at first slow to assert itself. This was still Brandenburg, but living the life of a generation ago – the narrow roughish road, broad fields, horse-drawn carts, red brick and sometimes wooden cottages. Through the woods I came to a small town, Ośno, formerly Drossen. It had preserved walls twelve feet high, brick on a rough stone foundation, and a couple of round towers. But within their ring lay a wilderness of rubble from which only a few old buildings rose. The story was the same everywhere in north and west Poland; a countryside long German, ruined by war in early 1945 and then put in Polish hands. Life is hard for the traveller, confused by changing names and disappointed to find some Junker mansion gutted, and for the topographer who fears to describe what may no longer exist.

This book tries to cover the architecture of the area within the present practical frontiers of Poland. No nation causes greater confusion in the history atlases, advancing, retreating, changing shape: in 1600 eight hundred miles across, in 1800 shrunk to nothing. There are thirty million Poles, as proud a race as any in the world. Yet only the triangle of Warsaw, Cracow, and Poznań is unarguably Polish. I have cut the knot and written nothing about the truly 'Polish' architecture of the cities of Lwów and Wilno which as Lvov and Vilnius now lie well inside the Soviet Union. In unequal exchange, the equally 'German' towns of Silesia and Prussia receive the attention their pride and beauty demand. The area I cover is what you get a visa for and where the Poles live now. There is no lack of precision in these definitions.

A minor problem which results is that of names. I have used Polish place names throughout, with the obvious exceptions of Warsaw and Cracow – I do not think 'Dantsic' qualifies as current usage, with respect to Baedeker and to British Rail's affection for 'Coblence' – and have given German (and Magyar) equivalents wherever they are likely to be useful. I have also in general stuck to the Polish forms of personal names; I have used Casimir in preference to Kazimierz, and St. Mary rather than the full Polish formula of Najświętniejsza Maria Panna, but I have eschewed the usual ludicrous Boleslauses and Ladislases. I hope the index will bridge the gaps this leaves.

More oppressive is the feeling that this is just a country on the periphery of what

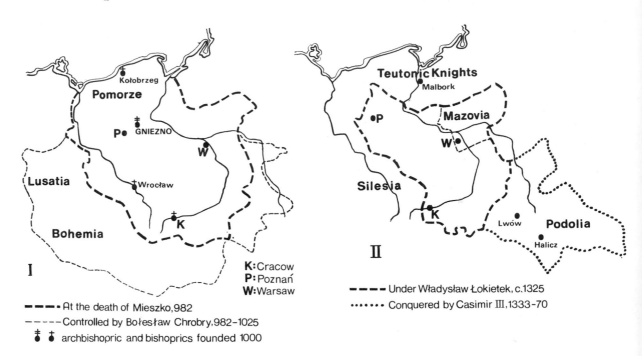

K: Cracow
P: Poznań
W: Warsaw

I

▬ ▬ ▬ ▬ At the death of Mieszko, 982
– – – – – Controlled by Bołesław Chrobry, 982–1025
☩ ☩ archbishopric and bishoprics founded 1000

II

▬ ▬ ▬ Under Władysław Łokietek, c. 1325
• • • • • • Conquered by Casimir III, 1333–70

III

───── At the Union of Lublin, 1569
– – – – Extreme limits of control in fifteenth
and sixteenth centuries

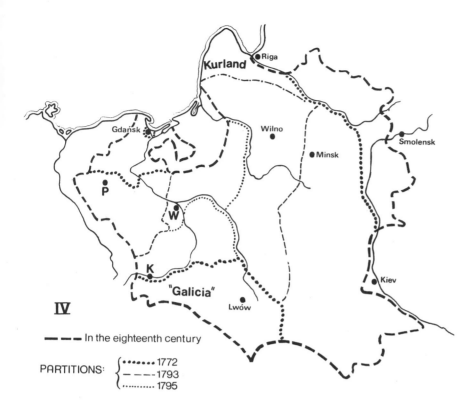

IV

- – – – In the eighteenth century

PARTITIONS:
- •••••• 1772
- – – – 1793
- ••••••• 1795

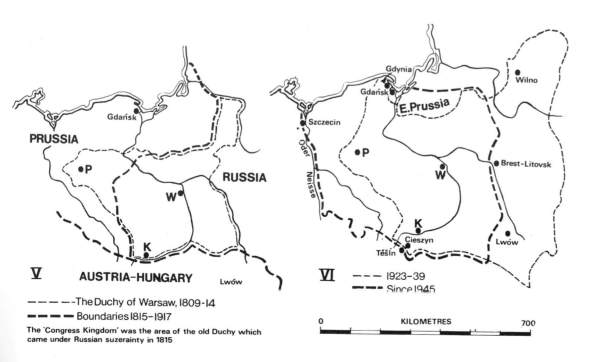

V AUSTRIA-HUNGARY

- – – – The Duchy of Warsaw, 1809-14
- – – – Boundaries 1815-1917

The 'Congress Kingdom' was the area of the old Duchy which came under Russian suzerainty in 1815

VI
- – – – 1923-39
- – – – Since 1945

0 KILOMETRES 700

Germans call German civilisation and others call that of Central Europe. Until two hundred years ago Poland depended on Germany, Italy, and the Low Countries not only for ideas – in that, it was not so different from may other European nations – but also for the architects themselves. No Polish peasant could rise to be a master builder, no Polish gentleman would stoop to it. Once one starts on this train of thought, everything seems to confirm it: the bare simplification of the few Cistercian abbeys; the arrogance of the castles the Teutonic Order built; the Italian extravagance of the great age of Cracow; the Flemish patterns of the tall houses of Gdańsk. Sometimes one can feel there is no such thing as Polish architecture. And a generation ago this was just what the Germans asserted. Their art historians drew up lists of the works of art that should be repatriated' to the Reich, and put them in as evidence of Germany's natural cultural dominance.

From this it was but a step to suppress any evidence to the contrary. Under the German occupation higher education was prohibited, libraries were closed, and many of the learned put to death. Himmler set out the limits of future Polish culture: 'Simple arithmetic up to at most 500; the writing of one's name, and the teaching that it is a divine law to be obedient to the Germans, and to be honest, hard working, and good. I do not consider reading to be necessary.' To this assault there was no answer but rebuilding, the pretty reproductions – and ingenious pastiches – which fill the centres of Warsaw and Gdańsk. They pose a relatively small problem for the historian. More awkward is the question whether Polish architecture has any distinctive Polishness. There is no simple and explicit answer, any more than there is to the search for a distinctive Englishness; this book is intended only to provide evidence.

The earliest Polish architecture is naturally of great interest to Poles. But to anyone else Polish Romanesque must seem rudimentary and often much over-restored. The country was first pulled into the main stream of European architecture by the great religious organisations: the Cistercians whose most important early foundations date from the 1170s and whose nunnery completed by 1219 at Trzebinca set the pattern for Silesia and Little Poland for a generation; the Teutonic Knights who arrived at Toruń about 1230 and similarly set the standard for the north. When in 1241 the Mongols retreated from a half ruined country, it was Silesia, the richest province, and Prussia, the best organised, that led the reconstruction. Poland was one of the busiest areas of mediaeval 'colonisation'; almost every town in those two provinces was founded in the thirteenth century and built a big church in the fourteenth; and almost everywhere they built in brick.

Thirteenth century Gothic is here still classical in idea, with measured plans and a severity which followed the universal example of knights, monks and friars. But in the second quarter of the fourteenth century Little Poland, Silesia, and Prussia were all involved deeply in the revolution in taste which for German scholars divides '*Hochgotik*' and '*Sondergotik*', and which in England is marked by the excitements of the 'Decorated'. About 1340 a great Wrocław architect experimented with asymmetrical 'spring' vaults on a big scale, and his successors and the contemporary builders of Casimir III in Cracow tried out Bohemian ideas like net vaults and the two-naved hall; but the inspiration somehow drained away. In Prussia the change was far more dramatic, for alongside the severe thirteenth century convent at Malbork the Grand Masters of the Order built a palace of splendid elaboration inside and out, a far greater contrast than that which the contemporary work of Clement VI produced at Avignon. Here, on the lower Vistula, we find a new passion for diagonals, for complicated vaults, for spaces reaching out and corners chamfered off, above all for the immediate visual effect. And decoration took on a new virtuosity in the brickwork we associate with Brunsberg and his school in Pomerania. In 1502 Gdańsk completed St. Mary's, the greatest church on the Baltic, a vast hall whose almost directionless space is ceiled with intricate nets and crinkly patterns of tiny cells.

At the same time the wandering masons of north Italy were bringing the Renaissance to Cracow. Some of their work there is of striking purity; but as they spread out into the country, Polish enthusiasm made their vocabulary serve wild and wonderful dreams of decorative glory in keeping with the zenith of Polish political power. The age is best commemorated in its sculpture, and one visits Cracow most of all for the grand tombs of fifteenth and sixteenth century kings and Stoss's great altarpiece. The merchants of Gdańsk were at their richest too, and they also imported architects, this time from the Low Countries, for the fantasies which the last generation has so painstakingly restored. The indigenous master almost disappeared.

After the political and economic collapse of the seventeenth century, the Poles became if anything more dependent on foreign builders, and lost much of their ability to mould their ideas and techniques into something distinctive like, say, the Renaissance churches around Lublin. The Saxon kings naturally brought in Dresden architects, though lack of cash restricted their opportunities, and alteration and destruction have left us little of their work. There were other north Europeans: Sobieski's Dutch architect Tylman van Gameren; Martin Frantz, born in Estonia, who imitated in Silesia the spatial experiments of Bohemian baroque; Jean de Bodt, the Huguenot who served the Prussian gentry. But the Italians are to be found everywhere, and though their vocabulary was generally conventional, there is real imaginative force in some of their work in Great Poland. I have, alas, had to deny myself the greater pleasures of describing the more virile baroque of Lwów and, most attractive of all, the extraordinary fluid half-rococo of Wilno.

But the torpidity of the mid-eighteenth century was followed within a generation by an astonishing outburst of creative energy. The accession in 1763 of a new king, Stanisław August, although himself a near nullity imposed by Russia, opened the way to constitutional reform, economic recovery, and the synthesis of Poland's most distinctive architecture – romantic neo-classicism. The king himself employed Italians, and imposed a compromise style; but the Polish gentry, as well as their architects of whom more and more were Polish born, travelled to England and to France and came back demanding crisp Palladian country houses and Anglo-Chinese picturesque parks. By 1780 the classicising movement had gone as far in Warsaw as anywhere else in Europe. Its masterpieces – houses like Natolin and Śmiełów, gardens like Arkadia and the lake setting of the 'Łazienki' Palace outside Warsaw – are something distinctive, all of a piece. And at the same time they inspired the simpler country gentleman's house which commands the farmyard with a neat portico and the unkempt garden with a bow that perhaps holds a domed saloon.

After the Napoleonic wars the leaders of the 'Congress Kingdom' tried to carry on as if Warsaw were still the capital of more than a Russian province. Their effort was crushed with the rebellion of 1830. Nineteenth century architecture reverted to straight dependence on other people's ideas, German neo-Tudor, 'Sezession' and 'Jugendstil' from Vienna; it was German Wrocław that alone housed a school of architecture of European importance before 1914. When the country was made independent again, the Populist regime of Piłsudski proved a far less fertile soil for architectural experiment than the bustling democracy of next-door Czechoslovakia. And after 1945 there was first a desperate need for any sort of building, and then the imposition of Russian 'social realism'.

Since 1956 I have been hoping that 1763 may have come again. The evidence so far can be read either way. Some rather wild experiment sticks out awkwardly from a great deal of bureaucratic mass construction, often as inhuman as that of France or Russia. There is still, as there has been for centuries, a desperate lack of skilled craftsmanship and good materials. But in Leykam there is a 'form-creator' in the Western individual tradition, and in industrial building a body of less personal work which is consistently good. There are real hopes still.

In the arrangement of this book I have tried to help the traveller with a compromise between history and geography. I have divided the country into six big provinces – of which each can be covered from one or two centres – and given separate chapters to the chief cities within them; I have then arranged these chapters in a sequence which corresponds to the chronology of their most important architecture. In Cracow, and in Little Poland round it, we can follow the rise of the mediaeval Polish kingdom and its Renaissance apogee. In Silesia, Pomerania, and Prussia the brick architecture of the late Middle Ages dominates, ending with the Renaissance show of the merchants' houses in Gdańsk. In Great Poland we can watch the appearance, first of a distinctive baroque, then of early romantic neo-classicism; and in Warsaw and the country round, the old Mazovia, we find neo-classicism's most distinctive achievements. Warsaw is, as one might expect, the best vantage point for a survey of modern building.

Within each chapter I have tried to keep to a generally chronological arrangement, while often hanging a description of a whole town on to that of its chief building, in the hope that something of its character will slip into the reader's mind, and that it may be easier for him to choose what he will himself visit. The state of the buildings I describe is in general that of 1961 and 1962, though I was able to revisit a great deal in 1967 and 1969. I hope that you will find the result more historically informed than a straight guide-book and at the same time easier to plan journeys from than a straight history.

1. Cracow

Until the fourteenth century there is hardly a Polish state. We first hear of a Polish ruler, Mieszko, in 962; he seems to have had some control over part at least of Pomerania and Silesia and the plain as far east as the Bug; in 966 he was baptized a Christian. He died in 982. Under his son Bolesław Chrobry (the Brave) Poland became a European force. His massive raids reached Prague in 1003 and Kiev in 1018. In 1000 he caused the archbishop of Gniezno to be founded, to control bishops at Cracow, Wrocław and Kołobrzeg. Cracow had been a fortified place for centuries; on the Wawel, embedded in the west wing of the inner castle courtyard, a little rotunda, later a church, goes back to the Czech occupation in the second half of the tenth century and may rank as the oldest remaining Polish building in stone. Beside it rose the church of św. Gereon, known as 'the first cathedral', a simple Latin cross with aisled nave, short apsed chancel, and eastern apses to the transepts. Like the first church of św. Salwator at Zwierzyniec up the river, it was both small and massive. Almost all Polish Romanesque has a rude fortress character.

1 Cracow: rotunda on the Wawel, 1:400

Bolesław's Poland was no more cohesive than the Ireland of his contemporary, Brian Boru. After his death in 1025 it disintegrated; Pomerania drifted loose for good, and only after decades could a younger son of Mieszko, Casimir or Kazimierz Obnowiciel (the Renovator), pull Mazovia and Silesia back. He, and not Boleslaw, is the likely founder of the Benedictine abbey at Tyniec. They have been digging for the original walls, and from the plain mediaeval cloister fragments of Romanesque pillars and doorways can be seen. What stands now is a convent shaken by the centuries and a plain baroque church distinguished by massive marble furnishings and a battered boat for a pulpit. But the site is lovely, a steep white rock above the Vistula, looking over a rude ferry and water meadows to the woods and the twin white towers of Bielany; a picture from the Poland of a century ago.

Casimir's son Bolesław Śmiały (the Bold) succeeded him in 1058. While the German Empire was weak he could interfere in Hungary, push his rule east, have himself crowned king in 1076. But three years later he had the bishop of Cracow, Stanislaw, put to death; we do not know the cause or that of the rebellion which drove him into exile to die. His brother Władysław Herman followed him without a crown, and the provinces drifted apart again. But from his time come the oldest buildings that still stand in Cracow, the much altered little church of św. Wojciech (St. Adalbert) on the present square and the towers and west end of św. Andrzej (St. Andrew), the chief church of the settlement of Okól which had grown up by 1100 between the Wawel and a small market place between the later Franciscan and Dominican churches. Św. Andrzej has changed hands many times since the Benedictines came, and inside is almost all rebuilt; there is another jolly boat, with a huge mast, for pulpit. But we can guess that it had a short apsed chancel and a nave of two bays with aisles whose eastern bays rose an extra storey like false transepts. Meanwhile, in 1075, the 'second cathedral,' św. Wacław, had been begun further west where the present cathedral lies. It was bigger, but still severe, with four towers and an apse at each end; its western crypt of about 1118 has survived with two rows of vaults on round columns and cushion 3 capitals to house Kosciuszko's tomb.

Twelfth century Cracow was no more than a provincial capital. But under the system of the 'Seniorate' by which Boleslaw Krzywousty (Crookmouth) regulated the succession among the Piast families it became the apanage of the senior prince, passing from Władysław Herman to Bolesław Kędzierzawy (Curlyhead) to Mieszko the Old, and Casimir the Just united it with Sandomierz to create the base from which the kingdom would be recreated. Meanwhile under Henry the Bearded and Henry the Pious, Silesia led the way, inviting settlers from the west, giving them untilled land to clear, laying out towns and the great checkerboard city of Wrocław (Breslau). They brought brick building with them, and it came to Cracow when in 1222 Cistercians arrived at Mogłia, a few miles down river, from Lubiąż (Leubus) on the Oder. In the same year the Dominicans came to Cracow, the Franciscans fifteen years later. The city spread north along the trade route; by 1224 we hear of St. Mary's, and a second market place to the east of it where the Mały Rynek now is. To the south, along the crossing over the marshy valley, two more churches stood on humps of rock, one of these the 'Skalka' where św. Stanisław should have met his death. Then in 1241 the Mongols came and burnt, and Henry the Pious fell in the battle which checked them at Legnica. All was to do again.

The new city shifted its centre of gravity well to the north. It had to leave the river to gain space for the symmetrical grid of market place and streets which by the 'location' date of 1257 was de rigueur in the developing countries of east central Europe. Only the old backbone running out to the south disturbs the system of square blocks of which four were merged to make a great new market place. On the old market to the south the friars built new brick churches. The Franciscans, to the west, used in about 1270 a Greek cross plan of which little now remains beyond the north transept. Today old vaults remain only in the long fifteenth century chancel and the cloisters; the fourteenth century nave supports a plaster tunnel; the walls are covered with arts-crafts pansies and vapid histories by the polytechnic Wyspiański, less inspiring even than the raucous colours of the modern glass.

The Dominicans did better to the east. After the raid, they rebuilt on a big scale along the south side of their existing cloister, leaving traces of their part stone church wall in its north range; in 1289 they consecrated the usual long simple church, dedicated to the Trinity, with a square ended chancel and many details in common with their slightly older one at Wrocław; in the next century they raised the walls, carved the excellent, sharp, leafy west doorway, and livened the silhouette with spiked and panelled gables. Inside it is quite imposing; arcade matches clerestory in height, there are star and net vaults, and the pillars have the odd T section, with a buttress towards the aisle, which Cracow brick building shares with Wrocław. The aridities of detail left by the restoration after the roof fell in 1850 are balanced by an uncommonly rich set of chapels. In the north aisle steps climb to that of św. Jacek (St. Hyacinth), originally of 1581, redecorated in about 1700 by Baldassare Fontana who is by far Cracow's best eighteenth century stucco worker. From the south open small gothic chapels, two with crazy rib vaults, and two pompous Renaissance

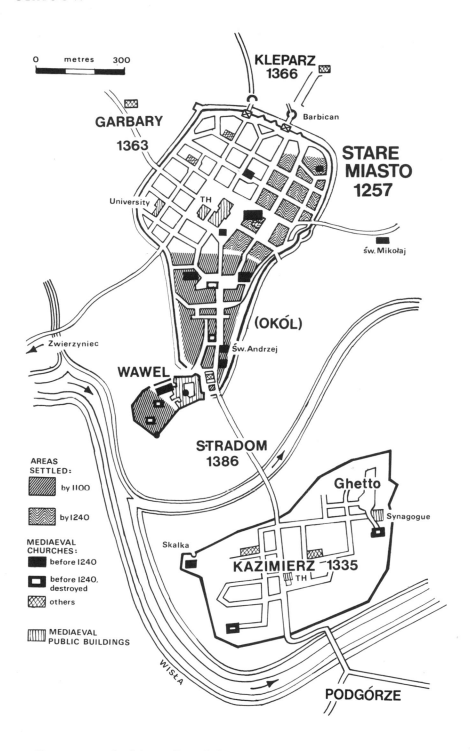

0 metres 300

KLEPARZ
1366

GARBARY
1363

Barbican

STARE
MIASTO
1257

University

TH

św. Mikołaj

(OKÓL)

Zwierzyniec

Św. Andrzej

WAWEL

STRADOM
1386

Ghetto

Synagogue

Skałka

KAZIMIERZ 1335

TH

AREAS
SETTLED:

by 1100

by 1240

MEDIAEVAL
CHURCHES:

before 1240

before 1240,
destroyed

others

MEDIAEVAL
PUBLIC BUILDINGS

WISŁA

PODGÓRZE

2 Cracow: growth of the mediaeval city

mausolea of 1614 and 1616. And at the east end of the chancel's south wall a small bronze tablet commemorates Filippo Buonaccorsi, Jan Olbracht's Florentine mentor, with mediaevally quirky robes and misdrawn Renaissance perspective. The combination will be explained when we describe the monuments of the Wawel.

Meanwhile a new Poland was taking shape. Bolesław Wstydliwy (the Bashful, fifth and last of a fine succession of cognomina) united all southern Poland east of Silesia. In 1308 the Teutonic Knights seized Gdańsk (Danzig) and blocked off the sea coast for 150 years. In 1306 Władysław Łokietek (the Dwarf) – Ladislaus the Short, if you prefer – became ruler in Cracow; by 1314 he commanded Greater Poland; in 1320 he was crowned king. On the narrow base the triangle of Poznań, Cracow and Warsaw afforded, a state at last appeared. His son Casimir turned it in a new direction, swallowing up Halicz (the original 'Galicia') and Lwów, reaching east to the Dniester. With Warsaw still the headquarters of an overmighty vassal Cracow was the natural capital, and so for three centuries it remained.

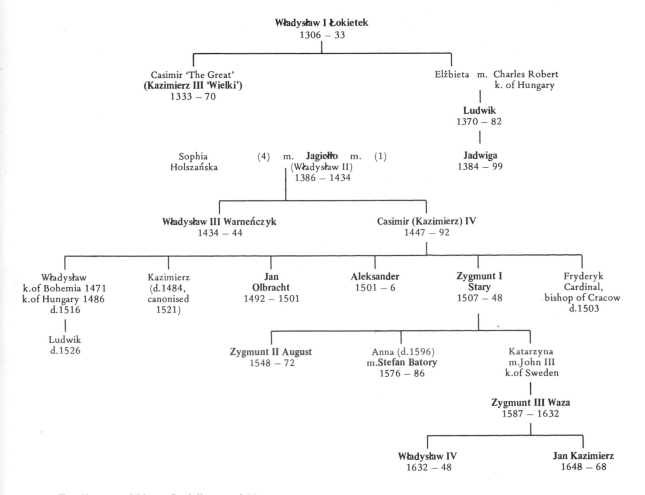

3   Family tree of Piasts, Jagiellons and Vasas

Under Władysław the bishop of Cracow was a Silesian, and his new cathedral followed in many points the example of Wrocław. In 1320 he built the little apsed stone chapel which has become part of the present sacristy. In 1322 work began on a new chancel, replacing half the Romanesque church and still attached to the rest, but slightly deflected from the old axis, perhaps to fit the buildings around it which included the new chapel. In 1331 the eastern Lady Chapel was consecrated, in 1344 the south-eastern chapel of św. Jan, in 1346 the high altar. The core of the plan is that of Wrocław, a brick basilica, of exactly the same breadth, with a square east end to the nave divided by one central pillar and embraced by a straight ambulatory; here, though, each nave bay matches one aisle bay instead of two. On the aisle sides of the piers rudimentary buttresses appear again, and 'Piast' vaulting, which matches two piers to three with groups of threesomes of ribs, heavily emphasises the eastern central pillar as it does again in the Lady Chapel. How this originated we cannot be sure. The very similar eastern chapel at Wrocław seems not to have been planned until 1354. But it brought to Cracow the new fashion for experiment in vaulting forms which, inspired in part by English models, spread all over central and eastern Europe in the fourteenth century. As they pushed west, the builders returned to the orientation of the old cathedral, and adapted its two towers, so that the very short nave consecrated in 1364 lies at an angle to the chancel. This opportunism persisted. Chapels were added of all sizes and facing all ways; a wall tower to the north was brought into the system and in the fifteenth century a new treasury went up beside it, looking out over the city; as late as the eighteenth century the greatly strengthened north-west tower sprouted a new top. It is just as confusing inside: the displaced centre emphasized by the huge baldacchino of św. Stanisław's tomb, kinks in the lines of the dark aisles, chapel doorways in unlikely places. But perhaps the tombs and altars, silt of history, should after all outface the architecture.

Casimir came to be called 'the Great' by starting venture after venture which the generations after him had to struggle to complete. Among them the University he founded in 1364 attracted few teachers, had to be refinanced around 1400, and was not properly housed for another century. But he codified the laws, created some sort of administration, left an example of justice. He also left no son. The crown passed to his nephew, one of the Angevin kings of Hungary. This man's daughter Jadwiga followed him, and in 1386 she married Jagiełło, the pagan overlord of the great unorganised territory of Lithuania which spread to the Dvina and the Dnieper. In 1410 at Grunwald (Tannenberg) he and his brother beat the Teutonic Knights, who after another war of eleven years gave up Gdańsk and the lower Vistula and accepted the suzerainty of Poland. With the annexation of the Ukraine the new empire, till 1569 only a personal union, became one of the chief states of Europe, and for a time a member of the family wore the crowns of Bohemia and Hungary. So the capital, Cracow, spread. In 1335 a rectangle between the channels of the Vistula was walled about and took its founder's name, Kazimierz; it governed itself and its own town hall, in structure of his time, still closes the line of the main street as you go south. Suburbs spread on the firm ground to the north, and in 1386 Stradom was enclosed in the gap between Kazimierz and the Wawel. At the end of the fifteenth century, the Jews moved into the north-east corner of Kazimierz and created there one of the most distinctive of all their European communities.

The Kazimierz area already had three small churches, of which only that on Skalka has a successor left today; two large ones were needed. In 1340 Casimir founded a new parish church north-east of the new market place, Boże Ciało (Corpus

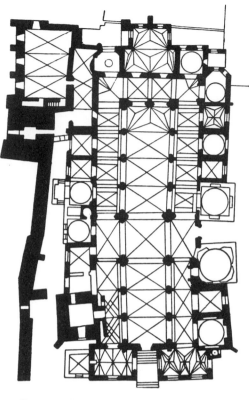

4   Cracow: the Cathedral, 1:800

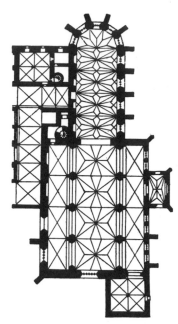

5   Cracow: św. Katarzyna, 1:950

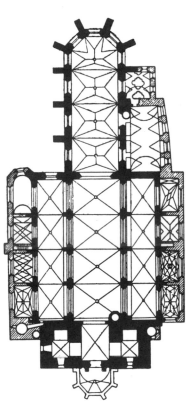

6   Cracow: St. Mary, 1:800

Christi). Its builders were the Czipser family, generation after generation, and things went slowly. The chancel was not finished until 1387, though Lateran canons from Silesia seem to have taken over a complete church in 1405. It has kept its original shape well, that of the great brick and stone basilicas of Silesia; its nave is more than twice as high as it is broad, the first Cracow example of late Gothic proportions, and outside this height is emphasized by the crowded buttresses of the long aisleless chancel and its apse. Inside it would have surprised a Silesian with its massive chancel arch, typical of Cracow, and the rough stone which covers the nave arcade and walls up to a sharp string course beneath the clerestory. The present simple and gently rounded vaults are later, and so is the pretty pinnacled western gable; there are sixteenth and eighteenth century chapels, the tower has a baroque top. It is picturesque, if a little shapeless.

In 1345 Austin canons from Prague began św. Katarzyna to the west; they com- 5 pleted the chancel in 1378, and probably the rest in 1426, but in 1443 the nave vaults fell and were replaced in wood; the present stone stars were put on the chancel in 1505. It has practically the same plan as Boże Ciało. There is no west gable and no tower, only a set of neat pinnacles to the chancel buttresses and a rustic wooden belfry in the churchyard. But inside it is just a little taller, two and a half times the nave's breadth. And the stone detail is much better, in the elaborate piers of the spacious cloister to the north, the two pillared chapter house alongside, the single pillared south west chapel, above all in the splendid south porch and inner doorway which must have gone up in the 1420's and bear the device of the great prelate and politican, the elder Zbigniew Oleśnicki. Nothing else Casimir began in Cracow – two churches now demolished on the Wawel, the tiny one of sw. Idzi (St. Giles), now half concealed and greatly altered, at its foot – so much expressed the ideals of architecture at the end of the fourteenth century.

The challenge was taken up. The Dominicans and the Franciscans, as we have seen, set themselves to extend; and the people of the Old Town completely rebuilt their parish church. St. Mary – the 'kościół Mariacki' – was a low brick hall. In 1355 6 they began to convert it into a basilica whose nave would be nearly three times as tall as broad. In 1384 the chancel was finished, by the end of the century the two massive western towers had risen, and a Prague builder, Mikuláš Werner, went on with the nave; in 1442 the chancel vaults fell, to be replaced by one of the Czipsers with four pointed stars. Fifteenth century fantasy reigns in the vaults of the aisle chapels, dim finicky spaces crammed with monuments, and best of all in the northern tower's top of 1478: an octagon of brick and stone, then a stage of eight angular projections carrying eight small spikes, from whose centre one huge spike thrusts heavenwards through a gilded crown.

Other mediaeval churches are inconspicuous and in general much altered. The Jesuits did leave standing the west gable of św. Barbara, behind St. Mary, and its very pretty stone doorway of about 1500. And, disregarded in a cold corner beyond the opera, the clumsy brick shape of święty Krzyż (Holy Cross) still rises. Its square nave of about 1400 is a small miracle; it is worth endless patience to get inside; one strong plain round column, sixteen spreading ribs, little canopy spaces to fill the corners. The present vault is a replacement of about 1530, but the idea has the simplicity of a century before. (See overleaf)

The city is still rich in mediaeval secular buildings, not to mention its synagogue. In the Square, no. 17 conceals the 'Hetman's Hall', a room vaulted in the same 'Piast' manner as the east parts of the Cathedral, probably late in the fourteenth century.

And on the Square a new town hall was begun in 1383. It grew into a whole clump of buildings, but almost all have gone; a carved stone doorway of 1593, copied from the patterns of Vredeman de Vries, was transported to the University; there remains only the tower, covered in restless stone panelling, crowned by an unimaginative double lantern of 1686. The Sukiennice or Cloth Hall beside it went up between 1340 and 1390; it was burnt in 1555 and its structure now wears Renaissance finery, Santi Gucci's attic and outsize savage masks and a busy parapet. It is a splendid long backdrop for the flower sellers and the birds and the café tables. The shops inside do not carry much conviction now, 'peasant art' for an urban market, but the coffee seems less gritty and there are horses and carts and old women in headscarves and at the hour the trumpeter in the church tower repeats his plaintive interrupted call.

About 1300 new city walls were started, and by 1473 they had seven gates and seventeen towered bastions. In the 1810s all was demolished to create the present ring of parks, save a few hundred yeards, with three bastions and a gate, that face north; much is of stone, notably the square Brama Floriańska, the old north gate, the Baszta Stolarska (Carpenters') has machicolations to show, and the Baszta Pasamoników (Trimming-makers') is decorated with zigzags of glazed bricks. In front of the gate, too, still stands the Barbican of 1498, much diminished by filling in its moat; it is a turreted and machicolated circle of brick, always full of small folding chairs, as if expecting a Punch and Judy show which doesn't happen. More intriguing still is the University, the 'Collegium Maius'. It hides behind almost unornamented stone walls in the Jagiellońska, and the ulica św. Anny, broken only by an oriel and two brick gables. The irregularity of its plan perpetuates the private houses in which it spent its first 130 years, until, in 1492, Cardinal Fryderyk, Jagiello, the king's brother, set out to rebuild it completely. He created a great hall at the angle of the two streets, and a courtyard inside; it has arcades with simple 'diamond' vaults, made up of faceted cells between the lines that would be ribs, a system thought up at Meissen and popular in Prussia and Bohemia; their intricate stone balustrade used to carry long wooden posts which bore the great projecting eaves of the roof, an echo perhaps of the top storey of the Wawel courtyard added after the cardinal's time, replaced in the 1830s by brackets.

By 1500 Cracow possessed sculpture too of European quality. In the north east corner of the cathedral ambulatory hangs the Crucifix of Queen Jadwiga, work of the end of the fourteenth century; large, graceful, a sheet of beaten silver silhouetting the soft outlines of the '*piękny styl*', the '*weicher Stil*' of German art historians. The first of a great succession of royal tombs are those of the 1370s to Casimir the Great in the cathedral chancel, handsome red marble which is no longer provincial, and of about 1440 to Władysław III at the east end of the north nave aisle, whose harsh realistic face and sharply observed details could be Italian work. The city was already accustomed to fine carving when in 1477 its German community sent to Nuremberg for a brilliant young sculptor to create for St. Mary an altar to outshine all the rest. Veit Stoss (Wit Stwosz to the Poles) worked at it for twelve years and on his way carved out a mannered but unforgettable personal style, part the soft curves of two generations before, part new fierce expressiveness which runs to great flourishes of crinkling drapery, all informed by an uncommon grasp of volume and space.

Even shut, his 'masterpiece' commands the whole church; the largest and richest thing in sight; all painted low reliefs of Christ's life, and gilded brambles above them. A crowd collects and to satisfy them a tiny hunchbacked man comes from the sacristy with a long boathook, and slowly and with agonizing creaks pulls back first one wing

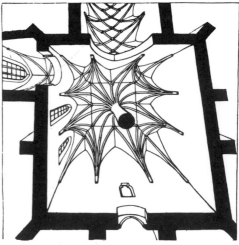

7   Cracow: św. Krzyż, nave vault

and then the other. This is what has drawn us to Cracow, it is a shock, and not pleasant. So much gilt. So many crowded figures. It is a struggle for the eyes to master it, and again and again we want to admire one figure by itself; consider the Negro king in the lowest panel of the left wing, and how good St. John looks photographed by himself against a plain background, the uncertain gesture, the smooth slightly flabby face. Surely the sandstone crucifix Stoss made around 1491 for the end of the south aisle is finer, with its arching chest and long emaciated arms and legs.

In 1492, perhaps while the king was still dying, he made the red veined marble tomb of Casimir IV which stands in the cathedral, almost invisible behind the locked 9 grille of its south-west chapel and under the canopy by Jörg Huber which swarms with angels and devils. You must get in to see the sweep of the stiff priest-like robe, the insignia of Poland's empire disposed as for a sacrament, the compassion which shapes the strong tired face. In 1496, a mature artist and the greatest sculptor north of the Alps, he went back to Nuremberg. He left behind splendid marble slabs to archbishops at Włocławek and at Gniezno and a school of pupils, his son among them, whose handiwork is plain in many altar pieces in southern Poland and Silesia. And when he reached home he seems to have given the famous Vischer workshop a design for a bronze tablet which we have seen in the chancel of the Dominican church. It commemorates 'Callimachus', the Italian Filippo Buonaccorsi, teacher and counsellor to Casimir's second son Jan Olbracht. We see him at his desk in a long gown with a Stoss loop of stuff defying gravity over one knee; under his feet the paterned tiles point inwards in rough perspective, a nod to the subject's new ideas. When Jan Olbracht died in 1501 his red marble figure was carved, probably by Stanisław Stoss, in the mediaeval posture and attire of his ancestors, an odd, short, large-headed man with an ironical expression. But in its chapel, the furthest east in the cathedral's south 10 aisle, it is surrounded by finicky symmetrical decoration of the Italian Renaissance.

Italian builders had arrived more than a generation earlier in Hungary and Russia, as engineers first and artists only afterwards. In 1475 Aristotele Fioravanti of Bologna had begun the Cathedral of the Dormition in the Kremlin, and in the 1480s Mátyás Corvinus of Hungary was employing a Florentine as his architect. In 1486 Mátyás was succeeded by Casimir's eldest son, Władysław, who may have sent 'Callimachus' to his brother, and very likely passed on to him the Florentine architect Francesco, perhaps surnamed della Lora, who was working in Cracow by 1502 and died there, an old man, in 1516. It was for Zygmunt (Sigismund), the fourth brother, who spent his early life at the Hungarian court, that this man designed the frame for Jan Olbracht's monument; and for him he undertook the creation of a Renaissance palace amid the congeries of buildings on the Wawel.

In the last two centuries a big residence had grown up round a courtyard less regular but as large as the present one. Many fragments of it remain. Oldest is the fabric of Władysław Łokietek's square north-east tower, which still holds a fine late fourteenth century ground floor chamber vaulted from one pillar. Just south-east of it lie two more Gothic rooms in a building which replaced the original keep in about 1400; like the 'Danskers' of the Lower Vistula, a tiny (now vanished) tower was pushed out to the north-west at the end of a raised gangway; two more towers which still face south and east mark the curve of Casimir's palace wing. The place was ruined by fire in 1499. Rebuilding started at the north-west corner; and there, in the second floor of the arcades, two unequal windows and a door mark the apartment of Zygmunt's mother with a splash of the same Italian arabesque as surrounds Jan Olbracht's tomb.

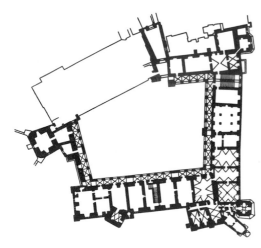

8   Cracow: castle on the Wawel, 1:4000

11   In 1507 Zygmunt decided to rebuild completely. Casimir's palace came down, and new north and west ranges went up, the beginning of a rectangular layout left half realised. In 1516 Francesco was succeeded by Bartolomeo Berrecci, a thirty-six year old architect from Pontassieve near Florence, and in 1524 Benedict 'of Sandomierz' was engaged to help him. Berrecci may in fact have been responsible for the handsome Ionic arcades, close to those of the Palazzo Strozzi in Florence and of the Cancelleria in Rome, and also for the peculiar decision to give the top storey double height; thus from the second balustrade there rise great poles of stone, marked half way up by curious bulbs where one would expect to reach capitals; and these carry no entablature but only the wooden substructure of a colossal overhanging roof. By about 1535 two and a half wings were complete. They must have been overpowering in their original colours, the red courtyard floor and columns, the blue second storey frieze, and the roofs painted blue, green, white and yellow. Zygmunt August built the short blank south wall; a characterless wing rose on mediaeval foundations in the south-west. The projecting north-east tower was replaced by an odd little belvedere, the 'Hen's Foot'. After a fire in 1595, the north wing was reshaped; Zygmunt III added a little Baroque tower at the corner of Łokietek's, and around 1700 Sobieski matched it with another at the north west corner. But by then the Wawel was hardly ever a royal residence.

In 1569 the Union of Lublin formally united Poland and Lithuania. It decided that the joint Seym or Parliament should meet at Warsaw. The fire at Cracow sent Zygmunt III there to live, and his new palace was ready in 1619. In 1661 Cracow was overrun by the marauding army of Karl X of Sweden. In the seventeenth century its population halved; it became a provincial town of many memories, and something of a museum. The Wawel served the Austrians as a barracks, and restoration has left much of it pretty impersonal. From the sixteenth century palace remain stone doorways which mingle Gothic and Renaissance, and painted friezes such as those by Antoni of Wroclaw in the east wing. The best interior is the Ambassadors' Hall at the south end of the wing. Here the coffers in the ceiling of 1535 hold not rosettes but a crowd of small carved heads, and you must crane your neck and read through a parade of inexhaustible wit and oddity. In the north-west corner Zygmunt III's apartments are lavish baroque; by 1609 Giovanni Trevano had reshaped the staircase, fitted up a little chapel and study in the new tower, and created an upper room in Łokietek's tower with marble doors and fireplaces and a gilded coffered ceiling from which toy birds once, but alas no longer, hung on wires. Among them the king dabbled in alchemy like his contemporary Rudolf II in Prague.

Zygmunt I had brought Berrecci to Poland for a project he valued more than his palace. In 1515 his first wife died and, though he was only forty-eight and was to marry Bona Sforza three years later, he thought of a mausoleum. He approved Berrecci's model in 1517, and wrote off to Jan Boner, one of the great Cracow family who were his servants and bankers, for plenty of the best Hungarian marble, 'for however much we may lay out on temporal buildings, we shall be ill advised to economise on that, in which we shall abide for ever'. An older chapel on the south side of the Cathedral was razed, and in 1519 the new foundations were laid; in 1529 Berrecci agreed with Seweryn Boner to provide the figure sculpture; in 1533 the chapel was consecrated, and in the lantern could be read BARTHOLO FLORENTINO OPIFICE. Beside his work on the Wawel, Berrecci designed only one more building that stands, the very simple little house of 1534 at Wola Justowska outside Cracow. In 1537 he was murdered. His chapel was to be copied all over southern Poland for

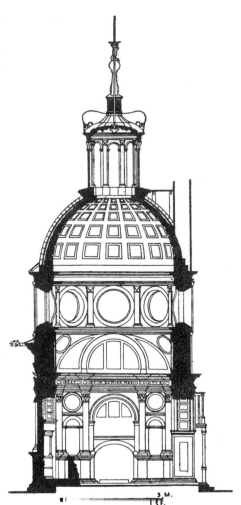

9   Cracow: Sigismund chapel, section 1:200

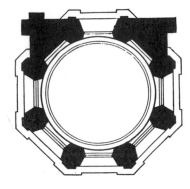

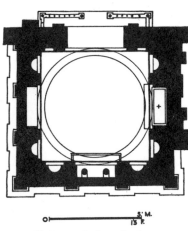

10   Cracow: Sigismund chapel, plans 1:200

a century; and if it were in Italy it would rank with all but the very greatest funeral chapels there.

The Sigismund Chapel – Kaplica Zygmuntowska – expresses without equivocation the architectural ideals of the Florentine Renaissance. Inside, its lowest stage is a cube, each wall regulated by pilasters into four units of which one central pair become an arched doorway or niche; a space of the same height is filled by the pendentives and the cylindrical drum with eight circular windows. The exterior is shaped by the same principles, but the units are about a third taller; again the base is a cube, informed by a pilaster order half its height on a tall plinth, and this time the same height is filled by the drum, octagonal outside, and the dome. Only the slender lantern with its angel spire thrust through a pretty openwork crown does not conform to the system. In essentials this is a miniature of Alberti's ideal church, a brother to the works of Florentines like the Sangallos from whom Berrecci may have learnt. But in visual effect it is the opposite of its near contemporary, Raphael's Sant'Eligio; for all these geometries are overlaid by a profusion of sculpture and decoration. The entrance from the cathedral aisle is blocked by the massy bronze grille the Vischers made in 1532. Inside, every pilaster and panel is dappled with arabesques cut in low relief on the grey-green Myślenice sandstone, some of them, as on the north wall, mere horror vacui. The best work is high up, for, in the beautifully shaped tympana between the pendentives, all sorts of things are going on; Adam and Eve bound to a tree, birds pecking fruit, satyrs fighting, sea-monsters that carry girls away, and in one corner a massive Neptune who in his turn obeys the shaft of love. This may all be the work of a Roman, Bernardo Zanobi. Its lusty delicacy would have held its own anywhere in Italy.

No major independent sculptor appears anywhere in the accounts. Berrecci and his assistants may very well have carved the impersonal red marble figures, the six standing saints and the roundels which, on Boner's instructions, matched the four Evangelists with himself as David and Zygmunt as Solomon. But it is tempting to believe, as many do, that the king sent to Italy for an outstanding sculptor to make the royal effigy; and that in 1529 Giovanni Maria Mosca, known in Poland always as 'Padovano', forsook the thriving business in marble reliefs and monuments he had built up in his twenties in Padua and Venice and came to Cracow. Thirty years later Italian gossip spoke of the extravagant offer he had accepted; and would he have travelled so far for the promise only of bishop Tomicki's monument and the four handsome medals of the royal family he was to strike? In the Solomon roundel Zygmunt's peculiar features, the sharp slanting lines that frame the mouth, the immense continuous eyebrows, only add up to a stiff, staring visage. But his full effigy has an extraordinary angular restlessness, and in spite of its half-shut eyes the face is wide awake, squinting round the room in pursuit of some displeasing servant. By comparison even the long forked beard his son wears below him seems convention; Zygmunt August himself commissioned his own figure from Padovano in 1571, but the sculptor was dead, surely eighty years old, in 1573.

Padovano's other work is all in Cracow or southern Poland. He probably finished Tomicki's monument before the bishop's death in 1535. It stands in the chapel of the south chancel aisle; arabesqued columns, a relaxed sleeping figure. In 1545 his workshop made an almost exact replica, the figure of bishop Gamrat in the matching north chapel, and in 1552 probably also the rather dull monument to bishop Maciejowski in the chapel off the north transept. Padovano carved three delightful monuments to children: to Rafał Ocieski, who died in 1547, in the Dominicans' cloister;

to Krzystof Herburt at Felsztyn; and at Pilica to Katarzyna Pilecka, whose head rests on a pillow, but her elbow on a skull. Away to the east in the Franciscan church at Krosno there is a flat but lively slab effigy to Jan Kamienecki, dead in 1560. But the workshop's best products are in the disappointingly rebuilt cathedral which presides over the decorative square at Tarnów. A mass of architecture, stage on stage, commemorates two Tarnowskis, one the famous general Jan who died in 1561, with women in niches and great reliefs of battles. And up on a wall grey and black stone coolly frames Barbara Tarnowska, in drapery as relaxed as Nicholas Stone's figure at Stanmore. Padovano's work was not just monuments, and in 1551 he made for St. Mary's in Cracow the tabernacle on the south side of the chancel arch, compact, with small medallion heads and two gentle angels, a spiritual safe. In the chancel it has brash competition from other hands, the near baroque stalls and effigies which commemorate the Cellaros and the Montelupi in full coloured stone.

Still the best monuments in St. Mary's are in bronze, and older, from the Vischers' Nuremberg workshop; the tablet in the chancel to Piotr Salomon, dead in 1506; the great severe slabs of 1538 to Seweryn and Zofia Boner in the north east chapel. In the Cathedral, on one of the southern nave piers, their slab of 1505 for Piotr Kmita is almost wholly Gothic: long legs, floating banner, hair falling to the shoulders, the ultimate in military dandyism. Then five years later they show cardinal Fryderyk Jagiełło kneeling in the chancel under lines of Trajanic lettering. The examples of Berrecci and Padovano created a whole Cracow school of sculpture, most of it too mediocre to list. Most prolific was Hieronimo Canavesi from Milan, easily spotted in places like Gniezno by the conspicuously carved name and address of the artist; the one Pole to make a name, Jan Michałowicz z Urzędowa, made two good tranquil figures for fussy Netherlandish looking tombs in the Cathedral, one of 1560 to a Zebrzydowski in one of the north chancel chapels, the other of about 1575 to a Padniewski in the Potocki chapel south of the nave. Then another Florentine arrived, Santi Gucci, to work for Stefan Batory. He built a grand house with an arcaded courtyard for him at Lobzów, now vanished; and fitted up the Cathedral's eastern chapel with its marble stalls; and, probably after 1586, set in front of the throne in the Sigismund Chapel the red marble slab to Batory's wife Anna Jagiełłonka. His figures are oddly mediaeval, half flying on their tilted slabs, cloaks blown stiff behind them by a gale of stone.

Stefan Batory was a Transylvanian noble famous for his valour against the Turk, and the Poles elected him because their empire was on the defensive. When Zygmunt August died, they first picked a Frenchman; he could face neither their manners nor his responsibilities and was home within a year. Under Batory, Polish arms had a brief golden age, when a man like the Chancellor Jan Zamoyski would raise 10,000 men for the Russian war out of his own pocket. Under his Vasa successors the state exhausted itself in both war and internal division. The European inflation made it as hard for Władysław IV to make ends meet as Charles I, and on top of this the Baltic food exporting countries seem to have suffered shrinking markets, which turned peasants into serfs and concentrated power in the hands of a few nobles. The rulers of Brandenburg were digging in in East Prussia; in the Ukraine the Cossacks rose, the Tsar behind them; Karl X of Sweden marched unopposed across the land. Jan Kazimierz abdicated and died as the abbot of St. Germain-des-Prés, and his successor, Michał Korybut Wiśniowiecki, was a nullity. Jan Sobieski took the credit for the relief of Vienna in 1683 but could do nothing in twenty years to weld a modern state together. Polish Liberty reigned, the Republic of gentlemen supposed free to rebel, free to dissolve a whole session of Parliament with one voice, and free to take ever greater bribes and promises from candidates for the crown.

The Vasas' decoration of the rooms in the north wing of the Wawel was Cracow's first taste of the baroque. In 1605 they began a chapel alongside that of Sigismund which mimicked its exterior, as if all the confidence of a century before was gone. Their architect Giovanni Trevano laid out the wall and the pretty gateways south and west of the Cathedral, and in 1626 designed the great grim baldacchino over the tomb of św. Stanisław in its centre. This is the last serious royal intervention in Cracow's architecture. Of their successors only Michał Wiśniowiecki and Sobieski are commemorated there, and then only in florid black and white achievements set by Francesco Placidi in the ambulatory in 1757. With the shift of capital Cracow had become architecturally as well as politically provincial, a school to be set alongside Poznań, Lwów, and Wilno, each at least as prolific and original.

The first of its baroque churches was naturally built for the Jesuits. They had come to Poland in 1565, when there was a real danger the country might turn Protestant, and were in Cracow in 1582. They began to build in 1596, but made two false starts; Trevano produced a completely new plan in 1605, and in 1619 his dome was finished. Its scheme is, naturally, close to Sant'Andrea della Valle; inside, nave with chapels but no galleries, domed crossing, chancel apse; outside, three pedimented bays on top of five for a façade; all very simple and large, the only decoration sharp architectural detail, not a flicker of fresco. It stands back grandly from the Grodzka behind a parade of hortatory saints. It has one imitator in the city, almost a hundred years younger, the University church of św. Anna, begun in 1689 to plans by Tylman van Gameren, the Dutch architect who was making a career under Sobieski and adorning Warsaw with far less demonstrative churches. It is a little smaller, but more elaborate, the nave divided into four bays instead of three, two odd small towers in the façade, and plenty of admirable stucco decoration. The best is the work of Baldassare Fontana, a craftsman, like so many, from Como who came to Cracow in 1695. His are the saints and angels round the altar and the medallions and fruit on the nave piers, done with the delicacy of a Gibbons. He worked also in the chapel of św. Jacek at the Dominicans', made the boat pulpit for św. Andrzej, and decorated rooms in private houses, like the Renaissance 'Hippolytus' on the Plac Mariacki, 'Pod Baranami' at no. 27 in the Square, and 'Pod Gruszką' at the beginning of the Szczepańska where a vaulted first floor room has miraculous putti in the lowest relief.

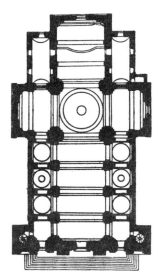

11   Cracow: św. Anna, 1:800

Altogether Cracow has more than a dozen churches of the baroque, half of them begun in the second half of the seventeenth century. Their fussy unmemorable shapes turn up in the suburbs, like św. Franciszek in the Krowoderska; size is not enough to redeem things like św. Bernard, south of the Wawel, or the Carmelites' St. Mary. The eighteenth century shows up little better; the Missionaries' church in Stradom, which Kacper Barzanka may have begun in 1719, seems disproportioned to no purpose, and the great block begun on Skalka for the Paulines in 1733 by Georg Münzer from Silesia is very ordinarily competent. The Capuchins score as usual by simplicity, with their Loreto chapel of 1712 in a treed courtyard on the far side of the boulevard from the University. Much more attractive is the great church which the Camaldulensians began in 1605 out on the wooded hill at Bielany, completed in 1642 with the help of Wallenstein's architect Andrea Spezza, and saw burn in 1814, so that only half its inside elaboration remains. It is white, very broad, severe, and behind it range the cottages which a few religious still live in. They gave us sour plums and talked about the problems of the Church.

The last and best baroque architect here was a Roman, Francesco Placidi. He had worked on the Hofkirche in Dresden, and for forty years until his death in 1782 he supplied Cracow with altars, chapels, and monuments. He is responsible for the façade, completed in 1759, of the pretty church of the Piarists which faces down the ulica św. Jana, a tall white wedding cake crammed into the bend of the street, the best view from the bedrooms of the Hotel Francuski. His showpiece is the little Trinitarian church, św. Trójca, built in 1752 south of the main square in Kazimierz. Inside it is just a good cut-down version of the usual chapelled box. But what a charming incident in the dull street; the door pediment turned outwards with the broken ends projecting forward on clumps of pilasters, the top stage of the tower with two long concave sides and two short convex ones, all informed by a sure sense of rhythm and by knowledge of Borromini's tower on the convent of the Filippini in Rome.

Kazimierz is poor in old houses. But there are unexpected pleasures round its edges. The wooded hillock of Skalka has on one side the convent's big garden and the formalised pool where św. Stanisław should have been drowned, his statue on a pillar in its centre, and, on the other, the broad waste area between city wall and river, alive with children on a summer afternoon. And in the opposite corner of the town the Ghetto survives. When the Germans came they pushed the Jews across the river to Podgórze before the Final Solution took charge and Auschwitz was built. They omitted efficiently to destroy the buildings left behind, and a clutch of synagogues survives, mostly plain street buildings firmly locked. The grandest, the Ajzyka, raises its vaulted hall of 1640 to overlook a small crowded market beside the Józefa. The Ghetto's market was the now half ruined Szeroka, and at its southern end they have rebuilt the Ghetto wall and beside it the old synagogue, a hall of about 1500, rib vaulted on two pillars in clear imitation of the Staronová synagoga in Prague. They have reassembled the Renaissance doorway which framed the Torah and the columns which carried a canopy over the outside steps to the women's gallery. In 1959 we found only a handful of the faithful, strangers from the Ukraine, to represent a community which was once a third of Cracow's population; now there is a neat, impersonal museum.

The old town proper has kept houses in almost every street, if not many are first class. North of the Square it is a matter of doorways; a hotel in the Floriańska, and at no.20 in the św. Jana caryatids which echo Prague and Vienna. Round St. Mary's there is a clump of pretty Renaissance things, the 'Hippolytus' house and the 'Prałatówka' decorated in sgraffito, or so-called scraper-wall, and with a bobbled attic of 1626. On the Square itself a lot is fake or plain ugly, but at the corner of the Bracka a Louis Seize shirt hides the Renaissance body of the Potockis' house, which still has a tiny arcaded courtyard. In the św. Anny are more University buildings, the classical front of the Collegium Physicum at no.6, the much altered courtyard of about 1640 of the Collegium Nowodworskiego at no.12. The Grodzka is the show street, and because of the pastel colours it is hard to distinguish true and false among the doorways and arcades. At no.53, opposite the Jesuits, the Collegium Iuridicum has another seventeenth century courtyard, and its rear presents Gothic gables to the Kanonicza. This is Cracow's best street, a procession of old doorways and attics on a gentle curve. The portal of no.18 is the work of Jan Michałowicz; no.21 is the Deanery, 'procul este profani' over the handsome door, the most complete of the city's arcaded courtyards inside; at the southern end, the house which belonged to the historian Długosz commemorates him in a carved tablet facing the Castle walls.

Cracow is not Prague; two centuries of decline have kept the streets plain and honest; but the scale of the place is easy on the feet.

Cracow was a 'Free City' from 1815 to 1846, and stagnated; under Austrian rule it began to go forward again. Its nineteenth century public buildings, notably the opera house of about 1890, are generally confident enough, and more than that in the case of Księżarski's 'Collegium Novum' of 1883 whose great staircase leads to an airy diamond-vaulted hall. The Teatr Stary which Stryjeński and Mączyński began in 1903 sprouts low relief Art Nouveau vegetation under its eaves – there is, alas, none to be seen inside – and is not the only good example of the eclecticism of 1900. The best, in fact, is the astonishing 'Jama Michalika', the café at Floriańska 45, designed in 1911 by Karol Frycz and recently restored; it combines Glasgow School tall-backed chairs and pseudo-historical stained glass with pastiches of every sort of folk art, and the result is irrepressibly jolly.

It seems to have been more difficult to come to terms with the twentieth century. Until recently the University persisted in the reiteration of rows of columns, and on the southern outskirts one church built since the war not only imitates fourteenth century brickwork but adds to it a pastiche of a domed Renaissance chapel. In the last ten years the usual international eggbox style has appeared in hotels and offices; the best large scale building seems to be out to the west, the sharp student housing on the Piastowska. North of it lies the most striking of the new schools, built by Józef Gołąb in 1960 in the Młodej Polski: parallel two-storeyed ranges which seem to have five in views of the north front, because of the violent repetition of projecting cornices. Further on, one can find in the Wojciecha Halczyna the sort of things Poles build for themselves if given a chance – notably no.14, with an extraordinary splayed-out balcony by Zbigniew Gądek.

But all this time a massive foreign body has been menacing Cracow from the east. At Nowa Huta a steelworks has been built, far from water transport or coal or iron ore, regional diversification with a political edge to it. Its plan, a half wheel of radiating avenues, is typical enough for Stalinism, and north and north-west the five-storey blocks march out across the land. Along the road to Cracow they have become less uniform, and now one finds the popular combination of ten- to twelve-storey blocks set north to south with four- to five-storey ones set east to west. In the Majakowskiego, beside the aggressively columned theatre, stands a school designed also by Gołąb in 1961 which is refreshingly relaxed, but there are few such oases. It is not one of Europe's more habitable looking new towns; and its people still have to travel to Cracow to go to church.

2. Little Poland

The triangle of Cracow, Kielce and Sandomierz is the core on which the late mediaeval kingdom of Poland was built up. It is a rich countryside, but over-populated and short of industry. Much of it is dull, gently rolling, but in the north around Kielce rise long wooded ranges of hills, and between Cracow and Częstochowa spectacular gorges wind through the limestone plateau. The sandstones and limestones are good enough for building to have made it the one large area in Poland to withstand the tide of brick.

All over Poland the Romanesque found its rough expression in stone. In Little Poland there is not a great deal of it, just a few box like churches or parts of churches; but there is a surprising splash of architecture at Kościelec near Proszowice, where the church founded in 1231, and since much rebuilt, has a triform, a rudimentary clerestory, and carved capitals. The one imposing twelfth century parish church is at Opatów, forty miles east of Kielce. Here everything is very tall, emphasized by fourteenth century gables, the ashlar south tower runs to half a dozen stages, and the short square chancel has long thin buttresses. Inside the first effect is all eighteenth century fresco and furniture, and not good, and the nave has a fussy sixteenth century vault. But the height and slenderness of the arcades are new. The north transept is full of monuments to the Szydłowieckis, a big bronze effigy of one, a chancellor, made in 1536 by Giovanni Cini, with a relief of an animated council meeting, a decent red marble figure of his wife, and frescoes of battle covering the wall above.

In 1140 the first Cistercians arrived, brought direct from Morimond, the Burgundian mother of most central European houses, by the bishop of Wrocław, in imitation of Otto of Freising's foundation of Heiligenkreuz five years before. The abbey of Jędrzejów, or 'Maly Morymund', has preserved the plan and structure of the church consecrated in 1210; four bay nave, transepts each with two chapels, short chancel to which an apse was later added. But of the convent there are only fragments; the four-pillared chapter house was pulled down in 1873; in the fourteenth century the nave arcade was altered, and given buttresses towards the aisles; everything is overlaid with baroque plaster and paint, delicate pinks and yellows, light and warm. The best architecture to be seen there now was all done after 1726. Between 1733 and 1742 the north transept was given a sharp, tricky new front and flanked by two symmetrical domed chapels; in 1751 a splendid tall east front went up, with two slender towers and odd blocked doorway as if a plan for a west front had been used. The detail suggests a

CLAIRVAUX → Esrom (Denmark) 1151

‹ 1172
Dargun
1209

Doberan
1171/86

Altenberg
1133

Lehnin
1188

MORIMOND

Schulpforta
1132

Bukowo
1248/59

Oliwa
‹ 1178/86

Pelplin 1258/76

(Byszewo)
Koronowo c.1250/1285

Chełmno 1267

Kołbacz
1175

Bierzwnik
1286

Łekno/Wagrowiec 1143

Owińska
1242

Paradyż
1230

Obra 1237

1175 Lad
1193

(Wieleń) Przemet 1285

Sulejów 1177

Lubiąż
1175

Trzebnica
(1203) 1218

Wąchock
1179

Krzeszów
1292

Henryków
1222

Jemielnica
1280

Jędrzejów
1140

Kamieniec
1247

Koprzywnica
1185

Ruda
1252/9

Mogiła
1222

Szczyrzyc 1245

Men's Convents ——●—— Women's -○- – –
Minor houses omitted
Two dates given where a foundation was revived

12 The Cistercians in Poland

competent Cracow architect with a Borrominesque vocabulary, like Francesco Placidi.

Jędrzejów is still Romanesque; there is not so much as a rib to be seen in its vaults. Its three sister foundations have the half Gothic character typical of Cistercian building when the order was expanding fastest. They were founded in ten years between 1176 and 1186, part of a burst of activity which involved Pomerania and Silesia too, and the tradition is that all the original monks came from Morimond, though one party cetainly went from Wąchock to help keep Sulejów going. In plan their churches are reduced, even more than that of Jędrzejów, to the barest elements; four bay nave, transepts with but one chapel each, one rectangular bay for a chancel. The plainest is Koprzywnica, founded in 1186 down by the Vistula near Sandomierz, the church begun in 1207. The piers are square, all the arches unmoulded, the chapter house vaulted from two short round columns; the half columns on the chancel arch seem an extravagance. Baroque additions hardly soften this earnestness.

Wąchock is a little more hospitable; it was founded in 1179 in a kink of the Kamienna valley and its striped brown and grey stone walls rise among great trees. The church is positively squat, for the walls of the nave are only as high as it is broad; but there are wall shafts and some outbreaks of carving, notably in the chapter house, whose columns have leaf capitals and faces on their feet. The now mostly seventeenth century mass of the convent holds only a few other mediaeval rooms, of prison solidity.

The best of the group is Sulejów. It was founded about 1176; in 1232 the church was complete, but the convent went on building, part in brick, and what stands now is of all ages. It lies in a bend of the Pilica, protected by a full ring of walls and eight towers which include an elaborate north gateway. South of the church is what remains of the convent, the east range only, with a chapter house, vaulted from one pillar and with another pillar awkwardly dividing its doorway. The church has at least achieved normal proportions, the nave twice as high as broad, with pointed vaults and more elaborate piers; and the round arched west doorway is three orders deep.

These abbeys had few children, and those sickly. In 1232 Wąchock founded one across the the Tatra mountains in the Spisz; in 1245 Jędrzejów sent monks into the hills who in time built at Szczyrzyc what is now no more than a simple village church. More serious was her creation in 1252 of Rudy (Rauden) in Upper Silesia, fifteen miles beyond Gliwice; the same scheme, but heavily achieved in brick, and now most ruthlessly restored. As we have seen, other Cistercians had already brought brick to Little Poland; in the 1220s the bishop of Cracow had settled monks from Lubiąż (Leubus), on the Oder, at Mogiła, and in 1266 they consecrated one of the largest abbey churches in Poland. It closely follows the Cistercian nuns' church begun in 1203 at Trzebnica in Silesia, with two aisle bays to each bay of the nave; its nave has the standard width, about 28½ feet, to which this whole generation of great brick churches conforms. It has been much rebuilt; the nave has only a painted tunnel vault, only the windows of the old chapter house remain, and the convent is mostly of the sixteenth and seventeenth centuries. But the very elegant cloister has survived, and there are still dome-like rib vaults in chancel and transepts, the best of them in the transept chapels. Opposite the west end lies a timber church as quaint as any in the hills, and to the north the flats of Nowa Huta march across the plain.

But brick became in a generation the equal of stone in serious buildings. By the 1250's Franciscan friars were using it at Nowy Korczyn, at the junction of the Nida and Vistula, and Franciscan nuns at Zawichost where their plain brick box now stands in a neglected garden on a hillside above the river. And in 1227 the Dominicans had begun their new church at Sandomierz in brick. It lies outside the

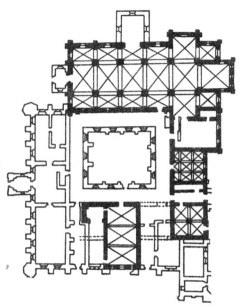

13   Wąchock: abbey and church, 1:1,000

town to the south-west, up a country lane, and outside it looks wholly Romanesque, with an elaborate round arched north doorway and glazed brick used to frame windows and as a frieze; inside, though, the nave arcade has pointed arches. There are no old vaults, and the best decoration is some lively plaster in a late Renaissance chapel. When the friars arrived Sandomierz was still a minor capital, but now it is an odd ramshackle town with an air of going nowhere. The castle down by the river is a mere barrack, too much rebuilt to betray any past. One tall square gate faces north towards a Benedictine nunnery of the seventeenth century whose builder created an eloquently well-proportioned courtyard with no formal order and a picturesque skyline with the minimum of effort on gables and turrets. In the square a pretty mediaeval brick town hall with an arcaded parapet and a slender octagonal 31 tower presides over dull houses. On the town's east edge the historian Długosz' other house, a little brick box of 1476 with stone windows, looks out over the valley. Among the trees besides it rises the big collegiate church Casimir III began about 1360. It has suffered much; outside there is an absurd rooftop turret and a west front of sorts of about 1670, and inside all kinds of undistinguished furniture, bad nineteenth century polychrome, and – most disconcerting perhaps – the much restored and wholly alien frescoes with which Jagiełło's Ukrainian painters darkened the apse. But the brick walls still display their glazed headers, and inside the stone skeleton is admirable, great square piers, crisp capitals with beasts and leaves, slender shafts, sharp ribs. It is the most ambitious of Little Polish hall churches.

The first hall church in the province had gone up in the thirteenth century in the nunnery founded in 1228 at Staniątki, south-east of Cracow, which still houses religious women; the heavy pointed arcades were all overlaid in 1760 with pretty rococo plaster and paint. The finest by far is that at Wiślica, on a hillock commanding 2

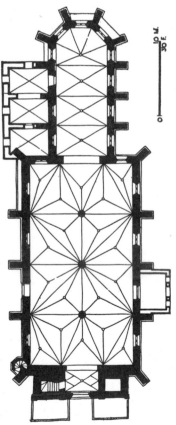

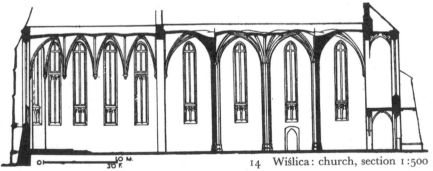

14 Wiślica: church, section 1:500

the flat Nida valley. This is an old inhabited place; there are the foundations of a Romanesque church under the present one, and until 1915 parts of its two west towers, shown on the plan, still buttressed the west front. Now a simple square bell tower and a mediaeval priests' house frame the Gothic collegiate church. It is a block of stone geometry, plain west gable, tall buttresses, a grand blocked north doorway, a tablet over the south one that shows the Virgin Mary and King Casimir. Inside it is a marvel. The chancel is three bays and an apse long, all tall slender windows, well over twice as high as broad. The nave is a hall vaulted like the refectory of some huge monastery from one row of three pillars, with a system of ribs that starts with twelve branches from the central shaft and absorbs their spreading force with ingenious corner spaces. Everything is very sharp and clear, rib profiles, carved bosses, pillars with as many sides as ribs grow from them. There are no tricks. Casimir seems to have

15 Wiślica: church, plan 1:500   refounded the college in 1346; this date would make the church as early a double

nave as any in central Europe, though long after those in France, and the equal of
any in sophistication and grace.

The system was naturally much imitated in the country roundabout. Sometimes
the nave has but one pillar, yet the church of about 1360 at Kurzelów almost equals
Wiślica in elegance; we find two pillars in those of 1350 at Niepołomice, south of the
river, of 1355 at Szydłów (now vaultless), of about 1362 at Stopnica, and of as late
as 1499 at Szaniec. There, a few miles east of Wiślica, stands an honest little building
whose master only copied and simplified, like most of his predecessors. But Stopnica
is a miniature of brilliance. Recent restoration has laid the pearl-grey limestone
rudely bare. The two pillars are slightly closer to each other than to the nave's end
walls, and share the radiating rib system, nine ribs each. For all its later accretions
this is less than ninety feet long inside. Its concise elegance matches anything created
in Bohemia by the architects of the Emperor Charles IV.

Szydłów was founded by Casimir on a half regular plan. It took a beating in the
war. But it still has a mediaeval aspect; to east and west its grey stone walls are
practically intact, towered, up to twenty feet high; to the south the Brama Krakowska
faces the road, a double gate which looks like a chair for a colossus; to the west chunks
of the castle stand; to the north a cinema occupies a late mediaeval synagogue. It is
sad that the church can be only in part restored. Another depressed town is Bodzentyn,
on a narrow steep ridge among the hills east of Kielce. At one end blurred ruins of a
sixteenth century castle rise from the rock. The church is a great, plain brick space,
built in the 1440s when bishop Oleśnicki of Cracow founded a college of priests,
vaulted in plaster in the seventeenth century. It is full of surprising brilliant objects
bishops have dumped; a red marble tomb for bishop Krasiński, dead in 1577; parts
of sixteenth century altar pieces, the best a very fine Death of the Virgin of 1508,
against the easternmost south pillar of the nave; biggest surprise, the pink and blue
and gold of the immense high altar made for Cracow Cathedral in 1545, which got
here in 1728. The oddest of Little Polish mediaeval churches is far to the south-west
at Krzcięcice. Here between 1531 and 1542 a master Albert built a replica of one of
the tiny brick village churches of Mazovia, gabled outside, inside a surprising riot
of star vaults, all varieties represented with four stars to each bay in the chancel. Thus
in this gentle valley one might be out on the harsh sandy plains of the Bug.

Castles start with Chęciny, on one of the steep narrow ridges south of Kielce. Miles
away you see it from the road. The rock it stands on is folds of pink and grey, the
walls and square gate tower of around 1300 rise pink and grey too, but the huge two
round towers have later brick tops. West of Cracow, at Rudno near Krzeszowice,
Tęczyn lies, ruined by the Swedes; inner castle with keep and chapel, outer curtain
wall with round towers and bastions, all remodelled about 1570 with Renaissance
parapets and a lost arcade for the open courtyard. Far to the north, almost in Mazovia,
Drzewica has a moated wall with four stone corner towers of about 1530 and a brick
gabled house inside them. The best of a mostly very dilapidated but picturesque
group is Pieskowa Skała, perched on a limestone rock above the Cheddar-type gorge
of the Prudnik. It is still watertight, and I found a film being made, with Robin
Hood characters mumbling over their lines in corners. There are seventeenth century
bastions, two gates, and a courtyard fitted up in the 1580s with rough arcades,
square piered, naked of balustrades, but whose spandrels display pretty masks and
shields. Crude architecture, but a setting from the fairy background of a Flemish
painting, these strange rocks and caves and forests.

North of the river there are almost no formal Renaissance houses, nothing like

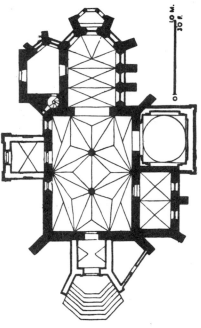

16   Stopnica: church, 1:500

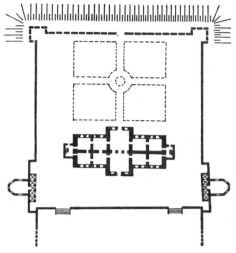

17   Mirów: original layout, 1:1,500

18   Klimontów: collegiate church, 1:800

Baranów south of it. The most striking gesture was made by a bishop of Cracow who in 1585 had Santi Gucci, a Florentine who may have learnt something from Bandinelli, begin for him the solid block of Mirów which from a bluff to the east commands the little town of Ksiąz Wielki. It is a plain rectangular mass, two storeys of banded masonry and one of smooth, the centre of each side pushed slightly forward, half-heartedly gothicised in 1841 by Schinkel's pupil Stüler; to the east of it, two pavilions with five bay arcades flank the view of an abandoned garden, their delicacy a disconcerting Mannerist contrast. Santi Gucci died at Pinczów, where about 1600 he may have built a tiny chapel of św. Anna on the hill above the unimpressive town; just a Renaissance cube and half sphere, the minimum of detail, one statue on a separate pedestal. Other such chapels are all stuck to churches: that of the Branickis added in 1640 to the Franciscan church at Chęciny by the local builder Gasparo Fodiga; that of the Tęczyńskis put up in 1613 at Staszów; best of all that of the Firlejs at Bejsce, a work of about 1600 in Santi Gucci's manner, with plenty of fully modelled plaster, a rosetted dome, alabaster Christ and Mary, great kneeling red marble gentry and tiny dead marble children.

In Little Poland the chief centre of the Baroque was Kielce. On a hill outside, Karczówka, the Bernardines began a two towered church in 1624. In 1632 the town church, now the cathedral, was rebuilt in earnest; it looks fascinating at first glance, but in general it is a lot of repetitous fuss, the interior relieved only by the excellent red marble effigy of 1553 for Elżbieta Zebrzydowska which for liveliness might be by Padovano. To the west lies the palace built in 1637 for bishop Zadzik of Cracow, 34 perhaps by Tommaso Poncino, perhaps by Giovanni Trevano. It has a central block still half Renaissance in effect, half detached hexagonal towers, an entrance 'loggia' of three arches, broken pediments over all windows of whatever size; not one pilaster, but the grouping, the arms that reach out to embrace the church, seem baroque. Beyond this Kielce is a dreary town of narrow, grcy crowded streets, a mean centre for the fine hill country around.

The most ambitious builders of this generation were Krzysztof Ossoliński and his architect Lorenzo Muretto from Sent in the Grisons, whom the Poles called Wawrzyniec Senes. In 1643 they began the collegiate church of św. Józef at Klimontów west of Sandomierz. It is an impressively full statement of early baroque ideas, clumsily clothed in dry, sharp, repetitive decoration which belongs in the previous century. A great oval dome rises from an ambulatory and a most odd octagonal arcade, with rectangular windows fitted in above the arches and huge recessed columns which support nothing. The façade is uninspired work of 1779, dry as the little town, with two passable towers. The thing is grand in spite of itself. But Muretto's biggest commission was eight miles away, north of east towards Iwaniska, the castle called 'Krzyżtopór' at Ujazd. In a fortified pentagon two hundred feet across, he laid out a 3 residence fit for a king. Low wings framed the outer courtyard, looking on the plan 4 like thin bent legs; in the centre of the main body a narrow passage leads to an inner, oval space, from which you penetrate to the seventy foot long hall which is the heart of the palace and the octagon tower which is its head. It is a passionately expressive plan, Caprarola cut open. The site adds to its effect; only four storeys tall towards the entrance, the building becomes six where it rises from the marshy lake beyond. The surviving detail is dry and flat, circles and quatrefoils in low relief, pilasters and panels, not a single column. Size was all. It took seventeen years to build, from 1627 to 1644; eleven years later the Swedes came and it was gutted. Now it is all for crows and small children.

The most famous baroque church in the province – if not in all Poland – is out on its western border at Częstochowa. The monastery at Jasna Góra was founded in 1382. Within a couple of generations its Byzantine looking painting of the Virgin was drawing pilgrims. Fourteenth century building survives in the chancels of the present church and of the chapel to the north where a replacement of the original image is now shown. The main structure was made up of the additions of the next two centuries, mainly of around 1460, which extended it to ten bays altogether and an immense west tower. In the 1620s the place was fortified; in 1655 it turned the Swedes back. Suddenly it became a symbol of national hope and regeneration. So far only the south wing of the convent had been rebuilt; now a maze of plain heavy buildings went up to north and west. After a fire in 1690 the church was all redone, its interior by 1725 one crumpled crust of stucco. The tower too was raised, and chapels added, and in the middle of the

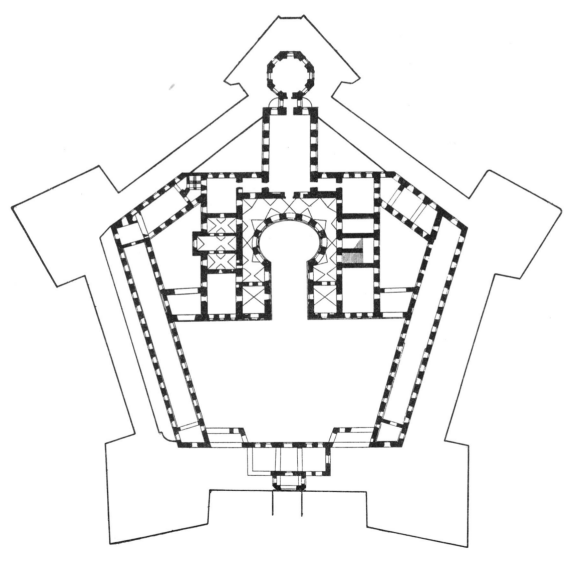

19   Ujazd 'Krzyżtopór' Castle, 1:1,000

eighteenth century the walls were all rebuilt, so that what we approach now is far more sophisticated than what the Swedes bombarded. The most recent addition is the south-eastern cloister Adolf Szysko-Bohusz built in 1920, a weird blend of rococo and art nouveau silhouettes. The walk above its arches leads to the treasury, history in miniature, with kings' sceptres and travelling altars and the Meissen figures Augustus the Strong gave. Today the whole place is a Polish paradox; the railway yards and furnaces down by the Warta, the town aligned on the endless tree-lined avenue that climbs the hill, the waste space ringed by souvenir stalls which on great feast days fills with hundreds of thousands to hear the Cardinal speak.

Of the great baroque houses that which Tylman van Gameren built at Łubnice in the 1690s is now wholly lost – as is also another he designed south of the Vistula at Przecław. But near Szydłow, at Grabki Duże we find cosmopolitan ideas which survive; 42 for here in 1742 an eccentric gentleman, one Rupniewski, built a small house, now empty but well preserved, on his return from an embassy to the Sublime Porte. Here he too would have a miniature harem, with a girl in each of the building's four splayed limbs linked by a hall under a swelling tented octagon. It is, they say, by Francesco Placidi from Cracow, who in the 1770s was still at work, reshaping the great country residence of the bishops of Cracow at Wolbórz with tall firmly modelled Ionic pilasters; it is certainly one of the most imaginative of the many successors to Fischer von Erlach's Althan pavilion in Vienna.

There is little originality in eighteenth century church building, even by Great Polish standards. At Piotrkowice south of Kielce a Loreto chapel was built on to the church in 1776, the usual Casa Santa wholly enclosed in a great simple pilastered octagon with an oval upper stage. The best church site of all is in the Bald Hills east of Kielce, where ridges rise and fall, villages strung out like wooden beads along them, and high on a spur of the main range which reaches 2,000 feet rises the Benedictine convent of Święty Krzyż. It has been endlessly damaged and rebuilt; the church is substantially neo-classical inside, cold, Doric; outside, it is still baroque, with a pretty bulging west front, begun in 1784. There are traces of the mediaeval cloister; but you come up here to gaze from the churchyard into the hazy forested distances all round.

There is little enough secular building of the neo-classical too, but what there is impresses. Białaczów, built by Kubicki about 1800, is a splendid example of the Napoleonic country house – the main block with southern entrance portico and northern saloon in a projecting octagon decorated inside with painted ruins, office wings joined on by quarter circle galleries. In 1802 he designed a much plainer house at Bejsce south of Wiślica, white banded walls, fluted Doric portico, oddly clumsy fenestration. And the same architectural manner informs the early nineteenth century ironworks around Kielce: at Samsonów, eight miles to the north, which has 4 the still grandly symmetrical ruins of the blast furnace and forge begun in 1818; at Sielpia Wielka further on, where the buildings of a rolling mill laid out in the 1820s and 1830s have been fitted up as a simple and fascinating industrial museum; most consciously imposing at Nietulisko up the Kamienna from Ostrowiec, where between 1834 and 1845 Karol Knake who had completed Sielpia dug huge canals and put up another rolling mill in grand but very ruined symmetrical brick and stone and fine Doric columned sluices at the head of the relief channel south of it.

In the established towns nineteenth and twentieth century building are in general undistinguished enough. The last ten years, though, have seen not only the harshly regular satellite town of Nowa Huta but also a completely new town rise at Nowe Tychy on the southern fringe of the Katowice coal basin. So far it looks all too much 4

20 Grabki Duże, 1:750

like one of the satellites of Paris, and again eleven-storey blocks aligned north and south alternate mechanically with five-storey ranges that run east and west. One can only hope that the more imaginative plans Wejchert's team have produced for the area south of the railway, with its woods and its lake, will prove more humane in execution. Meanwhile in this unbuilt area there stands a fidgety modern church of 1957 by Zbigniew Weber; the few modern churches in the province are better represented by that built in 1960 south of the Vistula on the northern outskirts of Tarnów, with parabolic arches, a sharp bell turret, and an east end like an upturned chalice, by Kozlowski, Seibert and Wolak.

But there is some good recent building in the great industrial complex. At its centre Katowice has the big monument to the Silesian Rising with Gustaw Zemła's sculpture of a pair of wings ingeniously related to a traffic roundabout by Wojciech Zabłocki. At Chorzów, Henryk Buszko built a neat tourist centre in 1962 and a very crisp Wedding Pavilion in 1965. Best of all is the Dom Kultury in the middle of the new 'Osiedle K' housing on the east side of Oświęcim (Auschwitz); in essentials a mere box, two thirds of glass, but in detail of a precision Poland seldom sees, a design of 1960 by Józef Polak which has true aristocracy.

SOUTH OF THE VISTULA

South of Cracow in the death-or-glory weekend traffic to Zakopane you are soon in a different Poland from the great familiar plain. Broad wooden ridges climb to three or four thousand feet; narrow valleys hold scattered villages; the hill people are shepherds who still come on feast days in their embroidered clothes. The tourists are hurrying to the Tatras, an eight thousand foot mass of rock on the Slovak border only ten miles across. There are ski lifts and bobsleigh runs; the Morskie Oko can get as crowded as Berchtesgaden, without the amenities; you can shoot the rapids of the Dunajec piloted, the book says, by 'highlanders who . . . wear the regional garb of one of the four ethnographical groups residing in the mountains'. The artistic effects are what one would expect; the knowing patronise the country woodcarvers, and the hotels and holiday centres, with some recent exceptions like the steelworkers' tall holiday house of 1958 at Szczawnica, art-craft the native timber vocabulary into something Swiss and nasty.

The Dunajec rapids start between two respectable castle ruins, Czorsztyn on the north bank and on the south Niedzica; when it belonged to the Paloczi-Horvaths the latter was called Nedeczvár, for this was once a corner of Hungary, and it is a typical spur castle of the fourteenth century, a triangle at the apex of a larger triangle, round flanking towers, battered Renaissance parapets. The family owned another castle up the river at Frydman, once Frigyesvágása; this is a complete Spisz village such as one finds to the south over the present Slovak border, its church a stone miniature of, say, Kežmarok, with aisled vaulted interior, tall parapeted tower, an odd squat separate belfry. But the showpiece of the Podhale is the timber church at Dębno. In its charming setting by a stream on the edge of the fields, it is typical of a dozen mountain churches. There is a wooden wall round the churchyard and its trees, a wooden gate, and little shingle roofs to both of them; nave and chancel make a tall plank box, the tall roof has out-curving eaves; small roofs cover rooms built on, and the tower is a big funnel of shingles with a smaller funnel perched on top but still hardly topping the roof ridge. Inside it is a delight. In the chancel every plank, every baulk of wood is painted; and the small figure on the Rood, his two silhouette attendants, the gilt relieved altarpiece, even the coach lamps the choir stalls are lit by, are overwhelmed by the circles, geometrical designs, and stylised leaves which run across or up and down like the traditional patterns of the country weavers. .

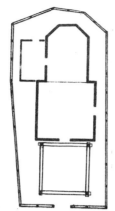

21   Sękowa: timber church

Dębno is of the fifteenth century, though naturally much renewed. But this timber architecture is almost as timeless as it would be in Japan; the sixteenth and seventeenth centuries register only trivial new details. And it spreads all across the hills, its examples far too many to list. Most of the internal painting in fact is eighteenth century, as in the unexpected little church across the road from the abbey at Mogiła, and it is not always very distinguished. Sometimes the roof comes down almost to the ground, spreading out in great irregular wooden skirts to make a covered way all round; a beautiful example is the early sixteenth century church down by the river at Sękowa near Gorlice, and there the whole ground floor of the tower is open, so that the closed space is but a fraction of the whole, like the cella of a Greek temple. In the eighteenth century architecture crept in. Szalowa, eight miles away, has a great wooden block of a church, all rustic rococo inside with painted ceiling illusions and the square pillars to the aisles coyly set diagonally. This kind of thing survives also out in the plains, like the dome and Greek cross plan of św. Krzyż at Buk, west of Poznań. There are even neo-classical ones, like the tiny church of the Transfiguration at Borowica far south-east of Lublin, which boasts fluted Doric columns in antis, the whole kit. Alas, high farm prices are quickly replacing the pretty but damp Polish timber cottage with neat concrete boxes; to see it you have to seek out deliberately preserved villages like Chochołów west of Zakopane or the open-air museum at Zubrzyca Górna further north.

The foothills of the Carpathians are temperate country, wooded hills, bowls of fertile, sheltered land filled with fruit trees, scattered tiny oilwells. Przemyśl is the most important town, finely set on a steep hill, badly battered in two successive world wars. The castle still has Renaissance tower tops; there are large baroque convents, not one of them a surprise; for that go into the heavily overplastered cathedral, where the chancel has been restored to its fifteenth century stone, very tall, a fully developed net vault, an unexpected elegance. Further west, Krosno has a nice square with very tall arcades, a parish church north of it now mostly of the seventeenth century which holds Renaissance looking painted stalls and two pretty stuccoed chapels, and a Franciscan church to the south-east where in 1647 the Oświęcim family were commemorated by painted portraits in their domed cavern of a chapel and where there are two good monuments, one the usual marble slab one would expect from Padovano's workshop for Jan Kamienecki, the other a fine effigy of 1609 to Jadwiga Firlej.

Biecz looks more mediaeval, stretched along a ridge, crusted with bits of old wall, spiked with the great 150 foot tower of the town hall and the round wall tower and detached belfry which frame the western approach; and, on its eastern outskirts, a Minorite convent is picturesquely disposed on its own secure hillock. The parish church is an immense hall, begun in the fourteenth century but not finished until 1521. Its comfortable brick gables belie the cold stone space within, where octagonal pillars rise a gigantic height to carry sophisticated net vaults like Parler built in Prague. Away to the west of Cracow, Żywiec (Saybusch) is much nearer to Czech and Silesian towns. For long it made the only Polish beer good enough to be drunk for pleasure

and not merely under duress of thirst. The church tower is topped by an open arcade
of 1582 in the Czech manner, as if at Olomouc not so far away, and there is a chapel,
neo-Renaissance outside and neo-neo-classical within, which the Hapsburgs built in
1929 to house them everlastingly. The original irregular core of the rambling, very
battered great house has an early arcaded courtyard of 1569, the lower arcades as
massive as if buttressed, cast iron columns set later in the topmost ones.

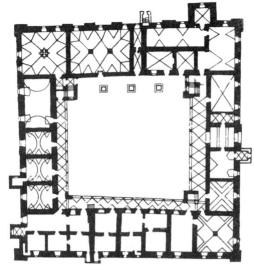

22 Niepołomice (reconstructed), 1:900

Away from the mountains few castles survive; at Dębno west of Tarnów that of the
1470s is just a brick fortified house, and a very attractive one. The first Polish Renaissance house with an arcaded courtyard was begun in 1550 by Tomasz Grzymała for
Zygmunt August at Niepołomice, east of Cracow, on the edge of a forest which now
shelters bison. It followed the scheme of the great house which Ferdinand, the first
Hapsburg king of Bohemia, had begun in 1549 at Kostelec and Cernými lesy west of
Prague; a plain rectangle, the courtyard framed in three ranges of arcades, Doric
columns above, square banded piers below. But more than a century ago the top
storey was burnt and the overhanging roof lost. Beside it stands the little double
naved church, which has lost half its vaults but kept the huge north chapel the
Lubomirskis built in 1640 and the handsomer southern one, neat circles and half
circles, designed for the Branickis in 1596 by Santi Gucci.

25   But Santi Gucci's manner – if he was the architect – is seen best of all at Baranów,
26 much further down the Vistula. There, between 1591 and 1606, Ondrzej Leszczyński
had a house built which is not large but none the less the most imposing of the Polish
Renaissance. In 1962 I found it all being restored; outside, the walls were grey and
yellow, the domelets on the corner towers green with golden balls, and fine new bright
red tiles all over. On the entrance side there are no rooms, and the loggias reach only
round three sides, an economy common in Bohemia. The double staircase above the
doorway, with its oblique colonnade like an outsize stair rail, is as clumsy as anything
attached to a church in Moscow. But the two storeys of Ionic arcades are admirably
elegant, masks on the ground floor plinths, a first floor balustrade, roses in the spandrels.
The contrast of this with the cold empty rooms, of ambition with poverty, is typical
of all the Slav Renaissance.

At Szymbark, south-west of Gorlice, the castle of 1580 is just a square mass with an
elaborately niched top storey and jutting corners and huge battered buttresses, ideally
picturesque on its low rock above the river. Much the proudest residence of this
generation is that which Italians such as Galeazzo Appiani, who also worked on the
7 castle at Przemyśl, built for Marcin Krasicki between 1592 and 1614 at Krasiczyn
nearby. Here the show is all outward. Inside, such arcade as the courtyard has is
modern, only fragments of doorways and an odd projection from the north wing are
of any age, and in 1962 I found the sgraffito ruined and military exclamations still
splashed in Russian on the walls. But three corners of this battered hulk are marked
by massive round towers, a dome marking that which holds the chapel, and above
the banded masonry of the west doorway a square tower rises to six storeys. And almost
all around the walls riot in attics and skyline balustrades, on the north-west tower
aedicules of different sizes, on the north-east one six little turrets, on the south wall
pillars joined by open circles with little spikes on them. A nineteenth century owner
began to collect rare trees here, and now it accommodates a school of forestry. There
is birds' song and the smell of pines, and a broken causeway reaches across the valley
towards an avenue diminishing in the forest distance. (See overleaf).

At Wiśnicz south of Bochina rises the greatest ruin south of the Vistula, a match for
Krzyztopór. The Kmitas fortified the hill in the fifteenth century, and in the sixteenth

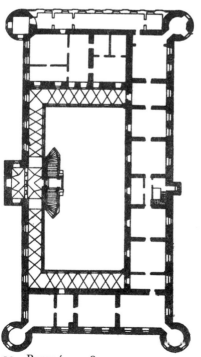

23 Baranów, 1:800

the Lubomirskis reshaped the central block as a Renaissance rectangle with three storeys, wooden posts serving for the uppermost. There is not much to see inside now, though the domed chapel has kept baroque sarcophagi and traces of Giovanni Battista Falconi's stucco decoration. But outside there is the splended bastioned pentagonal wall Matteo Trapola built all round the hill between 1615 and 1621 and his main gate with its showy scrolls and banded masonry.

Further west, beyond Cracow, the Zebrzydowskis began in 1600 a huge place of pilgrimage above a village now known through their efforts as Kalwaria Zebrzydowska. The first chapel is that of the Crucifixion; in 1603 Bernardoni, who had been working for the Jesuits in Cracow, began the Bernardine church and convent; in 1605 a second builder, Paul Baudarth, a goldsmith and by association tooth-filler from Antwerp, began the Sepulchre, and in time he took over all the work. All over the hillside chapels and monuments sprouted, to be surrounded by great trees and connected by two pilgrims' ways, the Sorrows of Christ and the Way of the Mother of God; the individual stations have names like 'Herod', 'Kaifasz', 'Pilat'. In 1617 the main building was fit for use, and in 1623 Baudarth completed his task by rebuilding the Calvary chapel as a picturesque three-lobed thing. Today it is still most welcoming. A great open court-yard framed by arcades leads up to the church from the east, and more cloisters lead round south and west of it; to the north the convent rises plain as a fortress, to the south stand three domed chapels. Everything is plain enough within baroque con-ventions, the only rich plaster is work of about 1667 in the chapel of the Miraculous Virgin south of the chancel. But it is one of the most attractive holy mountains of eastern Europe.

Baroque church building has a few other excitements, for all the disappointment of towns like Przemyśl and Jarosław that seem at first sight so picturesquely placed; the great attraction of Jarosław now is in fact the set of old houses on its square, including the astounding block the Orsettis built early in the seventeenth century, a square mass like a miniature castle, embracing a hall large enough to be a courtyard, spreading over the pavement on arcades, crowned with blank arcading and countless aedicules. But the road out to the west passes the grand bulk of a fortified Benedictine nunnery, and there is another picturesquely fortified convent, of the Bernardines, at Leżajsk to the north. And at Rzeszów is the quite unexpected Bernardine church of 1624, on an uncommonly Roman latin cross plan, no longer 'Renaissance' although the high altar within it is; to right and left of that altar kneel eight members of its founder family the Ligęza, life-size alabaster figures set in niches cut in the chancel walls.

The greatest house south of the Vistula is the Potockis' seat at Łańcut. Stanisław Lubomirski had Trapola begin it in 1629, a four-square house on a fortified base which once must have commanded all the country round. Now it is in its turn commanded by immense chestnut trees; the fortification is no more than a ha-ha that cuts across the half-hearted formal garden. The main fronts have vaguely baroque fenestration, and two corner towers have onion tops. From the south-west corner a big classical orangery projects westwards, added by Aigner, the favourite architect of the great families opposed to Stanisław August; the north-west corner faces a pretty semi-circle of columns he placed on a rise, but much too close, to catch the eye; in the park can be found the 'little castle' he built about 1800, with a corner tower, one of the first Polish examples of the Picturesque. Beyond a lane vast stables extend, still full of carriages, though the motor-cars, the Rolls-Royces which Alfred Potocki used to order three at a time, have vanished.

He managed to remove most of the pictures in 1944, so that much of the interior

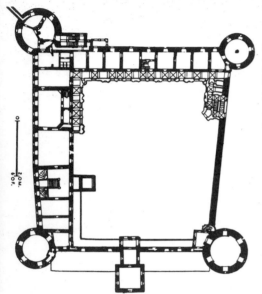

24   Krasiczyn, 1:1,250

is disappointing. Only one tower room has kept the stucco Falconi did in the seventeenth century. The first neo-classical hand was that of Vicenzo Brenna, the Florentine decorator who did so much to spoil Cameron's work for Paul I at Pavlovsk; he did up some of the small rooms in the ground floor of the north wing, and the Chinese room and the pergola-painted gallery upstairs on the south side. But the best work is Polish neo-classical, not only Aigner's orangery and colonnade but also the great rooms on the east wing. There is Aigner's dining room, and his huge saloon; the sculpture gallery whose silk-lined and columned apse fits into the south-east corner; best of all, the theatre of 1792, whose arc of great composite columns and white and gold plaster match in splendour Gustav III's theatre of 1781 at Gripsholm in Sweden.

About 1800 Aigner also built, to the common neo-classical plan with a circular saloon, a rather clumsy house at Igołomia, east of Cracow and north of the Vistula; and at Zarzecze east of Łańcut he put up in 1817 the grandest of his Picturesque houses, its corner tower now encircled with columns. But this manner comes out best of all in the little house Kubicki may have built about 1800 at Witkowice. An avenue runs north from the great road. Outside, there is just one storey, a pediment to the south, a curved central bay to the north, as cool as anything among the beeches of Sjaelland. Inside the curved bay lies a superb round saloon with mirrors and fluted Ionic pillars in antis and a ceiling which is one plain saucer dome inside a larger dome covered in plaster coffering; I found it all newly redone in white and grey-green, and outside white and pink, a tonic.

THE LUBELSZCZYNA

Between the Vistula and the Bug we are lost on the plain, spacious, endlessly rolling, almost without incident, vast fields in succession, broad forests; hills are events, towns surprises. People were slow to settle on this loess plateau and late to build permanently; as late as 1600 landlords were still busy chartering new towns. There is almost nothing mediaeval, and the eighteenth century did relatively little. So the dominant building manner is a provincial Renaissance, called after Lublin, distinctive and pretty, often with blank walls and buttresses topped by panelled gables.

Lublin itself should be handsome, and is a little disappointing. The site is admirable, a long spur along which Krakowskie Przedmiescie leads to the hump the old city crowns, and beyond that a hillock between rivers on which the castle stands. From the castle terrace there is certainly a splendid view, a tiny seventeenth century hospital huddled in the valley, and behind it the north gate and chunks of wall rising from the hillside and the massive chapels clumped around the Dominican church. The castle itself contains a round tower built on thirteenth century foundations and, concealed in a Renaissance exterior, a little two-storeyed chapel of the 1380s, vaulted from one pillar and painted in 1418 by Jagiello's eastern artists. But the rest was in ruins by the end of the seventeenth century, and in 1823 it was rebuilt as a prison by Ignac Stompf, in a vile neo-Gothic, neither inventive nor scholarly, which appears in some other official buildings in the town. In spite of its size it looks like a film set due to come down tomorrow. From the foot of the great flight of steps two streets diverge, the Kowalska eastwards between decent dilapidated classical houses, the Grodzka southwards to the town centre, underneath the plain Castle Gate which

Merlini reshaped in 1785. Between 1781 and 1787 he did the town hall as well, equally on the cheap, with dreadfully scrawny pilasters. The square around has much modern sgraffito and a few old houses, with sculpture or, at no.2, painted medallions; the Renaissance showpiece is the 'Żółkiewski' house of 1597 at no.12. 2

The area further south is more rewarding. From outside, the Dominican church of św. Stanisław is a pile of seventeenth century architecture jammed in an alleyway. But inside the baroque clothes do not wholly conceal the breadth of the fourteenth century hall plan. Beyond the chancel a strange space opens out, the domed cross oval of the chapel added by the Tyszkiewicz in 1645; and south of it the fluted pilasters of the square Firlej chapel of 1630 reach far higher to its dome than do the vaults of the aisle it closes. Not a great church but, as often in Poland, how kindly to come in on a cold spring evening and find it full of people and light. There are two good gates, the south-western Brama Krakowska, with its low crenellated forepart and domed tower behind producing the same chair effect as the south gate at Szydłów, and the Brama Trynitarska beside the Cathedral, absurdly reshaped in 1819 in Gothic; between them I found a great half round brick bastion being disengaged from ruined houses. The Cathedral was formerly the Jesuits' church, built between 1586 and 1596, perhaps by their favourite architect Bernardoni. Their convent lay west of it; when it had been pulled down and the present space created in front of the church, Corazzi was called in from Warsaw, and in 1821 he stuck on the present chill Doric portico. Nevertheless the interior is the best of any Lublin church, three very broad nave bays with shallow oval caps, arches to domed chapels, one chancel bay, an apse treated like five segments of an octagon; no galleries, a huge pilaster order, frescoes in warm colours, pinks, greys, marbling effects – mid-eighteenth century work like that in the great abbeys of Moravia where the painter came from.

In the fifteenth century the city was a royal residence, grander than merely ducal Warsaw, and spread west along the ridge. Here in 1412 Jagiełło founded the Brigittine convent, St. Mary of Victory, in memory of his defeat of the Teutonic Knights at Grunwald, and later in the century the Bernardines settled just to the east of it. St. Mary is surprisingly small and heavy, and the piers between nave and tall south aisle look like chunks of wall; a general rebuilding early in the seventeenth century gave chancel and convent refectory plaster vaults. The only evidence of the Bernardines' original church is the chancel's low ribbed vault; for after a fire in 1602 it was almost all rebuilt, a longer nave, pretty plaster patterns over all the vaults, and outside the multi-storey gables typical of the Lublin Renaissance.

Around 1600 Lublin had become the centre of the most characteristic local school of the Polish Renaissance. It is not sophisticated, and its passion is decoration which carries on late Gothic systems by Renaissance means but without the dependence on Flemish models typical further north. Outside, it accumulates eye-catching skylines, gables with row upon row of arched panels or shallow niches and plenty of finials; inside, the structureless nets of late Gothic ribs are translated into ingenious plaster patterns. In Lublin itself there are two splendid examples, św. Józef and św. Agnieszka. The first was founded in 1622 for Discalced Carmelite nuns; it went up slowly, and inside it is all mediocre baroque, but outside it is a postcard picture, as much because of the flash of green from the courtyard trees as of the artful combination of porch and bell-turret and gable. Św. Agnieszka was begun for the Augustinians in 1646 and finished in 1693; it is out to the east in the suburb of Kalinowszczyna, perched on the hillside above the Kijany road, and so less known, but not for that less attractive.

It has a very pretty separate open bell tower, and not only is the gable panelled, but the whole body of the church is covered in two storeys of pilastered panelling of the most rustic proportions.

In the seventeenth and eighteenth centuries Lublin declined. The baroque churches and convent are uncommonly modest; the best is the little church of św. Jan built about 1742 for the Boni Fratres on the Bernackiego in a north-western suburb; it is a short octagon, with four chapels on its diagonals and with the odd vault, a short arch-like barrel between two half-domes, attributed to Paolo Fontana who built the churches at Lubartów, Włodawa, and Chełm. The great families' houses make little more show; the largest, that of the Radziwiłłs, even as reshaped in 1829 hardly outfaces the feeble neo-Italianate of the office building next to it on the Płac Litewski. The nineteenth century gave Krakowskie Przedmieśsie its present busy, characterless face, and pulled down the parish church of św. Michał. The twentieth century has made few amends, although the local architect Tadeusz Witkowski is responsible for some decent University buildings and for the handsome glassy department store of 1959 in the Osterwy. One comes here to stay in the depressing hotels because of the vast countryside, the strange pretty towns, the feeling of a separate nation that is stronger than anywhere else in Poland.

The best country churches are Renaissance. The local manner prettifies the simplest of them, like Markuszów and Końskowola on the way to Puławy. At Uchanie the church was begun in about 1625 to serve a village its lord hoped to turn into a town; he failed, and the building dragged on to 1693; but it is a most sumptuously panelled box, with a hexagonal chapel stuck on for his family. At Radzyń Podlaski the church, dated 1641, seems overshadowed by the Potockis' vast house, described with other houses by the Warsaw Fontanas in the chapter on Mazovia. But towards the town square it asserts itself with pilastered buttresses and odd capitals, and absurd herms support its sacristy. There is one exception to this rusticity at Gołąb on the Vistula. This is a big church in exposed brick; the façade has two solid towers and is informed by tall shallow superimposed pilasters, and the reticence is broken only by a spiky central gable and by the odd vertical series of main door, round window, and arched rectangular window with their disparate frames. Just to the south stands a dignified Loreto, not too much sculptured, but panelled as if by a conscientious carpenter. Built between 1628 and 1636, this is the one successor to the grander architectural ideas of the group who, as we shall see, built Zamość.

At Kazimierz Dolny the 'Lublin Renaissance' reaches its apotheosis. Here the Vistula cuts through the limestone plateau; it carried the main weight of the grain exports which until the seventeenth century slump went through Gdańsk; where the current brought the boats to a landing between the cliffs, a little town grew up. Its merchants' granaries are scattered upstream and downstream along the bank, buttressed and gabled, some ruinous, some restored like that of 1636 on the way to the Janowiec ferry which is now a hostel, one dated as late as 1792. Its centre is an oblong market-place parallel to the river, with a well. On the slope to the north rises the church, another example of the Lublin manner, begun in 1586 and rebuilt in 1613 by an Italian called Balin; it has two pretty gables, a west belfry lower than the nave, and panelled plaster vaults; but with three memorial chapels, the best that of 1625 for the Górskis on the south side, it is a complete country effort at the Cracow ideal, with carved stalls, a dome with lunettes, and a most elaborate plaster vault where four angel faces gaze into the lantern's base.

The showpieces of the town, even so, are houses. In their emulation the local merchants remodelled their two-storey homes, adding attic storeys and then cresting that went as high as another storey still. Mikołaj Przybyła started the first example, on the square, in 1613; on the first storey St. Nicholas duly appears in a panel, the attic is all Evangelists and one odd goatlike figure looking across at the next house, and from it rise two and a half aedicules joined by the most brutal strapwork. Within a few years his brother Krzysztof had matched him in extravagance, slightly less preposterous alone the skyline but with Judith and Salome on pilasters facing a huge St. Christopher in very low relief with crayfish, to indicate water, flipping round his feet. The very restored timber arcades and roofs of the synagogue look most incongruous next door. Then to the west, in the Senatorska which runs down to the river, the Celejóws set out to outdo both. Their gateway has the date 1578, but the show above was put on in 1635, a monstrous iteration of blank niches in the attic and above it an indescribable skyline of statues in frames which sprout dragons and hippogriffs.

From a quarry half-a-mile upstream beyond the hostel a simple ferry poles across to Janowiec. It is a quiet dusty village now, far from the river, but in 1537 the powerful Firlejs set it up as a town in the hope of attracting the river trade, and rebuilt the little church; around 1600 it was reclothed in the Lublin manner after the ravages of Arianism – for this part of Poland once harboured a heresy as unsettling as any Anabaptists – by Stanisław Tarlo, whom a monument inside commemorates. On the bluff above, the Firlejs built a great house whose ruins still dominate the broad silent landscape and the great river; it has two corner towers and an irregular façade twenty-one windows long showing traces of the baroque remodelling Tylman should have given it. The Firlejs made another abortive colony north of Lublin, at Czemierniki. In 1509 they gave this now plain village a charter. In 1603 Henryk Firlej, Bishop of Płock, rebuilt the church with an ambitious west front; and about the same time he built a simple house, a block with two storeys and an attic, among the marshes on the north-east edge of the place. In 1852 it got an extra attic; now it stands on a walled island in a lake, its entrance a causeway commanded by a gateway with an octagonal top. The trees and the reflections invest it with magic.

The greatest of the sixteenth century colonisers had the most success. In the struggles over the election of a new king after the death of Zygmunt August in 1572, one man emerged as a leading supporter of Stefan Batory and as the champion of the lesser gentry against the magnates – Jan Zamoyski of Zamość. His rewards were great: Vice-Chancellor, Starosta of Cracow, Grand Hetman, Chancellor, leader of the Commonwealth's armies against Moscow and, later, the Swedes. In 1587 he was the chief mover of the election of the Swede Zygmunt III; in the next year he captured the rival candidate, Maximilian of Austria, and brought him prisoner to Zamość. For a decade he was virtual ruler of Poland, and in 1600 he raised ten thousand men practically at his own expense for a campaign in Wallachia. As early as 1578 he resolved to make a city of his birthplace. As planner and architect he engaged an interesting eclectic, Bernardo Morando of Padua. The formal foundation followed in 1580. In the next ten years 275 house plots were let, in 1584 Morando, now mayor, began to raise the church and in 1591 the town hall, and in 1593 Zamoyski founded the Academy which was to teach the humanities and his unfanatic brand of counter-Reformation. But his efforts were hampered by devaluation and plague; he had to threaten to take back the plots of tenants who did not build. In 1600 Morando died. In 1605 Zamoyski followed. It was the signal for his many enemies to rebel and reassert their 'golden liberty'. Zamość today is just a country town, but it still bears the stamp of its founder's passion for coherence in a crumbling age.

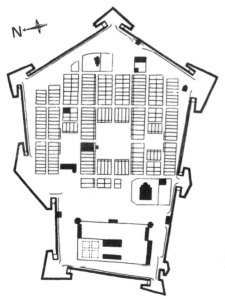

25   Zamość: town plan

Not that this was the only or the first planned town of its generation; a similar system had informed Głogów Małopolski, ten miles north of Rzeszów, begun in 1570. In essence the plan was mediaeval: a chessboard, none of your radiating Palmanovas. One idea, though, does link it with Italian Renaissance towns like Sabbioneta: the chief buildings are not segregated on island sites but pushed out to close the main axes, so that church, castle, and town hall all rise at ends of streets. Zamoyski's castle, abandoned by the family early in the nineteenth century, is a big plain mass with one elaborate gateway of 1594 in its north wing. Outside, the church is plain now, stripped a century ago of its Mannerist detail which framed the façade gable in volutes rising from finial to finial; the separate bell-tower was put up in the eighteenth century. But inside, apart from the plaster patterns put on the vaults after Morando's death, it is much more sophisticated than the 'Lublin' churches, with nave, aisles, and two rows of chapels all of duly graded height and the whole given a Palladian decency by its new coat of white and grey. Its gravitas is in fact Roman, that of Sangallo the younger. And this is Zamoyski's memorial, more than just the plain slab in the floor with his name; some say its mathematical proportions are reflected in turn in the plan of the whole town.

26 Zamość: original church façade, 1:800

The other churches are unremarkable; in the south-east part of the town what used to be the Franciscan church of 1637 still sports a colossally wide gable. South of the parish church the priest's house keeps a decent doorway of about 1620. North of the square there are battered remnants of a synagogue. The fortifications were much remodelled in the nineteenth century, notably by a Russian General Mallet, who pushed a battery out into the marsh and thus spared the pretty neo-classical south-west gate; of Morando's massive Sanmichelian designs there is nothing. The best building is all around the square. It has thirty rich men's houses, in groups of four above arcades, and there are a few more in the nearest streets. Some have baroque fronts, as one sporting a virgin on a dragon on the north side, but the founders' blend of Renaissance and mediaeval ideas still rules; on façades the fancy of Kazîmierz is constrained within architectural bounds, and down the east side behind the arcades carved stone doorways still lead to vaulted entrance halls. The whole is commanded by the town hall. Its core is Morando's original block, a tall plain base, two closely pilastered storeys, and above them a very restrained skyline by Polish standards. But in the mid-seventeenth century it grew a double flight of steps out of all proportion to its main door, and storey on storey was added to the tower, which swells now into two baroque bulbs. The classical mass its designer imagined has become one of the most romantic objects in Poland. Popular if Italian artists were, we see here that in this still mediaeval society their stricter ideals did not stand a chance.

In the two centuries that followed the area employed just one architect of character, Paolo Antonio Fontana, who came like his Warsaw namesakes from Castello Valsolda on Lake Lugano. We first meet him in 1735 working at Lubartów north of Lublin on a new parish church commissioned by the Sanguszkos. In 1741 followed the Paulite church founded by the Pociejs at Włodawa and in 1753 the parish church at Chełm, where he may already have been working on what is now the Cathedral. We have mentioned the tiny Lublin church of 1741 in his manner. His three attested works are all to a pattern: long oval nave, two west towers and a gable, chapels all round, a vault made of a short arch-like tunnel between two half domes which may derive from Ferrari's church at Leszno in Great Poland. Without special originality, they make the best of good sites; Lubartów in a clump of trees beside the broad street and a handsome eighteenth century house; Włodawa on a steep little spur above the

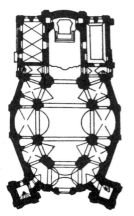

27 Chełm: parish church, 1:800

wide watery valley of the Bug, commanding an endless view into Russia; Chełm facing a steep busy street with briskly moulded concave-sided towers set on diagonals, much like Hildebrandt's St. Peter in Vienna, and very grand and gloomy with all its incurved pilasters inside. The Cathedral there was begun in 1735 as a Piarist church right on top of the hill. It has a separate bell-tower, and the solid conventional nave and crossing lead to an apsed chancel filled with detached columns jumbled under broken entablatures, a logical ground plan which led to visual disaster. What it contributes is another tower to the silhouettes on that steep little hill, making a miniature city a hundred miles from any other, as lonely in the enormous fields as if we were already half-way across the vast Ukraine.

3. Wroclaw

Silesia has been the shuttlecock of politics. In the tenth century it was part of Poland. Under its own Piast dynasty it became the richest of her provinces; its rulers brought in German law, and settlers in the thirteenth century created more than a score of towns. Henry the Bearded, who died in 1238, ruled also in Cracow; his son Henry II followed him as the senior Polish prince, and in 1241 fell at Legnica trying to stem the Mongol tide; then Polish leadership slipped away, and at the end of the century the poet Henry IV ruled a small independent state. In turn the Piast lordship crumbled, the land divided into family principalities, the Luxemburg kings of Bohemia took over, and in 1335 Casimir III abandoned all the claims of Poland. For four centuries Silesia was bound to Bohemia, for the last two under the Hapsburg Emperors. In 1741 Frederick the Great seized it and for two hundred years more it was part first of Prussia and then of the German Empire. Now it is Polish again. The new generation has colonised it all afresh, and the population is even younger than anywhere else in this young country.

Wrocław (Breslau) appears on the map in 1000 as one of the four bishoprics of Poland. Where the Odra was shallow and easily crossed settlements grew up on a chain of islands and on the largest a wooden cathedral was built. Around the beginning of the twelfth century the Piasts moved to the south river bank and fortified a small area there. In 1139 the abbey of Ołbin (Elbing) was founded north of the river by Benedictines from Tyniec outside Cracow; transferred to the Premonstratensians, and then demolished in 1529 in the panic after the disaster of Mohács lest the Turks use it to besiege the city, its place has been marked since 1871 by the church of św. Michał. Then the city spread southwards across the flat valley. When the Mongols came it certainly reached as far as the churches of św. Wojciech (St. Adalbert), where the Dominicans arrived in 1226, and św. Marie Magdalena; the walls of 1260 may well have followed the line of the 1230s, and beyond that a large community of Flemings had settled further to the south-west. In 1241 the people took refuge on the islands and the south bank town was left in ruins. It was rebuilt in the regular manner, perhaps of Roman inspiration, which had become the rule for Central and Eastern Europe since the first Italian and Austrian foundations of 1200 or so and which by the 1230s had spread as far as Salisbury and Rostock. Irregularities, such as the position of the Town Hall out of line with the huge market place round it,

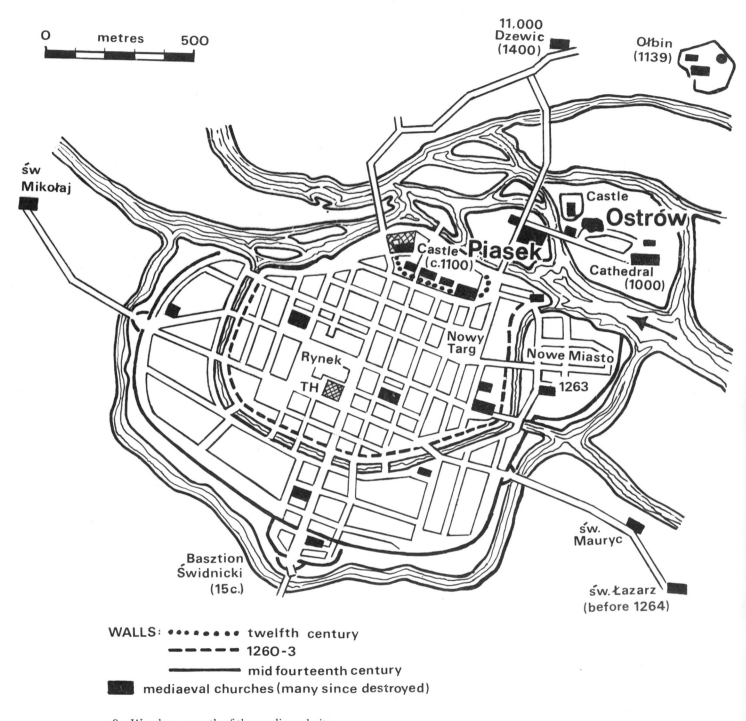

O   metres   500

11,000
Dzewic
(1400)

Ołbin
(1139)

św
Mikołaj

Castle   Piasek
(c.1100)

Castle

Ostrów

Cathedral
(1000)

Nowy
Targ

Nowe Miasto

Rynek

TH

1263

Basztion
Świdnicki
(15c.)

św.
Mauryc

św. Łazarz
(before 1264)

WALLS: ••••••• twelfth century

–––––– 1260-3

———————— mid fourteenth century

■ mediaeval churches (many since destroyed)

28   Wrocław: growth of the mediaeval city

suggest the present grid may have been superimposed on an earlier one. There were now three markets, with the Salt Market south-west of the main Rynek (Ring) and the Nowy Targ to the north-east. The new area was too small; almost at once new settlements sprang up to south and east, given legal incorporation in the 1260s, and in the next century a new and stronger moated wall went up, so that Wrocław was ringed with parallel walls and watercourses. At the Reformation it held some 20,000 people, not far short of London, and twenty-seven churches, which people already said was too many. Half a dozen of them are each worth travelling a hundred miles to see.

One great project was undertaken almost the moment the Mongols retreated. The stone cathedral of about 1150 was replaced in brick, chancel first, nave after, framed it seems by four square towers; of the old building only a statue of John the Baptist was spared to preside over a pretty fountain on the north side of the new nave. The only structure of so large a scale in Silesia was the church Cistercian nuns had completed in 1219 at Trzebnica and for their design the builders turned to Cistercian experience and example. The plan they got matched within inches those of great abbeys like Walkenried; the main vessel is 29 feet broad and 73 feet high, the proportion of 1 to 2½ the Cistercians had by then accepted. The aisles meet behind the square east end. The omissions of chapels and of a transept, apparently never planned in spite of the hint in the broad bay which joins chancel and nave, are the only functional changes in the system. But the builders were not conservative; the east window, a rose above two double lights, followed the latest French ideas at Amiens. Work had started in 1244, the chancel was consecrated in 1272, and already Silesia led Central Europe in picking up ideas from farther west.

Work on the nave went on more slowly, in earnest it seems only after 1300, and after political interruptions it was finished about 1350. Here the visual rhythm is brisker; instead of big six-ribbed vaults, one in the nave to two aisle bays, there is a succession of short cross vaults; there are no carved capitals or bundles of wall shafts, only a shallow 'gallery' on stone archlets above the main arcade and above that walls as bare and sharp as in a friars' church. This is the fully developed building manner of Silesia, plain brick masses articulated by coldly handled stone. In 1354 work began on a Lady Chapel modelled closely on that at Cracow, where as we have seen the new Cathedral had already aped Wrocław within inches. This has one broad bay, two narrower ones, and the odd tripartite 'Piast' vaults, and these reappear in the broad aisle bays created when nave and chancel were joined. An elaborately sculptured main west doorway followed, and in the fifteenth century the west towers continued to rise and the lines of buttresses were filled in with the usual rows of side chapels.

In spite of its ruination in 1945 the Cathedral has kept much of the monuments and furniture these centuries piled up. Bishop Przecław of Pogorzela, who completed the nave and began the Lady Chapel, lies in the latter in marble effigy, and there also is the brass slab Bishop Johannes Rot commissioned from Peter Vischer in Nuremberg in 1496, ten years before his death. The sacristy door of 1517 in the south aisle makes an extraordinary and precocious display of stuck-on Renaissance ornament; the white marble figure of Bishop Turzo has lost its Italianate frame, but still lies, massive and calm, in the apsed north-eastern chapel he had built in 1537. The high altar of 1590 sports scenes and figures in silver, and the baroque altars of 1711 against the arches at the west end of the chancel hold splendid earlier reliefs, the northern a silver Assumption of 1618, the southern a bronze St. Vincent, where

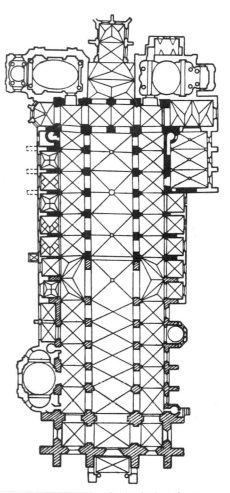

29   Wrocław: the Cathedral, 1:800

low relief is most skilfully used to gain more emphasis than high relief, made in 1614 by Adriaen de Vries. There are carved seventeenth century stalls in both chancel and Lady Chapel. And this is far from a complete tally of the objects that soften the uncompromising rectangularity of the building they adorn.

The nave has the usual rows of funerary chapels too, but the most ambitious memorials lie north and south of the Lady Chapel. In 1680 Cardinal Frederick of Hesse had Giacomo Scianzi design him the lavish chapel of św. Elżbieta, to the south. The plan is of Roman sophistication, with a stuccoed oval dome set athwart the axis, though provincial in execution; and between diagonally set columns the moustached Cardinal kneels, carved by Domenico Guidi, a pupil of Algardi, on a scale worthy of St. Peter's. Grander still, Cardinal Frederick's successor Franz Ludwig, Electoral Archbishop of Mainz, in 1716 called Fischer von Erlach from Vienna to build him a matching chapel to the north. Its grand pedimented doorway closes the north aisle. In essentials, its plan is just a box. But by ingenious stages – a concave bay in the middle of each of its longer sides, a big arch on Composite columns at each end – it rises to an oval cornice, which bears an eight-windowed drum and a painted lanterned dome. The main entablature goes on in a broken circle round the tiny altar space, framed by four smooth grey columns and lit from an unseen side window. Wall and dome paintings are gold and purple and blue, and over false doors sit infants, bouncing or squalling with rage, from the hands of the best Prague sculptor, Ferdinand Brokoff. The precise, tense manner of manipulating space is Borromini's, and nowhere is Fischer's debt to him more evident; but the quiet ease of the whole is Fischer's own, most of all in the simple exterior with the roof of the dome marvellously lightened by the segments cut from its rim. Except for Dientzenhofer's convent church at Legnickie Pole to the west, no other building of the Baroque in all Poland has the same distinction.

Ostrów, the former Cathedral island, is still a sort of Close with quiet tree-lined streets and spaces. One church, św. Idzi (St. Giles), is older than the Cathedral, put up just north of it by a man who was Dean from 1213 to 1228; in shape it is just a late Romanesque village church with an arched south doorway and frieze round the outside of the apse. East of it the chapter-house of 1520 has a spiral stair, a vaulted first floor hall, and doorways in half Renaissance shapes. By the bridge to Piasek stands św. św. Piotr i Paweł, late gothic, with an almost square nave no longer vaulted. To the north something of the old castle chapel survives in św. Marcin, which may go back to a thirteenth century octagon, progressively extended. Between the last two churches Blasius Peintner built a decent orphanage in 1702; otherwise the houses are not individually remarkable, beyond a couple of doorways of 1600 or so in the Katedralna. And in front of św. Krzyż stands an excellent big figure of 1732 of St. John Nepomuk, the most Bohemian of saints.

In 1288 Henry IV made up a long quarrel with Bishop Thomas. The Bishop marked this by creating two colleges of priests, to serve the duke's castle chapel at Racibórz and the great new collegiate church which Henry began to build in Wrocław within two hundred yards of the Cathedral. It has two storeys, possibly because of the danger of flooding, but more likely for sheer effect; the lower is dedicated to św. Bartolomiej because on his name day the duke won a battle, the upper to św. Krzyż, the Holy Cross. In spite of Henry's death in 1290, work seems to have started fast enough to produce, according to tradition, something worth consecrating in 1295, and in 1319 the sacristy was given an altar. Henry himself was commemorated by a grand painted limestone tomb, with the first example in Central Europe of weepers

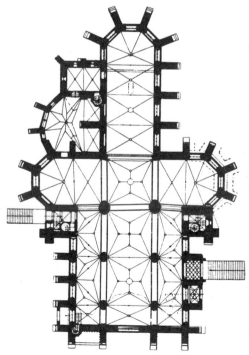

30 Wrocław: św. Krzyż, 1:700

in the French manner, which used to stand in the chancel and is now in the Muzeum Śląskie. But we cannot be confident that the whole building was complete until 1371. At least sixty years of building conceal a most awkward riddle.

The basis of the plan is a cross, with five-sided apses to the transepts as well as to the long chancel. The interior has not the great height the exterior suggests, and its proportions' near Cistercian correctness makes one expect the nave to have shorter bays and, perhaps, sexpartite vaults like those in the Cathedral. This is not so. Outside, each nave wall displays five tall windows, with admirable tracery, and five gables or short roofs which run north to south. But, inside, the nave has only two-and-a-half bays, the full ones practically square and vaulted with the stars which came into use towards the middle of the fourteenth century; the aisles rise to the same height, and groups of tripartite 'Piast' vaults are used to match the system of windows and buttresses to the discord of the arcade. Something quite unclassical has occurred.

There is a precedent for the combination of apsed transepts and hall nave in the Elisabethkirche begun at Marburg in 1235, and św. Krzyż, with its altars dedicated to Piast saints, had a somewhat similar inspiration. Although there are fragments of a corbelled blank arcade, now hidden by the roof, on the south and east sides of the northern tower, the brickwork preserves no traces of any checks to building or changes in the plan. But it is hard to believe that there were none. The nave has nothing to do with thirteenth century Hesse: the piers which look like pieces cut from a wall, the new types of vault, above all the use of the 'Piast' scheme to match broad nave bays to narrow window units are all common to two other great Wrocław churches, one begun in the 1330's and the other in 1351. The most reasonable supposition is that work petered out around 1300, with duke Henry installed in the chancel, and was resumed only in the fresh wave of building enthusiasm aroused a generation later by the example of Casimir III in Cracow and Charles IV in Prague. Perhaps the builders wished to match their contemporaries' grand ideas, but had not the resources to extend westwards off the foundations provided by the lower church, and therefore had to accept the present truncated plan and produce what seems at first glance a quite different kind of interior. For the classical proportions of the early work were kept, and the smooth verticality of the detail combines with the physical breadth of the nave space to make it feel oddly directionless, nothing to do with the long elegant chancel. Now only a few scattered altarpieces inhabit this large, cool, white space.

The two churches I have mentioned were both built for regular canons. St. Mary 'na Piasku', on the sand, was begun in the 1330s, traditionally in 1334, for an Arroasian college, and part consecrated in 1369. Św. Dorota was founded in 1351 for Austin eremites by Charles IV himself and part consecrated in 1381. Both were complete about the turn of the century. They are very close contemporaries of the cathedral at Kwidzyn (Marienwerder) on the lower Vistula, wholly rebuilt between 1344 and 1355; though it uses the octagonal piers of Prussia instead of the Silesian slabs of wall, it too combines elaborate stars in the main vessel with 'Piast' vaults in the equally tall aisles. It is impossible to establish that any of these buildings – or św. Krzyż either – was far advanced before the others were planned, and against the apparent Prussian leadership in the arts of vaulting we must set the speed with which Wrocław and the country round picked up the 'Piast' idea from work done at Cracow in the 1320s. Though attempts to give him a name have ended in academic farce, we may guess that in the 1330s and 1340s Wrocław housed an architect familiar with the buildings of the Baltic coast and capable of conceptions as imaginative and as

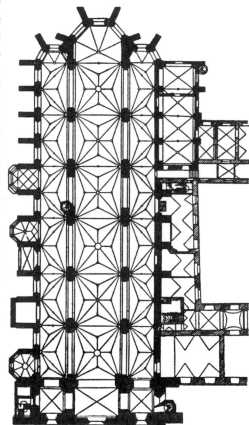

31 Wrocław: St. Mary 'na Piasku', 1:800

32　Wrocław: św. Dorota, section 1:800

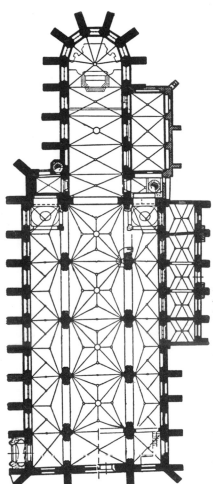

33　Wrocław: św. Dorota, plan 1:600

influential as those of Peter Parler a generation later in Prague.

St. Mary was completely gutted in 1945, but has been superbly restored. Its plan 49 is simple enough: the main vessel of six star-vaulted bays and a five-sided apse, the aisles half as broad, closed by three-sided apses, their bays adjusted to the breadth of those of the nave by their 'Piast' vaults. Walls are white plaster, pilasters and arch mouldings and aisle vaulting ribs red brick, the nave's stars grey stone; windows have tracery with all kinds of trefoils, quatrefoils, and wheels. The arcades are not so much part of an imaginary wall as in other Wrocław churches; they dominate by their proud rhythm and proportion, so that the whole space moves by great bounds to the high altar. And the aisle vaults, so bouncy and tricky when you look along them, from the nave seem only the natural complement of its stars, spreading their thrust on to the outside buttresses. This is the most majestic interior of all German brick church architecture. (See preceding page).

South of the church is the massive square of the Austin convent, later the University library, begun in 1709 perhaps by J. G. Kalkbrenner, without vertical organisation but handsomely divided into all sizes of window and wall panels and over the first floor windows displaying shells in sharp moulded forms as smart as anything in Prague. Over the road are more pretty remains; the former chapel of św. Anna, built late in the fourteenth century, afterwards a hospital, marked by a smart late Gothic entrance with two canted doorways separated by a projecting pillar; a plain convent of 1711, and beside it what remains of a gabled church built in 1688 as św. Jakub and rededicated to św. Anna later. But much is still rubble, and many of the fine trees which used to hang over the water are now lost.

To find our unknown master's work unharmed we must go down the Świdnicka to św. Dorota. To the street it presents an apse which is five sides of a decagon, slender 51 featured and imposing enough; but its size surprises most at a distance, for even now the huge roof and tall west gable can be seen high above the roofs on every side. Inside, the eye is rushed upwards, unhindered by the wall-like arcades, for this is the second tallest church in Wrocław and its tallest hall, more than eighty feet to the vault while the nave is only thirty broad. The simple vaults of the long chancel are rounder and more gentle, a deprecatory Bohemian gesture after this northern brilliance; Peter Parler's son came from Prague to work here. In Wrocław only St. Mary is more exciting. None of the contents match, and only the bombastic Spaetgen monument of 1753 even tries. The 'Piast' vaults find a last odd use in the church of Boże Ciało (Corpus Christi) which the knights of St. John began in the middle of the fourteenth century further down the street, inside the city's southern bastion. At first it had but a single vessel of three bays; the buttresses on what are now nave piers seem to have been those of external walls. Progressive enlargement up to the middle of the fifteenth century gave it seven bays in each low aisle to five in the nave, and the aisles were then vaulted with a maze of ribs in threes, the spring technique so ingeniously used that the eye hardly discerns the asymmetries of the plan. Disused after 1540, it is bare inside; but towards the street it sports an admirable brick gable of Prussian elaboration.

The earliest use of the star vault outside the great hall churches is in the crossing and transepts of the Dominicans' church of św. Wojciech (St. Adalbert). They took over the site in 1226, and in the generation after 1241 built a very plain cross plan church of which the aisleless nave and transepts remain. Early in the fourteenth century they lengthened their chancel and gave it an apse; it is a classic of its time, with central rose window and clumps of shafts corbelled into one and then fading into a plain bare wall. Nave and transept vaults were raised to match, and in 1492 the nave was extended westwards by one more bay and by Silesian standards a very rich gable. On the south side rise a slender tower and the chapel built in 1711 in honour of the first prior, the blessed Czesław, domed, rather dark, full of solid baroque stuff. Its builder, Müller, also added in 1717 the amorphous chapel of św. Józef north of the nave, where Polish services were held under German rule. A little to the north, a convent of Dominican nuns was founded in 1294, and in 1314 they began an odd ruined church of św. Katarzyna which had a two-naved lower storey and a single-naved upper one and presented a pretty baroque front to the street. The last preachers arrived in 1453, when a party of Observant Franciscans came under Capistrano to attack the Hussites. In 1463 they began św. Berndardyno, in the 'Nowe Miasto' east of św. Wojciech, and the oddly irregular nave was completed in 1502, one of the last Gothic churches of Silesia. It had nothing new to say, and in essentials is a typically hard and plain brick basilica, with the nave informed only by tall flat pilasters and refined star vaults. Of the convent there remain a net-vaulted west wing and, south of the chancel, a hall vaulted from one round pillar.

The original Franciscans had arrived like the Dominicans before 1240. But what we see of their church of św. Jakub, rededicated to św. Wincenty after its transfer to the Ołbin Premonstratensians in 1530, is mostly fourteenth century. There is not a flicker of display towards the market to the south, and, inside, the seventeenth century plaster does not conceal the plain earnestness underneath, no transepts, a tall narrow chancel. From the south aisle projects Hackner's Hochberg Chapel of 1723, three interlocked ovals with a central dome. Duchess Anna, the Franciscans' patroness, also founded about 1243, in imitation of Agnes Přemysl's foundation in Prague, the hospital and convent of the Knights of the Cross and Star which lies a couple of hundred yards west. Their church began in the thirteenth century as an aisleless box to which all kinds of parts, including transepts apsed like those of św. Krzyż, were added by instalments with no great final effect. Last of the city's remaining minor Gothic churches is św. Barbara by the west gate, an irregular object of the fourteenth and fifteenth centuries gutted in 1945 but distinguished by the pretty figure of the saint which stands under a twisting thistly stone canopy on one of the buttresses of its south-western tower.

Of the two great parish churches the older is św. Marie Magdalena. It should have been founded about 1226, when the Dominicans took over św. Wojciech, and there may be traces of the pre-Mongol church in the foundations of the northern tower. By about 1270 it seems to have been recreated, nine bays long, relatively low, and of this stage there is evidence all over the structure. The present building probably took shape between the great town fire of 1342 and the work on the vaults reported in 1359. The Silesian passion for the unbroken wall asserted itself again, for the nave piers that look so complex on the plan send up only the shallowest of pilaster strips and all the arches have sharp edges; the effect of a long rectangular box was heightened when in about 1470 the chancel was rebuilt as two bays double the length of those of the nave, closed by a straight east wall and a huge window full of tracery. Outside, the south wall presents the same uniformity, with ten practically identical chapels and porches built on around 1400; the north side is less regular, with the two-storeyed sacristy and library attached late in the fourteenth century; the same generation created the splendid slender western doorway. The one surprise is the south doorway to the chancel, wholly Romanesque, four orders, chevrons, twined foliage, figures of saints and of the damned, a resplendent work of the twelfth century brought from Ołbin when the Premonstra-tensians left and set up here in 1546. Of the monuments the church used to hold I could count only those on the outside walls, and I have had to describe the interior all from photographs and plans.

Its competitor św. Elżbieta (St. Elizabeth) was founded after 1241 and set in the usual place, a plot at the corner of the main square. After the fire of 1342 it was, like the Magdalena, wholly rebuilt; part at least could be consecrated in 1361 and in 1384 chapels were already being attached. It pushes the idea of the brick basilica a dramatic stage further. The means are the same as in the Magdalena, save for the three five-sided apses, but the dimensions are quite different, for the vaults reach not seventy-six feet above ground but eighty-eight, and the nave is practically three times as high as broad. It does not surprise one to discover that the nave arcades have both at one time or another fallen and been rebuilt. This sky-piercing ambition swells the tower too. Though its spire fell in 1529, it is one of the tallest of Gothic brick towers; and its stages increase in height as they go up, so that to the eyes of a spectator at the corner of the churchyard they should each subtend the same angle. Like other work of the late fourteenth century this is ruled by a new pressure for the greatest emotional effect; there are echoes of Prague, of the great south tower of the Cathedral and of the soaring interiors of Emauzy and Panna Marie Sněžná; but in the cold parsimony of detail we see the way Silesia was to go. In the war the church was little damaged, and inside it is now a lovely cool white space, still full of furniture and of monuments too numerous to describe. Up one pillar climbs the spiky superstructure of the tabernacle made in 1453 by Jodocus Tauchen; there are a fifteenth century font and gothic stalls, at least three fine gothic altars, and the Wolff monument put together in 1722, perhaps by Fischer von Erlach's son, to hold a fine Brokoff bust; across the west end spreads the huge organ built in 1750. Outside, the churchyard is now prettily approached by a baroque arch between two ancient gabled houses.

By 1500 the city possessed not only twenty-seven churches but also one of the showiest town halls in Europe. Outside its picturesque profusion bewilders, and to understand how it was built we must begin under the great roof which runs from the west tower to the richest of the eastern gables. This covers the area of the two-naved hall built in the third quarter of the thirteenth century, on a cellar most of which then rose above ground, and flanked by the present tower's base. In 1299 an oblong room was built across its east end to house the hereditary 'advocate' or bailiff whose jurisdiction the city shrugged off only in 1329. North of this a little tunnel-vaulted council chamber went on in 1328. Then between 1343 and 1357 the whole building was raised a storey, a central pillar set in the eastern room; vaults built in it, in the chapel above, and in the hall's northern nave; a new main entrance cut in the east wall; and the tower heightened. In the early fifteenth century more small rooms, north of the tower and west of the council chamber, were fitted into the space next to the market halls whose place has now been taken by rows of houses. And in 1440 they pushed out a miniature wing with two pert canted oriels to the south-east.

The last great building effort began in 1471 and lasted over thirty years. To set the building apart from Silesia's common brick the city brought load upon load of sandstone down from Złoty Stok on the Bohemian border. They started with the south-eastern corner building, a miniature tower with oriel and spire; the whole south and west side was pushed out, and ingenious brick-ribbed vaults with a rash of bosses set over all the broadened hall's three naves; then the east front fell to be remodelled, the chapel oriel was stuck on, and the flamboyant looking blank tracery and sixteen tiny flying buttresses above. There is a touch of the Renaissance in the

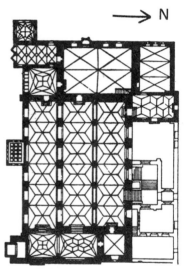

→ N

34   Wrocław: town hall, 1:800

doorway of the bailiff's room and in the pretty top put on the tower in 1558. But one neither can nor should describe the thing methodically, for this is true civic ostentation, so many showpieces stuck on as the means came to hand, looking like competition entries from the most practised masons of the late Gothic all over Saxony, Bohemia and Austria, thistly canopies and pinnacles over statues, brilliantly undercut friezes and panels of twirling vegetation, every silhouette unhesitatingly peppered with excrescences. At first the inside is surprisingly plain, the ground floor cold, the stairs modern, but upstairs there are doorways as elaborate as the windows outside, and filigree nets and stars cover the south-eastern rooms. As a whole it is nowhere near the impassive majesty of Toruń but, if you do not worry too much which parts are which, what fun.

All around it the evidence is being revived – with imagination and some invention – of how, as church building petered out, secular pride took over. The tallest houses are on the west side of the square, 'pod Gryfami' at no.2 with the gables Gross built between 1587 and 1592, the 'Seven Electors' at no.8, baroque of 1672 in front but hiding a courtyard in parts as old as 1503; on the east a modern replica of 'pod Złota Korona' raises a grand attic supposed to match that begun in 1521; scattered sixteenth century doorways survive all round and in the battered neighbouring streets. And there are surprises: an oriel of 1496 in the priests' house facing the east end of the Magdalena, a wooden statue of God the Father on a corner in the Mikołajska, and, inside the building on the corner of the Szewska and the plac Nankera, the late fourteenth century vaults of the town house of the Piast dynasty of Opole. There would be more but for the destruction of 1945; still, hardly so much that the city deserves complete reconstruction in the manner of Warsaw and Gdańsk. It was bizarre to see invented Renaissance gables going up in plastered brick.

In 1638 the Jesuits came; in 1659 they received a site in the remains of the old left bank castle; in 1689 they began their church of the Name of Jesus which now confusingly shares a dedication to św. Maciej with its next neighbour to the east. The Baroque was rapidly to transform the whole convent-crowded area of the twelfth century fortified town. Św. Maciej is the standard article, broad nave, chapels, galleries, begun by Matthias Biener, completed by his son-in-law J. G. Knoll. But inside it is dignified by splendid illusionist frescoes painted in 1705 by J. M. Rottmayr, the Viennese collaborator of Fischer von Erlach, which fill the whole rectangle of the nave with a swirling throng of saints, and by the sculpture and stucco work done by Christoph Tausch when he remodelled the chancel in the 1720s. To the north there remains still a little stone sacristy once part of the thirteenth century castle. Around 1700 Knoll rebuilt the Ursuline convent two blocks away; it is now a pleasant, irregular, much truncated group with an odd church which has two unequal naves for the nuns and for the laity. Further east the Premonstratensians' convent was rebuilt between 1682 and 1697 as an immense round-cornered three-storeyed pilastered box by Hans Frölich from Opava in Maravia; it recalls such late seventeenth century bombast as the Moravian archbishops' palace at Kroměříž, but in its courtyard the grandiose scheme is livened by surprising decorative inventions – shells, feathers, and so forth – in the harshly drawn window heads.

One building set a much higher standard. In 1675 the Knights began a new quadrangle in the north part of their space between Ursulines and Jesuits. Work went slowly; the river front was going up in the 1700s, the whole not finished until 1715. Various names of little repute appear in the records, but is is tempting to accept the belief that they got the plans from Jean Baptiste Mathey, the French

architect of their handsome church beside the Charles Bridge in Prague. It is as pretty
as anything else he did, three wings of three storeys, of which two present admirably
handled convex and concave sided gables to the river, and one low fourth wing, just
one banded storey and one of pilaster panels and a balustrade, above which a small
octagon rises to a dome. Its crispness and gentleness put the rest to shame. Here the
Ossolineum, the ancient library of the University of Lwów, has found a place to rest.

The greatest undertaking of all was the Jesuit College which is now the University. 5(
It was planned about 1700. But the first wing, the long range which runs west along
the river from the central gateway, was built only between 1728 and 1733, mostly by
J. B. Peintner; it is sheer repetition save for the central 'tower', which rises no higher
than the roofline, and for the absurd lantern. In 1740 Joseph Frisch completed an
east wing which extended the river front to a stunning thirty-eight bays. It was
followed by a handsome little south wing joined to the church by a two-storey vestibule.
The effects of this mass of plaster are wholly opportunist and not notably picturesque,
save for snatches of pretty detail, the sculptured doorway and balcony in the centre
of the main south front, the light and shade of the end wall of the south wing. The
interior offers some compensations – a double stair, long corridors with delicate
plastered and painted domes, the Aula Lepoldina decorated in 1731 by Mangold with 5'
stucco and by Handke with paint, a riot of caryatids and shaky amorini and standing
emperors amid the darkest architecture. The protectors of learning represented include
Frederick II of Prussia. In ten years he was to seize all Silesia. The province was
taxed and conscripted to keep Prussia a Great Power, and building languished. The
Jesuits began a plain seminary south of the church in 1734 and could not finish it
till 1755. And Silesia never produced a great architect of the Baroque.

Prussian royalty came to Silesia often enough, but left little mark on Wrocław.
The Royal Palace began with the adaptation of the Spätgen house, whose pleasant
courtyard begun in 1750 by Jan Boumann faces north to the Kazimierza Wielkiego,
flanked by his pretty Lutheran church of 1747 with its gabled front and galleried oval
preaching room, an example of half rococo reticence which helped to redirect Silesian
taste. But the one attempt at grandeur, the vast featureless south wing built in 1846
by Schinkel's dull pupil Stüler, is now an empty shell, and the parade ground which
it faces a car park. Other palaces have fared as badly, worst of all the Hatzfeld house
in the Wita Stwosza, begun in 1765 by K. G. Langhans, which combined still rococo
interiors with classical façade and courtyard; to see the family's work we have to find
the Pachal house in the Szajnochy, grimly refronted by his son K. F. Langhans in
1810, and north of the river the church of the 11,000 Maidens (Jedenastu Tysięcy
Dziewic), with an uninspired *Rundbogenstil* front of 1821 and a big dome carried inside
on arcades over galleries. K. F. Langhans also designed in 1824 the Old Bourse
(Stara Giełda) on the south side of the Płac Solny and in 1843 the Theatre in the
Świdnicka, both pleasant enough but below Berlin standards of distinction. My
nineteenth century favourite is the Main Station Grapow designed in 1856, lively, !
picturesque, rhetorical, in an unscholarly Gothic with turrets and battlements and
detached pavilions and a main entrance which is a delicate chicane of cast-iron
pillars.

In the twentieth century the city pushed to the frontiers of architecture again.
Hans Poelzig, Professor of Architecture here from 1903 to 1916, created a 'workshop
school' which was one of the powerhouses of the 'expressionist' architcture of part of
the Deutscher Werkbund. Of his own work there survives the 'stripped classical'
exhibition buildings of 1910 in the east of the city off the Curie-Sklodowskiej. In the

59 midst of them swells the immense Hala Stulecia (Jahrhunderthalle) designed at the
same time by his pupil Max Berg; the whole structure is 315 feet in diameter, and
within it six huge arches describe a circle 220 feet across which is covered by a dome
described by thirty-two concrete ribs. It is an enormously solemn space, the boldest
use of reinforced concrete before Nervi. Just as German industry was then leaping
ahead with steel and synthetic dyes while England clung to coal and cotton, so we see
German architects, many of them inspired by Victorian England, leave behind the
ebbing confidence of the England of Lutyens and Blomfield.

This leadership was kept up between the wars. In 1927 Erich Mendelsohn built the
60 Petersdorff store, now a clothes shop, at the corner of the Oławska and the Szewska;
like his Schocken stores in Nuremberg and Stuttgart it is all horizontals, bands of
glass and concrete, projecting sills and cornices and a rounded corner dramatically
cantilevered out, and unlike them it has been mercifully preserved. And in the park
behind the Hala Stulecia, at the junction of the Kopernika and the Dembowskiego,
61 can be found the hostel which Hans Scharoun built for a housing exhibition in 1929,
now half hidden in trees, a school for factory inspectors. It has two roughly aligned
three-storey wings, one of them slightly curved and with balconies facing the sun,
linked by an irregular group of entrance and service spaces. There are porthole
openings in the balconies' flanks, and the north fronts alternate thin continuous
window strips with little window holes punched in the cement; at first glance one
simply cannot guess how many floors there may be inside. The master's wilfulness
is already very clear. It at least has found no imitators in the steady revival of building
standards since 1960; there is no time to be more than workmanlike. But the neat
recreation of, for instance, the Nowy Targ market-place shows that such workmanlike
design has its rewards.

4. Silesia

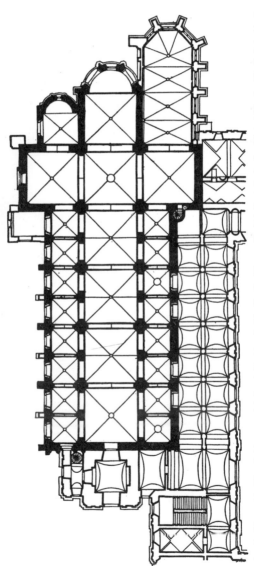

35 Trzebnica: abbey church 1:625

All round Wrocław the ploughed acres roll away, north and east into bird-filled marshes, south into the grand hills of the Czech border. This is one of the favoured provinces of central Europe; Frederick the Great knew it. It is as rich in fine buildings as all of Little Poland, yet hardly anything of value is beyond a day's round drive from Wrocław in a heavy car. By the beginning of the thirteenth century flocks of colonists were settling here from Germany and the Low Countries, creating massive farmhouses that present blind whitewashed gables to their village streets. But for the Mongols we might have had a solid inheritance of Romanesque building. As it is, Silesian town churches form a peculiarly coherent group of fourteenth and fifteenth century brick buildings, products of a local tradition quickly created and slow to give way before late mediaeval ideas. Nowhere in central Europe did the basilica hold out longer against the hall. Then, with the Renaissance, Silesia declines into an undistinguished picturesqueness; the best baroque works are in truth outposts of Bohemian design; only the romantic castles of Prussian royalty bring her to the front again.

The first stone buildings we have any remnants of are little round buildings, modelled on those on the Hrad in Prague and on the Wawel in Cracow. The best documented is in the earnest looking town of Cieszyn (Teschen), distinguished 6: otherwise only by moderate eighteenth and nineteenth century buildings around a market-place; it stands on the old castle site, now a park that overlooks the river and the Czech frontier post, and has both an internal gallery and a semi-circular apse, much restored but probably in origin eleventh century. There are some box-like parish churches. Only foundations remain under the baroque of that at Sobótka (Zobten), but it incorporates one of the splendid granite lions which go back to the earliest lodgments of Chrisianity round the heathen holy hill of Ślęża. A little to the west at Wierzbna (Würben) a tiny grey sandstone church, with two square towers of remarkable presence, survives as the entrance of the present one. There are slightly more elaborate thirteenth century stone churches at Świerzawa (Schönau), where the 'lower church' has an apse with columned windows and a leaf carved west doorway now inside the tower, and at Gościszów (Giessmannsdorf) where columns are awkwardly set at the corners of the three-sided apse. And that really is all.

Building of an international standard arrived with the Cistercians who came from Saxony in 1175 to take over an abortive Polish foundation at Lubiąz (Leubus) on the Odra. But almost nothing remains of their first church there. Their influence begins with the foundation in 1203 by Henry I and his wife święta Jadwiga (St. Hedwig) of (the nunnery at Trzebnica (Trebnitz), which came under Cistercian rule in 1218. By (

1219, it seems, most of the great church could be consecrated; a Cistercian cross, short apsed chancel carried on a crypt above the falling ground, a chapel to each transept, a nave of four big bays with sexpartite vaults and twice as many bays in the aisles. In plan and details it is singularly eclectic; everywhere round and pointed forms combine, the vertical proportions go right back to French abbeys like Pontigny, the sculpture recalls work on the upper Rhine, the dimensions of the plan come from central Germany, and the now lost western narthex, altogether unusual, follows closely that begun about 1210 at Maulbronn. It has been much altered. In 1754 the sculptor Mangold was let loose to fit it up with opera-box nuns' galleries round the transepts, stalls, altars, pulpit, two large cheerful figures of św. Elżbieta (St. Elizabeth) and św. Jadwiga; the huge west tower continued till 1785 to rise where the narthex had been. But the original leafed and columned doorways and their carved tympana survive on the north transept and half hidden behind the north flank of the tower, and inside the rhythms of the massive piers and the domed vaults run clear under all the plasterwork. The church seems to have survived the Mongols with little injury and, as the plan and dimensions of the chancel of Wrocław Cathedral show, it set the standards for thirteenth century building.

36 Trzebnica: chapel of św. Jadwiga

Święta Jadwiga died in 1248 and was canonised in 1267. A new south transept chapel was built in her honour, probably in the next ten years; the size and odd shape of the northern buttress of its apse has suggested that the builders may have planned to open out the whole east end of the church. They worked in stone, and in a graceful, sophisticated manner, with dozens of slender verticals reaching to a surprisingly rounded vault, which recalls contemporary Hesse and the Rhineland. After the heavy approaches, the convent begun in 1697 with its pilasters on pilasters, the tower whose bulk almost conceals the church, the Romanesque gravity of the nave, this confection is as refreshing as a water ice. In its centre rises the huge dark marble tomb made for the saint in 1679. The light floods in high above and all around. Delicacy and transparency like this are rare in this brick province.

The oldest Cistercian men's church that remains is at Henryków (Heinrichau) south of Wrocław. The convent was founded in 1222, the eldest daughter of Lubiąż; Romanesque columns have been dug out of the southern walls of the present church, which we must assume was begun after the Mongols had gone. In many dimensions its plan is very close to Trzebnica. But its elevations are all Gothic. The nave is classical enough, a little more than twice as high as broad, but by comparison the aisles are uncommonly tall, forty feet or two-thirds of the nave. It seems that like the Order's German churches of the same generation, such as Walkenried, Henryków may once have had an eastern ambulatory where there are now only the ante-rooms of rococo chapels, and the effect must almost have been that of a hall church. The details of the masonry which informs the usual brick are rough; put up rapidly and simply, this must be the first major church completed in Silesia after 1241. (See overleaf).

Today the surroundings are charming; village and abbey folded together in the green valley; a gateway, comfortably wide for the car, above which two saints survey the village street; then a big courtyard with trees, storehouses, a fountain, and an immense and unprepossing plague column of 1715. The convent is a large block with jolly corner turrets in the repetitious and awkward baroque of the 1680s; the west end of the church sports a scrolled and pedimented gable in the same manner, while in front of it a domed entrance chapel looks a generation more sophisticated; a huge plain buttressed tower dominates all. Inside, the church's cool grave lines are enlivened by all sorts of work done at the end of the seventeenth century. In the aisles hang five big dark semi-circular paintings of the life of Jesus done mostly between 1676 and 1678 by Michael Willman, the superb artist we shall meet again at Lubiąż and **Krzeszów**. Best of the usual furnishings are the fantastic choir stalls, Dehio's description '*recht unruhig*' an understatement for these contrapposto Fathers. The east end now leads into three decent domed chapels, of which one holds a good mid-fourteenth century monument to Bolko II of Ziębice. The pretty sacristy still keeps the monstrance Christian Menzel made in 1671 in the shape of a Tree of Jesse. And to the north of the chancel two sixteenth century chapels open out, in the most elegant of latest Gothic, one vaulted by ribs spreading from a central pillar.

At Lubiąż the Cistercians rebuilt later; they were at work on the present church in 1307 and may have consecrated it in 1340. They kept to the established rules and their plan, possibly older than the present building, matches the dimensions of Wrocław and Cracow Cathedrals. But their elevations are superbly elegant. The nave is only twice as high as broad, but one would think it higher because of the shortness of the bays and the steepness of the vaults. The new ideas of the fourteenth century break in with star vaults in the transepts and with a very pretty north-eastern chapel with three apses, by contrast sheer self indulgence, yet the result of a foundation made as early as 1312. The baroque turned the aisle arcades into processions of solid round arches but did little other harm. But the Russian occupation after 1945 was shattering. Old photographs show stalls which riot with sculpture like those at Henryków and the great gory paintings of martyrdoms to which Willmann set his hand when he came to settle here in 1660. He had been born in 1630 in Königsberg, a city better known for metal work; had travelled in the Low Countries and caught the eye of the Great Elector in Berlin; secure in the abbot's patronage, he lived at Lubiąż from his conversion to Catholicism to his death in 1706. Now all it can show of his are the tiny scenes from the lives of St. Benedict and St. Bernard he painted in fresco in 1691 on the domes of the corner spaces in the eastern ambulatory, and how fresh and pleasant they are – a whisper of Tiepolo. All else is gone; I saw carved fragments, arms, legs, heads, piled in a transept; and a tablet ironically described the place as '*Wiedererstanden unter dem Kanzler Hitler* 1934'.

In 1672 the abbey undertook a rebuilding plan as ambitious as any of the dreams the high tide of counter-Reformation conjured up. Two great courtyards, 400 feet deep, were to flank the church to north and south, making a west front 750 feet long. There was some economy on decoration; the only accent is the conventional two-towered front of the church, with its lanterns and its stepped pilasters; all the rest is inexpensive shallow panelling. Construction petered out in 1729, but furnishing went on inside. In 1962 I found the south wing an inaccessible storehouse; it should contain the refectory with paintings of 1733 by F. A. Scheffler surrounded by painted illusions of rococo plaster and the library with small carved bookcases and an immense and all-embracing ceiling painting done between 1734 and 1738 by C. P. Bentum. At the same time Bentum painted the ceiling of the spacious Sala Rycerska (Fürstensaal) which occupies two storeys at the east end of the north wing. I could hardly see his work, for the windows had been painted over and only a few were broken; it seemed full of damp and in the middle gaped a hole. All round stood huge white statues, heroes, empresses, emperors trampling Turks into the ground, made strangely expressive by a chiaroscuro of fine grey dust. Lubiąż was once a madhouse, and now seems the greatest of follies.

The other Cistercian churches in Silesia have little original character. Of Lubiąż' daughters, Kamieniec was rebuilt as the least monachal of halls and Krzeszów is

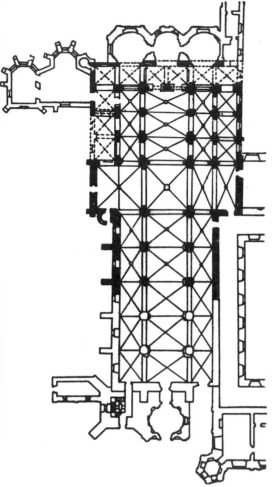

37   Henryków: abbey church 1:800

wholly baroque. We have mentioned Rudy (Rauden), a child of Jedrzejów, a dark disappointment with its over restored interior and silly unproportioned front of about 1790. Its child Jemielnica (Himmelwitz) has an odd little fourteenth century basilica with no transepts and an apse; everything was plastered over after a fire in 1733. By the middle of the fourteenth century, Cistercian building had lost its individuality.

In the thirteenth century towns appeared all over the province. Some, like Kłodzko, Legnica, Racibórz, grew up beside existing castles, the seats of government. Of the others the oldest lie along the old road from Dresden and Görlitz to Legnica and Wrocław. Men came to Złotorya (Goldberg) and Lwówek (Löwenberg) to seek gold in their rivers; the first received German town law in 1211, the second in 1217. Wrocław itself followed some time between 1215 and 1226. And between it and Legnica, Środa Śląska (Neumarkt) was laid out in 1214, one of the first planned towns of Europe, twenty years younger than Wiener Neustadt which it much resembles – a formal rectangle of walls, but the market place still easily enough recognised as the old village street. Its church still has its Romanesque nave, early brick building of about 1200; at one end rises a vile nineteenth century façade, at the other the tall chancel begun in 1388 with an elegance worthy of Wrocław. At Złotorya the stone church still has a columned south doorway and sections of wall older than 1241, and its eastern parts were rebuilt close to their old plan, apse and all; but around 1300 a new nave went up, four bays, rich in shafts, low but roomy in proportions, a small country masterpiece of building in the Cistercian manner. Later work, like the galleries put in in 1609, blurs the effect, but there are more good doorways, and the lanterns on the east and west towers add to the little town's quaint picture. In places like these which have kept the streets they had before the Mongols came we see villages tidied up; the many chessboard plans, of which Namysłów (Namslau) is an example, belong to the next generation.

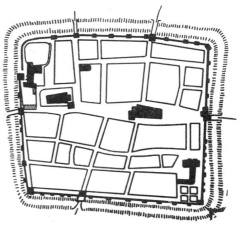

38   Środa Śląska: town plan

Lwówek (Löwenberg) had something of this grand formal character. Its walls are almost complete, with a western stretch beside the Baszta Lubańska which is roofed and galleried and all. Just behind them rises the great stone front of the church, an almost windowless rectangle of Romanesque solidity from which two octagonal towers rise in the manner of Brunswick and Magdeburg. The carved columned doorway with the Coronation of the Virgin added late in the thirteenth century still stands. But inside it is a desert. In the 1860s the once elegant hall church was robbed of every other pillar in its nave, and a flat ceiling set over all but apses and chapels; the misguided space this made is certainly large, but evidence of only the most perverse sort of imagination. The rest of the town has suffered abominably in war. In 1962 a few old houses stood here and there among the ruins, notably in the square and the Kościelna, and in one alley old stone arches braced the houses apart. But in the centre still rises an immense slender tower, marking what is after Wrocław the most exciting town hall in Silesia. After a fire in 1518 it seems very likely that the town turned to the master builder at Görlitz, Wendel Rosskopf, a man who, like Benedict Ried at Prague, commanded both a sophisticated Gothic and a crude early Renaissance; the bust of a mason set in a wall inside may be that of his assistant Hans Richter. They created within the plain mediaeval block a series of rooms, now a kawiarnia, vaulted like halls at Meissen and Prague with ribs which describe loops and ovals and in the eastermost rise from one shaft like leaves from a stalk. And they framed its southern windows with pilasters and friezes most barbarically carved, shown up by the far more Italianate detail of the first floor oriel added in 1546. It is a rich showpiece for so small a place.

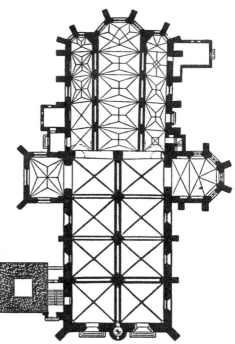

39   Ziębice: church, 1:715

The best surviving thirteenth century parish church building in Silesia is the nave at Ziębice (Münsterberg). Work must have started on it at once when the town was 67 founded in 1252. Outside it looks a muddle, mostly brick but for the rough stone tower. But the west end has two rose windows side by side, and the nave proves to be two naves separated by three becolumned, richly solid stone pillars. All the arches are heavy, the vaults seem tall almost pointed domes. In all but a few details the colonists had brought this architecture from Westphalia with them. In the late fifteenth century the town began to rebuild, but only completed the chancel. It is basilican; the outside walls continue the old lines, making everything very narrow, and the aisle vaults rise to the height of the old nave, making everything very high; it has three apses, star vaults, and the usual Silesian emphasis on the wall. It excites by the shock of its pillars facing the centre of the old naves and the contrast of its light with their dark. It is sad to find the double nave, so expressive in Bohemia, here so rare; only a handful of village churches, like Bystrzyca Kłodzka (Habelschwerdt), have it.

Racibórz (Ratibor) was the seat of a local ruler at the southern end of the province long before it got a charter in 1299. South-east of the square, the parish church has a most elegant chancel of about 1300, besides a late gothic nave with plaster vaults, a mass of jolly rustic furniture of the seventeenth century, and a monstrous modern tower. West of the square the town museum occupies the hall church the Dominicans built, also in about 1300; on the square itself a row of houses has been rebuilt with Renaissance attics and the war has spared the plague column of 1723. The town's jewel lies across the river in Ostróg, in what used to be the castle and since 1859 has been a brewery. It hides the chapel of St. Thomas à Becket founded in 1288 jointly with 6 św. Krzyż in Wrocław. It is simple: two-and-a-half bays, odd arcaded niches round the walls too small to have been seats, and shafts that run right up to sexpartite vaults. There are some parallels with work in Wrocław, but most of all this elegant little room recalls the royal chapels, like Zvíkov and Bezděz, of contemporary Bohemia.

Legnica (Liegnitz) became in time the second city of Silesia, fortified as early as 1000, the seat of a Piast family down to 1675. But it has really nothing left so ancient. In 1333 the citizens made a contract with master Wiland to begin the rebuilding of their chief church, św. św. Piotr a Paweł. He may not have got further than the south tower; work continued until the close of the century, parallel with that on the parish churches of Wrocław. The plan is close to that of św. Elżbieta; three apses, three bay chancel, a longer bay for punctuation, but the nave has three long bays with two cross vaults to each arch. The elevation is strange: aisles so tall the rows of chapels seem like further aisles beyond them, and only a windowless space between nave arcade and vault, whose ribs spring from corbels along a string course just above the arcade's points. It would look like a hall but for the usual wall-like shapes of the arcade. The aisles burst into spring vaults as they go east, with odd consequences for the southern apse. How the church got like this we cannot be certain; the vaults are mostly sixteenth century replacements, and in 1893 the whole was so rudely restored by Johann Otzen that from outside it seems so much shiny neo-gothic. There are many decent epitaphs and a south chapel with an elaborate vault. It is sad that the whole is not more inspiring.

Alongside stands the little town hall of 1737, with concave sided tower and curved flights of steps, decorated in green, yellow, and dirty orange, but still pretty. To the north a line of miniature sixteenth century houses, much restored, makes one side of the square. There are eighteenth century fronts to the east in the Rosenbergów. But the best group of baroque buildings lies to the north-west around the Jesuits' great church. The ulica św. Jana runs up to it between the Nobles' College of 1726, large and honest, and the house of the abbots of Lubiąz of 1734 with its pretty sculptured doorway. The end of the street is closed by the Jesuit College itself, begun in 1700, its nice bulging doorway dated 1706. Św. Jan lies just to one side, on the site the Franciscans used to occupy; of their church only part of the chancel remains, converted in 1677 to an oval domed mausoleum for the last Piasts' brass sarcophagi which now opens off the Jesuits' south aisle. The first plan for the new church was made in 1700 by J. G. Knoll, who had completed the Society's church in Wrocław. But the interior – the bulging piers with superimposed pilasters, the swing of the galleries, and even more the first vaults, with broad band-like arches dividing them into domes, which were replaced after they fell by the present inexpressive ceiling – all belongs to the inheritance of the great Jesuit church Christopher Dienzenhofer began in 1703 in Prague. And in fact work did not start until 1714, after Knoll's death. In 1727 Martin Frantz, one of the Dientzenhofers' chief Silesian imitators, completed the two huge towers, which speak the same language: concave sides, two fragments of a bulging balcony over the doorway, crisp windows from the Borromini vocabulary.

The town's third church is St. Mary at the east end of the old centre. In 1828 Schinkel rebuilt it as a big-box line brick hall, rather like the Friedrich-Werdersche Kirche he began in 1824 in Berlin; all sharp horizontals made by parapets and string courses, and fronted by a rectangular mass topped by two small towers just like Lwówek. And in 1835 the old crumbling sixteenth century castle with its pilastered courtyard was replaced by a long, hard neo-gothic block designed in his office; only the two tall, round mediaeval brick towers were left. The dry strictness of the design, the rectangular windows in rows, the unconvicing irregularities, leave plain the neo-classical bones under the Gothic beard. It makes a second-rate ruin, but in its surviving east gate is preserved one very early showpiece of the Piast Renaissance. It is dated 1532, and may be the work of Georg von Amberg; three shockingly ornate and disproportioned columns, an entablature with arms and medallions of princes, none of that tasteful Italianising that went on in Bohemia: a brutish German job.

To find this Renaissance in full fig we must turn to the Piast capital next in importance, Brzeg (Brieg). Here a complete rebuilding of the mediaeval castle began in 1535 and left untouched little more than the simple, tall apsed chapel of about 1370. Its show-piece is the gateway of 1552, a feast of applied Italian detail; three storeys, two entrances, restlessly carved pilasters applied with many a solecism; above the second storey, the bearded and hatted busts of twenty-four Piast rulers in relief along a double frieze; in the centre, a huge coat-of-arms flanked by free standing figures of Jerzy II and his wife. This object of fun is also the target of experts' attempts to prove its proportions as correct as anything in Cracow. Certainly its builder, Jacopo 'Parr' or 'Bahr', came from Milan. He first appeared in Brzeg in 1547, and he remodelled much else of the castle, giving its windows neat rectangular surrounds, its courtyard arcades which survive only in a corner, some of its rooms plaster ceilings to match the cruder doorways of the 1530s. The whole group has suffered much in wars and has been adapted as a museum.

Parr also built the Gymnasium on the south side of the little castle square, whose doorway bears arms and the date 1569. The Jesuits' pretty little church nearby, now used by the parish, was begun only in 1735 by Joseph Frisch, got its towers in 1856, and inside is content with architectural spaces painted all up the front and and across the ceiling; a very grand chancel that would be, if it really had a dome. And in 1570, after a fire, Parr and his son-in-law Bernardo 'Niuron' from Lugano began to rebuild the town hall. Its gables and its partly wooden arcades along the west front look festive in the ruined square. This became a dynasty of builders; of Parr's five sons, Francesco built the great house at Güstrow in Mecklenburg and worked for John III of Sweden at Uppsala and Stockholm, while Christoforo appears at Nyköping, and Giovanni Battista at Borgholm, Kalmar, and, if ambigious records can be trusted, at the fortress of Kexholm, now Priozersk, on Lake Ladoga, the confines of Russia. Careers like their show how international the emigrant Italian builders were, and how readily they adapted to their patron's tastes – to Polish panache and German arrogance and the cool fastidiousness of the Czech nobility.

The plan of mediaeval Brzeg is another checkerboard of streets, fixed in 1250 and two thirds laid waste by war. South of the square, in the Mleczna, the Jabłkowa, and the Armii Czerwonej, a few old houses stand, and on the north side of the square a modern block intelligently embraces a pretty baroque doorway. Above them towers the parish church, św. Mikołaj. It was begun at the west end in 1370; a contract of 70 1371 specified that master Günther should model the window tracery on that of św. Krzyż in Wrocław; in 1383 masters Heinrich and Peter were entrusted with the removal of the old chancel and the building of the new; contracts were exchanged for the chancel vaults in 1414 and for those of the nave in 1416. The plan was crude, a nave of five short oblong star-vaulted bays followed by a chancel of three longer practically square ones and an apse. But the dimensions were unequalled, for the nave is 27 feet wide and 95 feet tall, three-and-a-half times as much. The restorers have left it all the usual white plaster and red brick, but it is made more expressive than its contemporaries by its pilaster strips and the sunken panels that hold its immensely tall clerestory windows. These expanses of clear glass make it far too light, a steep narrow corridor to heaven.

Of the chief towns in Silesia, Świdnica (Schweidnitz) is left. There is no record of its foundation, nothing to prove that its almost regular plan is other than chance. It suffered much in the wars of the seventeenth and eighteenth centuries, little in the last. Its old houses, unusually in Silesia, are mostly country baroque, undistinguished on the square apart from the smart and pretty house of the Hochberg family at no.25, surprisingly elaborate elsewhere as at no.24 in the Pułaskiego to the north-east and no.16 in the Świerczewskiego to the north-west. In the Marksa there is an attractive Ursuline church begun in 1739, and odd remnants of history persist on the western edge of the old town: a doorway of 1537 from the castle embedded in a Capuchin convent, and a bastion with a little chapel of św. Barbara attached. The town hall was much reshaped after a fire in 1716, but the baroque fronts and the pretty chapel oriel conceal a mediaeval structure and Renaissance doors, and above it rises a tall, slender tower whose octagonal body, right up to the balustrade, was built in the fifteenth century and topped up in 1548 and 1734. There are works of sculpture in the square all round, the usual plague column, four fountains of which the best bears a Neptune made in 1732 by a local sculptor, Johann Leonhard Weber.

The Thirty Years' War brought the town one strange gift, the Peace Church (Kościół Pokoju, Friedenskirche). In the treaties of 1648 the Emperor Ferdinand III conceded to his Protestant subjects in Silesia the right to build churches at Świdnica, Jawor, and Głogów on condition that they should have no solid foundations and lie a cannon-shot beyond the walls. Nothing is left of that at Głogów. Both the others were built by Albrecht Saebisch, son of a Wrocław engineer, and that at Świdnica, though begun in 1656 and younger as well as smaller, is the finer one. It lies to the north, up the Kościelna which prolongs the Bohaterów Ghetta, hidden among great trees in an ample churchyard; in a cottage on the south side I found a Norwegian organist who kept the key. At first one can gauge nothing of its size, confronted by so much exposed timbering and by the ring of chapels of all shapes, and countless doors, all dappled by the ceaseless movement of the leaves. But the cross shaped space inside is packed with galleries, so that there is room for 3,000 to sit and another 4,500 to stand. Generations of proud, determined burghers carved and painted everything, arms of guilds, portraits of benefactors, a great organ of 1666, a little one of 1695 opposite it above the towering altar of 1752, a jolly pulpit of 1729, and in one transept the opera-box made in 1698 for the Hochbergs, the church's princely protectors who had given 2,000 oaks towards the building. It is quiet and disregarded now, but smells in a peculiar pleasant way of wood.

At the town's south-eastern corner the parish church rises from the hillside, high above the main road junction. The present building went up after its predecessor was burnt in 1313, probably in the second half of the fourteenth century, fast enough to put a roof on in 1385. Like św. Elżbieta in Wrocław it is a basilica with three apses; they are built out over a crypt where the ground slopes, and put on a splendid show of Silesian verticality – four endless stepped buttresses, two stair turrets, five tall slender windows. 250 feet away rise the stone west front and the 340 foot tower whose un-Silesian square stone body and octagonal upper stage were completed only in 1525 by Peter Zehin from Annaberg in Saxony. The vaults inside once stood 105 feet high, out-topping Brzeg, but in 1532 they fell, and one Lukas Schleierweber blocked up the clerestory and put in a much lower series of restless three-dimensional stars. The space is blurred further by the rows of chapels, some high as the aisles, and the accumulation of rich dark furniture. In the distance one discerns a huge columned and statued high altar arrangement by Jan Riedel, a Silesian who studied abroad and worked in the church off and on from 1690 to 1735; and the fine organ angels and saints along the nave pillars are the work of Johann Leonhard Weber from 1704 to 1710. Of its generation, this is the most sumptuous decorative effort in the province. But in the upper part of a big south chapel the light falls on an altar of the Death of Mary, made in 1492 almost certainly in the Stoss workshop in Cracow, and the best thing here.

We have a clue elsewhere to the chief author of this church. Nine miles from Świdnica lies the in comparison tiny town of Strzegom (Striegau). It was the seat of a Commandery of the Knights of St. John. In the second half of the fourteenth century they too caused the parish church they used to be rebuilt, and, encouraged by a convenient quarry, they built wholly in stone. The records show heavy payments between 1382 and 1390 to one Jakob who is to be found, described as a builder, in the Świdnica town records between 1377 and 1391. At Strzegom as at Świdnica we find three eastern apses with enormously tall, thin windows separated by a pair of stair turrets. In most other respects the Silesian brick vocabulary is just translated into stone, with the wall still triumphant over the arcade and the usual flat pilaster strips in place of shafts; and the drive on and up is just as strong, the nave a fraction longer than Świdnica, and only 31 feet wide although 87 high. Yet, unlike its fellows, the church has fully developed transepts and displays decorative sculpture of excellent quality, the tympanum of the north doorway, the west doorway with its sharp pinnacles and crowded figures which recall the work of the Parler school in Prague. And in the nave the net vaults follow closely those, probably of English inspiration, which Parler designed for Prague Cathedral, while those of the chancel use his principles to produce a scissor pattern such as we find in the churches that follow

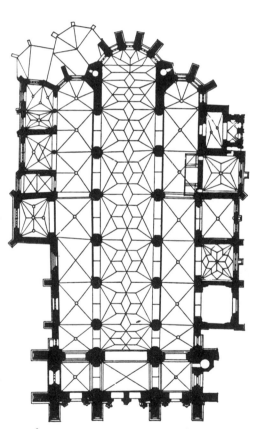

40 Świdnica: parish church, 1:780

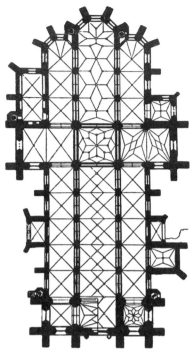

41   Strzegom: church, 1:900

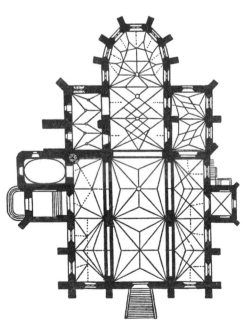

42   Paczków: church, 1:600

Prague traditions at Landshut and Maastricht. There is almost no furniture. Everything is greyish white or grey. The big cool space reposes in an absolute confidence that stone must be more graceful than brick. And its steep-roofed bulk dominates not only the little town but miles of the surrounding countryside.

Czech influence combines with stone again in the great church which Arnošt z Pardubic, archbishop of Prague, founded, just before his death in 1362, at Kłodzko (Glatz), which used to be the capital of a half independent country within his diocese. Outside it is all ashlar, with flowered niches and window heads and elaborate coats-of-arms on the chancel walls. But inside the early fifteenth century body is all but lost; the vault is a net of 1555, and about 1670 Prague builders moved in again and covered the walls up to the vaults' spring with low quality plaster architecture. In 1727 Tausch put in a well designed three-dimensional high altar; and archbishop Arnošt is commemorated as a neo-mediaeval lump of marble complacency. The town's character is mostly in its fortress site on a rock above the eastern Nysa, but many houses have eighteenth century plaster fronts, and a bridge that dates from 1390 is ranged with statues in the manner of Prague.

Of the remaining basilican town churches, that of Chojnów (Haynau) west of Legnica is all one piece, five tall bays and an apse, proportions nice enough for Strzegom, the thick Silesian arcades, well shaped star vaults of 1468, and a jolly Renaissance pulpit; its distinction is its single tower, a buttressed brick square of fortress seriousness which suddenly ends in a giggle of semi-circular battlements and a funny octagonal hut. There is a wall tower north of the square with a half-timbered Renaissance top; where the west gate used to be stands a handsome eighteenth century house; south of it a fragment of the castle displays Renaissance busts and shields and relief panels put together anyhow; at the west end of the square, house no. 43 has a doorway of 1544 in the same country manner. This may be the work of some Parr, here in 1546, or of G. B. Quadro from Poznan who was here in 1553. At Grodków (Grottkau), south of Brzeg, the thirteenth century chancel was kept, almost Cistercian with its big transverse arches and groups of stone shafts; the fifteenth century nave vault is a simple net that springs from unusual triple colonettes. Right beside the church, one of the gates, the Ziębicka, of about 1600 sports machicolations and jolly battlements.

Most barely and brutally Silesian of this line of churches is that at Dzierżoniów (Reichenbach unter der Eule) south-east of Świdnica. Once this was a stone hall, but stage by stage they heightened it in brick so that the nave is three times as tall as wide, the apse seven-sided like Swidnica, the slender buttresses and windows all in detail spare and hard. The only concessions are the pretty vaults, the nets of 1555 in the nave, and the spring pattern on the outer south aisle. The Protestant church at the north end of this plain town is just as grim – a grey block of 1795 by K. G. Langhans – now shut and apparently abandoned, a relic of regulation Prussian piety.

So ambitious and so coherent is this series of great basilican churches that it seems to set Silesia apart from her hall-building neighbours. Yet in fact among her town churche halls are in the majority, and after 1400 the tide set strongly towards them. The earliest of the new generation may be at Paczków (Patschkau) between Kłodzko and Nysa, for it bears the arms of bishop Przecław, dead by 1376, and was receiving indulgences in 1390. Its nave is a towering cube, only two bays long inside, but with its three vessels clearly separated by heavy Silesian arcades; the long aisle-less chancel, a more Bohemian piece of planning, bears what look like the results of many experiments in vaulting. North of it rises a massive brick tower, and the whole body of the church carries a blind storey pierced by what should be arrow-slits and topped by an attic with the split semi-circular shapes of the Czech Renaissance. Altogether this is a warlike little town, which has preserved a late mediaeval ring of brick walls almost complete with its simple gate towers and its half round bastions.

The bishops of Wrocław resided to the east at Nysa (Neisse) itself. The town has suffered sorrowfully in war; the young Frederick the Great once wrote to his father that 'we are preparing in all Christian charity to bombard Neisse', and in 1945 four-fifths of its buildings were destroyed. But in 1962 I found roofs and towers already rebuilt, and from the hill on the road to Grodków the town seemed to lie peaceful and unharmed in its broad vale; to the east, on the left, the Jesuits' twin towers, on the right those of the Knights, and between them, like an immense tent through whose horizontal ridge one pole stuck up, the great church of św. Jakub. They had restored some simple gabled houses on the square, and the weigh house of 1604 had risen again in brick, though it had not yet got back its statues, plaster architecture, and painted garlands; the tower finished in 1499 still rose beside the plain town hall; and this small rich area was still bounded by the remains of the centuries' fortifications, with a couple of sixteenth century gates, the Wrocławska sporting an ornate parapet.

83 Over to the east a new roof covered the shell of the bishops' palace, built in 1729 by Christoph Tausch. Its eleven repeated bays, stepped Composite pilasters which embrace two storeys but carry nothing but projecting eaves, banded basement, and two balconied doorways all echo dutifully the headstrong baroque of Prague. The two baroque churches also are provincial enough. The Jesuits' was built rapidly, between 1688 and 1692, and shows it in the reduction of the usual scheme to essentials: grudgingly pilastered front, dull stuck-on porch, obligatory chapels and galleries inside. Pilasters three storeys high lead along the rambling front of their College down a narrow street to the other, that of the Knights of the Holy Sepulchre. It was begun in 1719 by Michael Klein, a builder from Hungary who had settled in the town, and after his death the twin towers were finished in 1730 by F. A. Hammerschmidt. The plan is the Jesuits' again, but in detail more sophisticated; all the shapes are cham-fered off, clumped pilasters and undulating cornices show knowledge of the Dientzen-hofers' work in Prague; but both inside and out there is too much repetition, and, for all the near rococo enthusiasm of the Scheffler brothers' ceilings, it dulls the senses.

71 Nysa's first parish church was built before the Mongols came. We do not know exactly when the decision was made to replace it; it is possible that work had already been going on for some years before the superficially obvious occasion for it, the fire of 1401. Certainly the six western bays of the nave were built by 1416 and the chancel vaulted by 1431. The tower stands apart, begun in stone in 1474 and never finished, an oddly unlocated stump overtopped by the church's roof line. The fifteenth century also filled in chapels between the buttresses all round, and the sixteenth century saw installed in them a handful of serious bishops' monuments of which the best is the Cracovian looking red marble slab to Balthazar von Promnitz who died in 1562. In the nineteenth century a showy porch was put on the west end, and between 1889 and 1895 new cross vaults replaced the original net, a disaster. The Poles have put bright new red tiles on the roof and a Cracovian dome on one south chapel, and inside they have painted red the already sufficiently solid looking pillars of the nave.

This church attempts a range of expression unknown elsewhere in Silesia, for it is a hall of eight clear bays whose vaults rise 90 feet above ground and which ends in a three-sided apse inside a six-sided ambulatory. The plan follows buildings of a genera-tion earlier: the Austrian abbey church of Zwettl begun in 1343, the chancel at

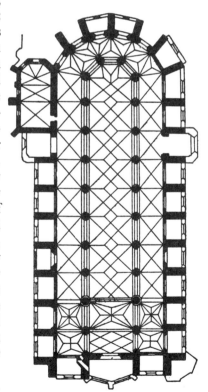

43 Nysa: św. Jakub, 1:800

Schwäbisch Gmünd which Heinrich Parler started in 1351; the original vault copied much more closely than that at Strzegom the net which Peter Parler completed over the cathedral at Prague in 1385. But these are all stone, and for similar conceptions in brick we have to go to Hinrich Brunsberg and his connection, to Brandenburg and to the huge basilica of St. Mary at Stargard where again we find a pillar in the ambulatory behind the central arch of the main apse. The architect of Nysa spoke an international language. But somehow his work is not a complete success. The mass of the octagonal columns, emphasised by their stone bands, dominates too much; in spite of ample light, huge windows, one might be in a cavern cut from soft pink rock. The fault cannot all lie with the restorers.

Almost as large, and quite unexpected in the Cistercian tradition, is the church of their abbey founded in 1247 at Kamieniec Ząbkowicki (Kamenz). Its plan is almost 200 feet long, a three-bay chancel with no apse, small transepts, and a six-bay nave; the dimensions are so close to those of Lubiąż and Henryków that it is tempting to suppose that the late fourteenth century rebuilding followed earlier foundations. It is still a very Silesian church; the arcades are too marked and the octagonal pillars too massive to create a spreading Bohemian kind of space; the transepts are not big enough to produce the excitement of Pelplin. The furniture is a decent rococo. The convent is all but gone, and now the church stands in a big farmyard, overlooked from the bluff beyond the little river by the castle Schinkel planned centuries later. It is grand enough, and would suit a small town, but its builders forsook Cistercian spirituality to no advantage. The one place in the province where Czech ideas were used to advantage is Gliwice (Gleiwitz), a sprawling town among the coalfields with a reputation in the last century for artistic ironwork and with a neat chessboard centre on thirteenth century lines. The church lies west of it, in the Raciborska. It has been much renewed, and all in pastel shades inside. But it is a real try at a brick version of a Czech hall – broad four bay nave, deep chancel, net vaults on solid octagonal pillars – and it is interesting and handsome.

The other hall churches in the south of the province betray no such singleness of purpose. That at Jawor (Jauer) is broad enough, and its structure is all stone from the Strzegom quarries; but the pillars are as thick as ever, and well-carved corbels and pastel colours cannot much reduce the oppressive feeling of the whole interior. The little town has other old buildings, a late gothic town hall with a gargoyled tower, arcades in the square around, a Renaissance doorway in the Legnicka, and best of all, the second of the 'Peace Churches' set like Świdnica's in a forlorn graveyard outside the walls and built between 1654 and 1656 by Saebisch. It, too, should have carved galleries and a painted ceiling, but it is very disregarded. At Ząbkowice (Frankenstein) the church is more cramped still, a small basilica turned into a hall without success, enlivened only by rich vaults, the best of them the net or star or some other pattern spread over the chancel in 1562. In the town's south-western corner hides the shabby ruin of its castle. Between 1524 and 1530 Benedict Ried, the great architect of the kings of Bohemia, remodelled much of it for Karl von Münsterberg, who had succeeded Ried's patron Lev z Rožmitála as Burgrave of Prague. Within the old foundations he tried to create a regular courtyard house with 200-foot sides, two round towers at opposite corners, and a square gatehouse tower. Now there are only fragments of the half and quarter circle parapets and a few windows framed in fluted pilasters like those of the Vladislav Hall in Prague. It demands too much of the imagination to see here a milestone in the spread of the Renaissance in the North.

In all Silesia only two or three places followed the splendid example of the Wrocław

churches of St. Mary 'na Piasku' and św. Dorota, though there is in addition an
excellent miniature of the type over the Czech border, the Augustinian church built
about 1404 at Jaroměř, just three bays and three apses and spring vaulted aisles.
Lwówek may have followed the system in stone, but that is now all lost. At Namysłów
(Namslau) the new brick church was begun in 1401, but progressed uncommonly
slowly; it seems that the three western bays took forty years and it is possible that the
chancel and its three apses were the product of ten more years' work after a fire in
1483. Yet the town was hardly ambitious, for the nave is only twice as high as broad
and there is no attempt to match the grandeur of its exemplars in the capital. The
aisle vaults match six arches to eight windows with deliberate irregularity, and the
stars of the nave grow richer as they go east and develop cross arches which create a
small grove of palm-trees and remind me of churches in England. The town lacks
other character; a formal plan, scraps of walls, ruins of a castle, a big plain town hall.
At Opole (Oppeln) the inspiration is weaker still. Only the plan, reduced to five bays,
follows Wrocław, and the vaults are stars in the aisles and the Strzegom scissor pattern
in the nave. This was all done after a fire in 1446 and remade in the nineteenth century
in the hardest of machine brick. It lies north-west of the old town square; to the south-
east there is the Minorite church, a fourteenth century hall later plastered over; and
on an island in the river the squat, round tower of the castle was attached in 1929 to a
modern but featureless block of government offices by Lehmann.

At Góra (Guhrau) away to the north-west we are half-way to the hall churches of
sandy Brandenburg. The church was rebuilt in brick after a fire in 1457 and in one
place bears the date 1552. Here the hall has much less distinct arcades and the
octagonal pillars bear pilasters that are almost buttresses. An enormous dull baroque
altar tries to hide a peculiar east end that needs to be drawn rather than described.
It is a six-sided apse which embraces the whole width of the building without creating
an ambulatory; instead, the arcades defining the central nave converge slightly to
conform to the apse's two central sides and the aisles make the best shift they can with
the rest; everything is glossed over with ingeniously irregular vaults. Outside, a big
blocky west tower presides over a few old brick houses; today this is hardly more than
a village. At Szprotawa (Sprottau), on the other hand, everything was done in order,
and the seven-sided ambulatory has a five-sided apse inside; but this was a rude, low,
clumsy version of the great apsed churches of Pomerania and the Mark. Finally at
Żagań (Sagan) the Augustinians' long fourteenth and fifteenth century building
effort produced a huge semi-hall with a still elegant chancel and a west front of
portentous, indeed obese, breadth, which contrasts preposterously with the neat and
jolly arcade of 1603 in front of it.

The chief town of this district was Głogów (Glogau), laid out in 1253 at a key
crossing of the river, the Cathedral in a suburb on an island in it. In 1900 it had 22,000
people; now it has dropped out of the guide-books. By 1962 it had a new steel bridge,
by 1969 a whole avenue of flats and shops had risen along the skyline south of the
mediaeval town. But in the space between them and the river hardly anything still
stood. In the north-east corner the Jesuits' church, the usual solid early eighteenth
century shape with two towers, has been under slow restoration since 1958, and beyond
it rose fragments of a once huge pilastered convent. I went to and fro with my ancient
Dehio in hand, skirting collapsed cellars, wondering what might have been the town
hall, what the neo-classical theatre, which church had left the mighty shell half way
up the slope. Down by the bridge the remains of the castle have acquired an incongruous new tower top; and beyond the river rises the great shell of the Cathedral which

was once a splendid hall, vaulted in 1466 with ribs fanning into stars from tall octagonal pillars; this had kept a chancel arch that rested on massive half columns of the thirteenth century.

The remaining Piast residence is Olesnica (Öls), north-east of Wrocław. Here the churches are of little account; the 'Castle Church' is a conventional basilica which was greatly restored after the vaults fell in 1905; in the eastern part of the town a second church has been oddly assembled out of two adjacent ones. I found much war damage and some old houses reconstructed. But the castle is impressive enough to rival Legnica and Brzeg. It still has much mediaeval substance in it, but outwardly only the huge tower, round below and octagonal above, shows through the Renaissance adaptation. Rebuilding began in 1559 with a small picturesque extension, the 'Wittumstock', north-east of the tower and after 1585 embraced the whole original four-sided court-yard, which got a pair of galleries on corbels, the upper roofed from a timber colonnade. There are gables of all sizes – concave, convex, involuted. And best of all is the entrance; first a real show of 1603, large and small gates side by side, lions carrying three shields of arms above, masonry made to look inordinately massive with star-patterned rustication; secondly a smaller gate, but with more heraldry among leaves and an imposing statue of a bearded warrior.

The hills have best preserved mediaeval castles from later adaptation. The Bolko princes of thirteenth century Świdnica left a whole cluster. The oldest may be Świny (Schweinhaus), mentioned in 1108, but Bolko I abandoned it for Bolków and later owners created a Renaissance house beside the great round towers. Bolków (Bolkoburg) 72 is typical, perched on a rocky ridge above a stream, and on its other side a tiny pretty town (on German maps Bolkenhain); its core was built between 1277 and 1293 and contains a round tower, too solid to hold more than stairs or dungeons, and a rect-angular living wing; down to the middle of the sixteenth century people went on adding chambers, gates, and walls, so that the whole is now almost 500 yards long. Others have wilder situations, like Zagórze Śląskie or Grodno (Kynsburg), south-west of Świdnica in a loop of the Barycza; its core is a courtyard block, with one remaining tower, of the fourteenth century; between 1545 and 1587 the Logau family extended the walls and bastions and added gables and carved doorways and sgraffito decoration like the two much renewed but splendid lions that frame the outer entrance. The last of the Bolkos, who died in 1368, may have begun Chojnik (Kynast) which commands from its bare peak the valley south of Jelenia Góra. In origin it is a mere guardhouse, a tower and a courtyard, but later it spread down the slope; walls with round gables crown the vertiginous rock.

Almost alone among these castle owners, the Pless family, otherwise the Hochberg-Pszczyńskis, went on living in Książ (Fürstenstein) for generations. The start was 7[made by Bolko I again, but much greater additions came in the sixteenth and eighteenth centuries, and early in the twentieth the whole, in Baedeker's words, was 'entirely altered and sumptuously fitted up'; in 1941 the interior was pulled out and a huge bunker built so that Hitler might reside there, which he never did. It still has a delightful setting – the baroque entrance wing, the park with its great trees, the little domed eighteenth century mausoleum 500 yards to the south-east, and glimpses through the leaves and across the steep valley of the 'Alte Burg' built as an eye-catcher in 1797. At their other seat, Pszczyna (Pless), the family, alas, replaced their old house in 1870 with a monstrous conflation of Louis Quatorze and German Baroque by the architect of the Rothschilds' Waddesdon, Hippolyte Alexandre Gabriel Walter Destailleur.

Another castle that was long inhabited is Sucha or Czocha or Zschocha near Gryfów, which goes back too to about 1300 and has touches of the sixteenth century; but the steep roofs, spikes, and snatches of half-timbering which look so romantic from the lake the Kwisa forms beneath are work of 1908 to 1912 by one Bodo Ebhart, a sort of Silesian Lorimer. He was responsible, too, for the remodelling, with fancy windows in almost cardboard tracery, of what, as architecture, might have been the most convincing of all these castles: Grodziec (Gröditzberg), on its solitary proud hill out in the plain. Its plan is the result of complete rebuilding between 1473 and 1522, the eastern wing by Wendel Rosskopf of Görlitz, the rest by obscure Silesians. They composed an almost symmetrical entrance with a great square central tower and rounded flanking bastions, and the other turrets and bastions all match; the Renaissance detail, since then so much 'improved', must be as early as any in Silesia.

Church building of this time is rare, but decoration plentiful. At Małujowice (Mollwitz) west of Brzeg the whole inside of this plain brick building with its grand porch and stone-framed doorway is covered in paintings, officially running from the fourteenth century to the beginning of the sixteenth but, to judge by the wigs, frequently retouched after that. Between 1597 and 1604 its Protestant congregation repainted and refurnished the very pretty church at Żórawina (Rothsürben) south of Wrocław, and in 1967 I found the museum people busy restoring it. At just the same time the walls of the chancel at Szklary Górne (Obergläsersdorf) north of Legnica were covered in an astonishing parade of memorial slabs, on each side eight lords and ladies and nine dressy columns with little gabled Biblical reliefs balanced above them. In 1587 Bernardo Niuron, whom we have met at Brzeg, began to reconstruct the church at Oława (Ohlau) for Protestant use as a sort of three-naved hall leaving, mercifully, the well-proportioned chancel of about 1300. Best of all, I think, is the chapel of 1615 in the castle at Siedlisko (Carolath), a box-like space, but with a tall apse on one side and, on the other three, three tiers of arcades covered in country carving. The rest of the place is half ruined – the hall with its stuccoes, the east gate Valentin von Saebisch built in 1611 – but it has a marvellous site on a bluff commanding a broad curve of the Oder and in the spring I found it drowned in the smell of lilac.

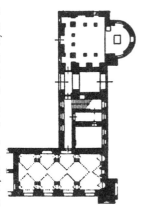

44 Siedlisko: castle, east wing

The first foothold of the baroque was the house Albrecht z Valdštejna, the Wallenstein of history, began in 1629 at Żagań (Sagan), whose Augustinian church has already been described. His architect was Vincenzo Boccaci, his objective size. In 1632 his death stopped work, and it resumed only in 1674 under the Lobkowicz family. The foundations testify to the ambitions of the original plan, but the rest only to the dullness of their architect, Antonio della Porta, who, as at Libochovice in Bohemia, clothed the three wings of this great block in tall pilasters, heavily banded like the window surrounds, which as usual then support nothing but a plain roof. Its full scale appears only as you walk round it, into the huge neglected park, and the ditch opens to reveal a rusticated basement as high as any of the storeys above. A close contemporary of the Lobkowicz' house is that begun in more rustic manner by the Colonnas at Pietrowice Wielkie (Gross-Peterwitz) north-west of Trzebnica. It is a compact four-storey block, covered in decoration, broad oddly spaced pilasters charged with panels of fruit and flowers and stucco ceilings inside bravely resisting neglect and broken windows.

The first baroque churches are basic too. The Hungarian Michael Klein's first job in Silesia was the pilgrimage church he started in 1686 at Bardo (Wartha), in the splendid gorge which lets the eastern Nysa out into the plain. Like the parish church of św. Józef at Krzeszów (Grüssau), which he completed in the 1690s, this is just a box with towers and galleries; there is none of the Bohemian sophistication we have already seen in his Knights' church at Nysa. There is a lack of the many pilgrimage spots which knowledge of neighbouring Bohemia makes one expect. Góra św. Anny, away south-east of Opole, has pretty chapels scattered on its wooded hillside, but the central church is far too mean for its splendid site; it is outfaced by the monument to the Silesian Rising, a great amphitheatre well set in the hill's west side and crowned by rather blockish sculptures by Dunikowski. But at Wambierzyce (Albendorf) the 7 pilgrimage has embraced the whole village, has filled it with chapels and gateways, and dominates it with the huge processional flight of steps to the church. The way is longer than you think, too, for it is the east front that displays all these paired pilasters and balustrades and gables so intensely decorated that they might be in India. Doors in the wings lead to a warren of passages, chapels, and at the far west end rooms that hold Biblical tableaux enacted by wooden figures which once, though no longer it seems, used to move mechanically. From this end you enter the church, an octagonal nave with a shallow dome, a smaller oval chancel whose dome dominates the group outside, all very light and in the organ case rising above country standards of decoration. All this took a couple of generations, for the first church, begun in 1695, became unsafe and rebuilding was not complete until 1730. It is sad it should be so awkward to get to.

There are seventeenth century churches in timber too. At Czarnowąsy (Kloster-bruck) near Opole a small dark cemetery by the main road holds św. Anna, one of those timeless churches we have seen in the Carpathians, with steep roofs and under their eaves open galleries, renewed in 1684; north of it the Premonstratensian nunnery raises the long block of the convent Hans Frölich began in about 1682, and beside it the church has kept a pretty almost rococo interior. A greater surprise lies away to the north-east at Olesno, where a straight-forward timber church of 1518 was extended in 1668 by one Marcin Snopek by the addition of a chapel of św. Anna far greater than its parent; a long connecting arm, a central hexagon surrounded by a gallery borne on posts with twisted flutings, five sharply pointed arms; a great wooden starfish. And at Duszniki (Reinerz) east of Kłodzko, where the village church sports a splendid pulpit of 1730 in the form of a whale, is an older timber building yet, a paper mill of 1605 that claims to be the longest preserved in central Europe.

Silesia's first baroque architect of real accomplishment was Martin Frantz. He was born in 1679 in Tallinn (Reval) on the Gulf of Finland, where his father had gone in 1677 from Dresden to become Master Builder to the city. After seven years of travels he settled in Legnica, where we find him at work on the great Jesuit complex after Knoll's death in 1704. His work there is in the international Jesuit manner, but influenced specially by Christopher Dientzenhofer's Jesuit church in Prague, and he was always quick to pick up the latest ideas from Bohemia. He secured such commissions for houses as the modest ideas of the Silesian gentry afforded. Between 1705 and about 1710 he rebuilt Pieszyce (Peterswaldau), west of Dzerzoniów, for the financier Bonik von Mohrenthal so that it boasted a pilastered front, an oval domed chapel, an ample staircase, and an entrance framed by columns and broken entablature as if in Vienna or Prague. In 1718 he probably began the neglected pretty, rather awkward 'pałac' at the foot of the hill at Grodziec (Gröditzberg) which displays a broken rhythm of pilasters and a rather unfeelingly used Borrominesque vocabulary of detail. He may be the author of the very expressive and well preserved house of 1723 at Chróstnik (Brauchitschdorf) north of Legnica, with its deeply recessed and

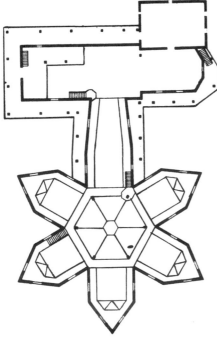

45   Olesno: timber church, 1:500

triumphantly gabled three-bay centre flanked by six-bay wings each of which throws two middle bays forward and upwards to make a kind of tower crowned with trophies. And in 1728 he certainly rebuilt the disappointingly solid and much damaged house with a big tower at the west end of the village of Chocianów (Kotzenau) further west.

His next church commissions came from the Silesian Protestants. In the Convention of Altranstädt in 1706 Karl XII of Sweden, self proclaimed '*Guds fiskal pa jorden*', had not only made August of Saxony give up the crown of Poland but also caused the Emperor to agree to another six churches beyond the three conceded in 1648. Three of them were mere half-timber copies of Jawor and Świdnica, the fourth, at Cieszyn (Teschen), a Jesuit box adapted by the insertion of three tiers of galleries. In 1709 Frantz undertook the Grace Churches – 'Gnadenkirchen' – at Jelenia Góra (Hirschberg) and Kamienna Góra (Landeshut). Born under Swedish rule and inspired by a Swedish champion he turned for his model to the Katarina Kyrka which Jean de la Vallée had begun in Stockholm in 1656 and which had not yet suffered fire and alteration. His plans have the same square chambers set in the angles of their Greek crosses and topped by turrets, even the same number of windows; hipped roofs rise towards a central block, at Jelenia Góra crowned by two lanterns; it has a lengthened eastern arm, Kamienna Góra a western tower. Both churches are crammed with galleries; Kamienna Góra has kept its original two tiers with their 'marbled' columns, and an excellent pulpit, but it is unused and neglected; Jelenia Góra is more crowded, plainer, has a heavy Romish altar stuck in its eastern arm's extra bay, and is in use. It is made picturesque by its broken silhouette and its treed churchyard; and in the walls round it Frantz set in the late 1710s elaborately baroque family vaults designed from a much less Protestant vocabulary which includes concavities informed by pilastery things whose Ionic capitals sprout faces. The town has a rather characterless late gothic church and a square whose gabled houses I found in 1969 half-way through a reconstruction from the ground up.

In the 1730s Frantz probably built the parish church, formerly the 'Weinbergkirche', at the end of the long village that straggles north from the abbey at Lubiąż (Leubus). It is a simplification of his church at Legnica, with gently undulating piers and galleries and a chancel framed by columns; the whole ceiling is one handsome fresco. His last church was begun in 1736 at Siciny (Seitsch) for the same patron, the abbot of Lubiąż, and with the same painters, Axter and Felder. It is centred on an octagon whose oblique sides have become big two-storeyed niches framed by columns and whose dome rises straight from the entablature. This system had appeared in Hildebrandt's Maria Treu in Vienna and had been worked out in a profusion of designs by Kilian Ignaz Dientzenhofer; Frantz could not go badly wrong with it. He created a handsome, solid, comfortable space that is the most satisfying produced by the local Silesian baroque.

His mentor, Kilian Ignaz Dientzenhofer, had by then built one great church in Silesia. Between 1723 and 1731 he completely reconstructed the convent at Legnickie Pole (Wahlstatt) whose foundation commemorated the checking of the Huns in 1241; it was the largest of his many commissions from Othmar Zinke, the abbot of Broumov just over the Czech border. It rises on a low knoll beside the Berlin-Wrocław motorway; its front has a great reticent Ionic order and above that two towers almost joined into an upper storey by a tall niched and statued gable; on each side extend convent blocks, gently shaped with fine fluid doorways but no more than banding for decoration, which I found sadly ruinous. Inside, it is a surprise, for the main vessel is a hexagon, the only one Dientzenhofer built and rare in others' work. Its

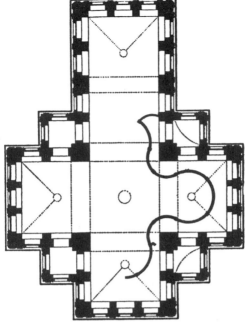

46   Jelenia Góra: Protestant church

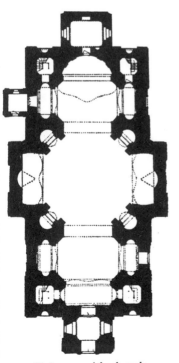

47   Siciny: parish church

walls are left plain; six great pillars framed in four columns each bear individual chunks of entablature, and the oval dome thus becomes a kind of baldacchino, standing clear on its six arches from the windows and the wall – another unique device for Dientzenhofer. With perfect calculation a short cap-domed space leads the eye on into the oval chancel. All the fittings are to these high standards; Hiernle's sculpture, Reiner's altar paintings, Casparini's organ, above all the main ceiling allegory of the missionary Church in the finding of the True Cross, which Cosmas Damian Asam came from Munich in 1733 to paint. This noble building is not large. But its assurance, its richness without repetition, its plastic substance and still more plastic handling of space, set standards Silesian architects never met and which Dientzenhofer himself seldom attained.

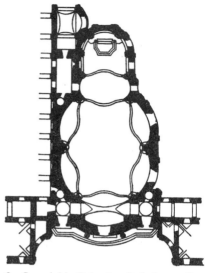

48   Legnickie Pole: św. Jadwiga, 1:800

In 1692, 400 years after its foundation, the Cistercian abbey of Krzeszów (Grüssau) began to rebuild its conventual buildings. In 1728, perhaps inspired by Othmar Zinke's activities, it undertook a completely new church, one of the few grand 8. baroque gestures in Silesia, with two tremendous towers and 230 feet long inside. The plan is ascribed from time to time to Dientzenhofer, but there is no mention of him; a local man, Jentsch, was in charge, and the conception is a straightforward enough development of Prague ideas to come within the capacities of a Dientzenhofer follower like F. M. Kaňka or Martin Frantz. The detail certainly denies Dientzenhofer with vehemence. The front has all the vertical iteration of provincial Austria; two storeys and a third on the towers jammed with disproportionately long pilasters; a main entablature frowning with more wrinkles than the forehead of an oriental sage; tower tops which are so much inflated ormolu furniture. The interior has more proportion, for the architecture is a straightforward adaptation of Christopher Dientzenhofer's procedures to a Latin cross plan, though with blockish over-pilastered piers. Its best part is the two-domed eastern chapels, the 'Princes' Vault', which have apses, broad arches, and plenty of smooth columnar architecture. But what rescues the church is its decoration, not so much Neunherz's frescoes or Brandl's altarpiece as the splendid figures on the façade begun by one Prague sculptor, Brokoff, and finished by another, Braun, and the internal stucco by a group under Anton Dorasil. Light floods in sideways through the ample side chapels on to clumps of putti and on to the supererogatory population of the choir stalls, whole plaster arguments and entertainments, most agitated at the west end of the north side where three gesticulating apostles barely keep contact with the architecture; among the false marbling of the Princes' Vault stand big, eloquent saints. This work gives life to the 8 building's broad, unaspiring repose.

Inside the church work went on until 1775, and by then yet another new convent was going up, meant to be huge and never completed. Its main body is the twenty-three-bay south wing Fellner began in 1774, with five-bay corner pavilions for main accents and a central pediment of proportions quite inadequate to so many coupled pilasters. The cross wing Rudolf began in 1788 would have been yet more grandiose. But the abbey courtyard has preserved its charm: the big trees which make the church towers so hard to photograph, the fragment of the plain 1692 convent, the farm buildings, the simple front of Klein's parish church of św. Józef in the north-east corner. And this holds the finest painting in Krzeszów, the cycle illustrating the life of the saint set on its walls between 1692 and 1695 by Michael Willmann. It was his last important commission and here his palette is lighter and his handling looser than in those solid chiaroscuro compositions for Henryków and Lubiąż. His best designs, such as the 'Rest on the Flight into Egypt', have figures that are hardly more

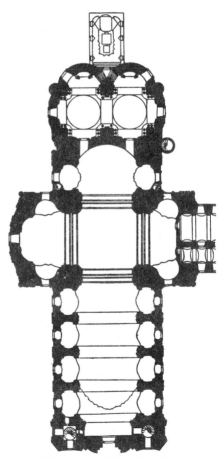

49   Krzeszów: abbey church, 1:1,000

than sketched and yet seem solid, and in this the corner of the darkening sky is tiny, yet huge. In 1694 he had made a portrait of his patron here, abbot Bernhard Rosa, now in the Silesian Museum in Wrocław, which is a rapid and brilliant exposition of hard character. For all his brief touches of Venetian assurance or of Rembrandt's penetration, Willmann is a provincial painter, but to discover him is a reward and an excitement.

The province has plenty more churches in the Dientzenhofer tradition. Most splendid in scale is that of the Benedictine nunnery at Lubomierz (Liebenthal) east of Gryfów, which commands the little town with a simplified version of the common Bohemian scheme of a hall with chapels and galleries, built between 1726 and 1730 by J. J. Scheerhofer and dignified with elaborate piers and cap domes painted by Neunherz. And at Rodziądz (Radziunz), beyond Żmigród, Christoph Hackner began in 1727 a particularly elegant little parish church, bare of all decoration save whitewash and the expressive concavity each pier's pair of Doric pilasters describes. In the half destroyed small town of Głogówek (Oberglogau) south of Opole, with its simple Renaissance town hall and castle, the mediaeval structure of the church was reclothed in paint and plaster between 1776 and 1781 by two Moravian artists, Schubert and Sebastini or Šebesta; they created a riot of white figures and a great, pale ceiling that recalls domes by Tiepolo. I found it sadly neglected when it could be so pretty. And then we reach the hard classical boxes of K. G. Langhans, that I have mentioned at Dzierzoniów and others of 1785 at Syców (Gross-Wartenberg) and Wałbrzych (Waldenburg) and of 1802 at Rawicz, all to the same plan with an oval dome carried by Ionic columns inside.

In country houses the shift to classicism is just as slow, despite Berlin's example; it is often more a shift to plainness. The very pretty but sadly ruined house begun in 1750 at Goszcz (Goschütz) opposes the round-headed windows and rococo details of Potsdam to a pilastered and statued centre which preserves the solidity of a generation earlier. Langhans, the pioneer of neo-classical planning, may have begun in 1780 the house with an inset portico at Samotwór (Romberg) west of Wrocław. Full-blown classicism appears in his pupil Geissler's remodelling in 1797 of the house at Milicz, an odd group with a most severe Ionic portico and the steepest of roofs surmounted by decorously garlanded dome. The contrast is resumed a generation later in the park at Brzeg Dolny (Dyhernfurt) downstream from Wrocław, which holds both Langhans' still rococo pavilion of 1780 and Friedrich Gilly's very severe Mausoleum of about 1800, a miniature Greek temple in fluted Doric. Geissler worked also on spa buildings at Cieplice (Warmbrunn), a little neo-classical place of rest with Rudolf's big solemn house of 1784 and a Doric Gallery of 1797 and a stripped post-Schinkel classical Theatre of 1836.

In all this one place stood out, not for its buildings but for its plan. At Pokój, out in the plain east of Brzeg, a roundabout with seven roads off marks the site of Carlsruhe. The first hunting lodge was built here in 1748, and that which stood till recently was begun in 1752; it was square, of two storeys, with round corner turrets and a domed lantern in the centre of the roof – a lookout like that on Ashdown House in Berkshire. It was surrounded by eight low pavilions, each with a small portico and a row of dormers. The idea of the court permanently encamped in the country went back to Louis XIV's Marly; the radial plan was that of the much greater Carlsruhe in Baden, laid out in 1715; the likely direct inspiration was the work of two Wittelsbach huntsmen, the vanished wooden pavillions put up in 1734 at Fürstenried in Bavaria and the beautiful group of brick ones built by Schlaun between 1736 and 1750 which still

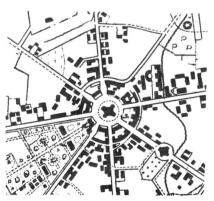

50   Pokój: town plan

stands at Clemenswerth on the Hümmling. Now almost nothing stands of the Silesian Carlsruhe. I found the central site a pile of freshly crumbled brick and learned that only in the last few years had a shrug of the shoulders somewhere let it fall. Down one avenue the Lutheran church begun by Schirmeister in 1765 still stood, solitary and shut, preserving a very simple white and gold rococo oval with organ, pulpit, altar, galleries, and the big opera box of the Duke of Württemberg. Otherwise, among the cottages and the big trees there reigned the sad peace of indifference.

The Gothic Revival arrived in Silesia with uncommon emphasis. The first examples are follies and park buildings, the 'Alte Burg' of 1797 at Książ and the 'Abbey' of about 1820 in the park at Kostrzyca (Buchwald) south of Jelenia Góra. By then English influence, alongside political prestige, was at its height; formal gardens were razed to make picturesque landscapes; and all over Central Europe buildings began to rise that claimed to express the Tudor style. Silesia got its 'Windsor' when, in 1851, the Duke of Brunswick-Lüneburg began the house at Szczodre called 'Sibyllenort'; its vast extent has shrunk to a tower and one wing that recall Wrocław railway station, lost in a big park now a holiday centre.

The prophet of romance was that strange architectural dreamer and dabbler Frederick William IV of Prussia, and his architect was Karl Friedrich Schinkel. In 1831 he bought the estate at Mysłakowice (Erdmannsdorf) whose lake reflects the 5,300 foot mas of Śnieżka. In 1836 Schinkel made designs, little used in the execution, for its church in Italianate round-arch style; in 1841 his pupil Stüler reshaped the house with finicky battlements and dripstones, charming now the whole modest rambling building has been repainted pink. And in the same year the king bought the carved doorposts and the great timber pillars from the demolished thirteenth century stave church at Wang in Valdress in Norway, and the lady of Kostrzyca had them set up again in an 'ideal' form, all shingles and lead-roofed apse, 3,000 feet high on the mountainside at Bierutowice (Brückenberg). Frederick William was always at heart the youth who had written home in 1815 on his first sight of Cologne Cathedral '*Ich war Halali . . . entzückt, ganz hin*'. But his visions shrank from his grasp, like the great new Cathedral for Berlin. Someone tried to assassinate him. And in 1841 Schinkel died, the man whom he had trusted to give him '*ein gutes Ja, ein gutes Nein*'.

So Schinkel's Gothic masterpiece was designed in 1838 for Frederick William's brother Albert and built after its designer's death by Ferdinand Martius. It is a great near symmetrical castle which stands on a wooded bluff above Kamieniec (Kamenz) overlooking the broad valley and the abbey I have described. The drive leads up, it seems interminably, through overgrown woods and along the top of the ridge behind; suddenly one is driving through a labyrinth of ruined stables and arcaded passages, with small trees springing up all about them; one is led round the flank of the house to the splendid double-track vaulted carriageway on the main west front, whose depth and spaciousness the photographs conceal. A covered way leads across the broad four-storeyed courtyard, a double stair up to the first floor where brick vaults stand to show how elaborate all the interior was. Every material lies about – rough stone, ashlar, plain and glazed bricks, cracked and collapsing plaster. In front, twenty-three broad steps lead down to the cramped terrace garden, and the sheer retaining wall, and the view. This Prussian ruin is eloquent of vanished glory

5. Pomerania

From the Odra the plain goes on east and north. Lakes there certainly are, and woods, and the broad marshy valley of the Warta, and the Baltic dunes. But the landscape lacks the delicate riches of the beechwoods of Mecklenburg and Rügen and the remote spaciousness of the Mazurian Lakes. It is poor. Villages are scattered, towns few. This very poverty long preserved mediaeval work such as other districts lost, notably a splendid collection of town walls. But the desperate fighting of March and April 1945 has rubbed whole towns off the map, and I have had to take special care not to describe what is no longer there. Most of the area was German for centuries. The Slav rulers of Szczecin, like those of Wrocław, brought in German settlers; and further south the Margraves of Brandenburg kept pushing east from their sandy domains across the Odra, clearing the Ziemia Lubuska (which takes its name from the bishop's seat at Lubusz or Lebus) and calling a whole stretch north of the Warta the 'Neumark'. The coast, bare and cold, was the last refuge of the Slav Pomeranians; a handful of families in Kluki are said still to speak the language of the Słowińcy.

The first church founded here was at Kołobrzeg, but nothing earlier than the thirteenth century remains. In 1173 the bishops settled finally at Kamień (Cammin) where the easternmost arm of the Odra reaches the sea, a town now hardly more than a pleasant overgrown village. The cathedral was begun in stone – the granite which in places crops out of the sand and gravel. Work seems to have gone slowly; we cannot be sure the main structure was complete until the middle of the thirteenth century, and that in brick; only in the north transept does the stone rise far enough to frame a plain round-headed doorway. It was a basic church, single-bay chancel with round apse, square transepts, nave of three square bays with aisles each of six. It gives nothing away; outside, the windows are plainly moulded, the south transept displays blank panels with trefoil heads; inside, ribs cross on broad dome-like vaults, creating the comfortable spaces of Westphalia. There is sparse furniture, some mediaeval sculpture, a charming seventeenth century grille round the font, but the fascinating Swedish eleventh century Cordula reliquary of carved horn has vanished. The northern brick cloister is plain and handsome too.

The surprise is the south nave aisle added between 1388 and 1438. Inside, it has star vaults; outside, it displays with a flourish a superb brick cresting of the least possible structural relevance. Above every wall buttress rises a pair of spiky finials, joined by a gable and a pair of arches; in between these, a bigger gable is filled by a circular rose of brick intricately moulded and glazed; below it, two little groups of columns and gables each describe what seems like the projecting half of a brick giant's six-sided crown. Here we see, as never in Silesia, stone forms not simplified or suppressed but replaced by forms of equal riches natural to brick. We are in the great stream of brick design which flows eastward from Magdeburg and Lübeck across Poland and all round the Baltic coasts. Its fantasies look strange to eyes accustomed to the limestone and sandstone amenities of central Europe, and just as much to eyes from England where brick won acceptance only in the fifteenth century. I have to beg the reader to clothe grey photographs in a great range of colours, dusty pinks and deep red-browns, glittering glazed greens and browns and blacks, above all the rich response to light of handmade brick's natural rough and sparkled finish. The tragedy is that so much in Pomerania and Prussia has been restored with the harsh machine-cut products of the last century.

As in Silesia the Cistercians came along among the first colonists, though here in tiny numbers. Their only large house is Kołbacz (Kolbatz) south-east of Szczecin, where a party arrived in 1175 from Clairvaux's Danish daughter, Esrom. It is a large plain exposition of the Cistercian plan, in strict proportion. Its core – the transepts, one bay of the chancel, and two bays of the nave – belongs to the beginning of the thirteenth century; the small round-headed windows, the solid unbuttressed height, closely resemble its near contemporary, Sorø in Denmark, founded in 1161 and completed about 1200. As the century went on, perhaps up to a consecration in 1307, the nave was lengthened to an imposing eight bays and given an odd asymmetrical west front with a great blind rose in its gable, in the more decorative manner of Brandenburg abbeys like Chorin. Finally, before 1347, the chancel was rebuilt, no longer, but with much larger windows and a five sided apse. The crossing got a star vault about 1500. Then the decline began. After a fire in 1662 all the aisles and chapels were pulled down; the nave became a storehouse; of the convent only a very grand barn with blank arcaded walls remains. Now little but the church's sheer size tells.

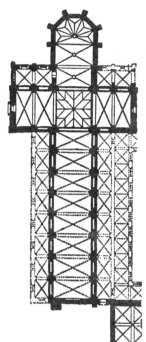

51   Kołbacz: abbey church

The plan and scale of Kołbacz were repeated by both her daughters. Oliwa in Pomerelia, later much altered, is described in my chapter on Prussia. Even before the war Bierzwnik (Marienwalde) had almost vanished, and only the elaborately apsed chancel and a fragment of nave served as a village church. But further south, at Gościkowo near Świebodzin, Paradyż (Paradies) was founded in 1230, probably from Lehnin in Brandenburg. The foundations of a north transept suggest that the thirteenth century builders built, or at least intended, a cross plan. Perhaps the example of churches like Lubiąż with eastern ambulatories made them give it up, leaving a four bay stump of a nave, with very low aisles each of eight bays, and, on the transept foundation, a round north-eastern chapel with a ribbed domed vault. The nave's vaults have kept the strict proportions of the thirteenth century, but much of the rest is under baroque plaster, and stalls and pulpit are neo-classical white and gold. Last of all, Bukowo (See-Buckow) was founded on the coast in the 1250s by the combined efforts of the Mecklenburg abbeys of Dargun and Doberan. It never prospered much. The convent has gone without trace, and what is left is a neat village hall church, four bays, partly star-vaulted, a broad apsed chancel; everything rather square and plain. In the fourteenth century the hall church won a victory here far more complete than in Silesia.

Between Szczecin and the Warta the relatively fruitful countryside bears a crop of ancient parish churches, often still substantially Romanesque granite, and brick town walls. The church at Banie (Bahn) is a stone box with narrow aisles and wooden ceilings which, like Kamień, echoes Westphalia. Trzcińsko Zdrój (Bad Schönfliess) has a part granite hall church, fitted later with richer vaults, an an old but plain

town hall, and splendid walls with towers and with south and west gates topped res-
pectively by octagonal and hexagonal turrets. At Gryfino (Greifenhagen) the church
begun when the town was founded in 1254 was in stone, on a singular Greek cross plan; by putting 'Piast'-vaulted aisle bays north and south of the nave's single star-vaulted space, the fourteenth century turned it into a kind of hall; there is a pretty Renaissance pulpit, and, odd though it is, the whole space is very comfortable.

The first big, wholly brick church is at Gorzów Wielkopolski (Landsberg). The town was founded in 1257 on the steep bank of the Warta; the church's dark red mass and broad panelled tower rise above scraps of old wall and the wide river. Inside, the aisles are very narrow, the nave a little taller than they, but dark for the lack of a clerestory; the chancel ends in a handsome apse. More intriguing than any of these is the tiny church the Templars built on their estate at Chwarszczany (Quartschen), now in a farmyard east of the village. On the thirteenth century stone base rises a neat fourteenth century brick box of three bays, with apse, two round west turrets, simple tall windows, but a sophistication and finish that at once betray in this distant province the presence of a European Order.

As all over Brandenburg and its dependencies, the commonest church shape here is the hall whose aisles run in an unbroken ambulatory round its apse. Examples are as big as św. Jakub in Szczecin, a match for św. Jakub at Nysa, and as small as the three-bay church on the south bank of the Warta at Słońsk (Sonnenburg). One of the prettiest is at Pyrzyce (Pyritz); a slightly higher nave, a five sided apse in a five sided ambulatory, and over the easternmost bay of all a splendid extra show front, a five-light window framed in blank panels and topped by a lantern as if it were another tower. But to imagine the old effect of this showpiece town in its toy fort walls you have to pass on to the grid of streets, circle of walls with two handsome gates and a round tower, and Dominican church with diamond vaults of 1500 or so in the west wing of the convent, that you can still find at its neighbour Myślibórz (Soldin).

Even Pyrzyce has not suffered so much as Chojna (Königsberg in Neumark). There the church was one of Pomerania's showpieces, now thought to be Brunsberg's work of 1389 to 1407. It is a great hall; its five sided apse is ringed by a nine sided ambulatory; ambulatory and aisles are all deepened by rows of chapels between the buttresses; everything is tricked out in green or black glazed brick. But in 1967 I found only the vulgar nineteenth century tower intact. There are, too, a plainly restored Augustinian church of about 1300, and the shell of a showy town hall, and round the rubble plenty of fragments of walls; and, set in those, two gates, south and west, the latter the Brama Świecka (Schwedter Tor) with octagonal top and four turrets and quatrefoil frieze.

South of the Warta it is rather the same story: scattered about, ancient red masses catch the eye in the forests' unending quiet green. Ośno (Drossen) has walls, a twelve foot ring of granite lumps, and a fifteenth century church of intensely red brick, broad and blockish with the squat tenacity of the Mark, low and star-vaulted inside. In the sixteenth century the late Gothic passion for vaulting took charge completely at Świebodzin (Schwiebus); the south aisle is two storeys, and has one patch in a diamond cell pattern; the nave carries a mad mass of ribs which loses all direction as it goes east. The oddity is reinforced by sober white and brown restoration; and outside there is a huge blank 'window' as centrepiece to the façade. Some villages around, like Klępsk (Klemzig), used to have timber and half-timber churches with old furniture.

To the north, there are more walled towns like Maszewo (Massow), which has a full ring, and Goleniów (Gollnow) which has three grand gates, one round-topped, one octagonal, and one elaborately gabled, and more eccentric churches. At Drawsko (Dramburg) the south doorway sprouted such grotesque reliefs in terracotta, griffins, mitred dwarfs, and so forth that one half expected a sheila-na-gig. There were Renaissance houses, too, notably at Pęzino (Pansin) east of Starogard, moated and gabled and made still more picturesque in 1853; Starogard (Stargordt) had quite a serious baroque house, the centre of 1717 a block of two pilastered storeys and a tactful three-bay centre under a mansard roof, and matching wings added in the 1740s. And at Kostrzyn (Küstrin) the castle still presents a huge ruined eighteenth-century front to the broad Oder. But one can drive through the town without noticing more than bushes growing from low brick walls and a dog-leg in the street, it is so destroyed.

Near the coast the Hanse tradition asserts itself; among the big town churches the hall is now outnumbered by the basilica. But the full east end of Lübeck is rare; the big angular bare church at Świdwin (Schivelbein) had an ambulatory, but almost all the others have an aisleless chancel closed by a three-sided apse. Most are small; at Sławno (Schlawe) and Białogard (Belgard) the nave is only three bays long, at Koszalin (Köslin) four; they all have plain octagonal pillars, the standard eight pointed star vaults already long established in Prussia, and great west towers, the most imposing that of Sławno whose surprisingly grand interior has eight pointed stars and where the ruined town runs to two fine battlemented gate towers as well. But however ambitious their thirteenth century street plans these towns could never afford to compete with Wismar and Rostock and Stralsund, and their churches often spent a couple of centuries building and remained as earth-bound as those of the Mark. The best of them is at Słupsk (Stolp). It has the largest scale and the richest detail, moulded arcades, an apse on five sides of a decagon with tall windows above low blank arches, star vaults elaborately run together in the chancel, plenty of light. Its huge block of a tower faces across a paved churchyard-market to the equally broad and confident New Gate. The castle, down by the river on the east side of the town, has gone but for a tower and one wing, still a pretty enough group with the Mill Gate nearby, and beside it rises the tall plain 'Castle Church' built by the Dominicans in the fifteenth century, aisleless, with seven star vaults and two pierced gables; inside it has been divided into two unequal rooms, of which the eastern one contains the eighteenth century pulpit and the grandiose black-and-white marble monuments to the last members of the old native ruling house.

The hall churches are just as broad and solid. Their standard plan is a three- or four-bay nave, an aisleless chancel, and again a really big west tower, as, say, at Gryfice (Greifenberg). At Lębork (Lauenburg) the sacristy still has cell vaults, and the tower is finely informed by pairs of tall blank panels which deepen into pointed blank arches half-way up; but the other vaults are modern, and the town much damaged. The tower at Trzebiatów (Treptow) is still taller, richly panelled, crowned by octagon and spire; restoration and ugly glass have not robbed the interior of its breadth, best expressed in the five-sided display of windows in the apse; the town is unspoilt, quiet streets and plain old houses. The villages hold a surprise or two; at Sarbia (Zarben), just north of the road from Trzebiatów to Kołobrzeg, a tiny but complete hall church has an apse as broad as the whole building, vaulted with an amusingly ingenious system of ribs focused on one big boss; a delightful piece of rural fuss.

Oddest of all is a group of centrally planned late gothic chapels. The best is at Darłowo (Rügenwalde), otherwise a quiet place, with a standard basilican church and the brick carcase of the castle where Eric of Pomerania, acclaimed king of Denmark, Norway and Sweden at Kalmar in 1397, carried on his career of piracy after his deposition in the 1430s. On a hill outside stands the cemetery chapel of św. Gertruda, fifteenth century in origin, a hexagonal centre under a star vault surrounded by a twelve-sided vaulted passage, full of carved and painted wooden furniture, and roofed with a shingled tent that rises to a disproportionate spike. At Koszalin there is an eight-sided chapel of 1383 with a star vault, and at Słupsk a simpler vaultless one; and at Wolgast, west of the Oder and the border, the cemetery in the Neustadt holds another St. Gertrude chapel of about 1500, twelve-sided, prettily vaulted from a massive central pillar.

Kołobrzeg (Kolberg) was the area's chief port, at times the seat of its bishop, in the nineteenth century its watering-place. It has suffered worst of all, for in 1945 nine-tenths of it were ruined, and in 1967 its old centre was still a wilderness. The great church of St. Mary was probably begun soon after the town got its charter in 1255. Its grand remains are those of an ambitious but simple hall, completed about 1300 with plain rib vaults and slender shafted octagonal pillars and with a long chancel with a seven-sided apse, built on probably in the 1330s, which has already been restored to use in all its elegance. Late in the fourteenth century an apsed Lady Chapel was built on to the south, and in 1410 it was extended westwards into a whole outer aisle with four stars to each vault in the manner of the great church at Braniewo (Braunsberg) in Prussia; a star-vaulted outer north aisle followed it. The church was full of furniture, sculpture, painting. Across the chancel arch stretched a fifteenth century screen whose slender stone pillars carried brick arches and a frieze of gables in glazed and moulded brick; from the nave vault hung a carved wood 'crown' of 1523 with Mary and John the Baptist under a rich canopy; of fourteenth century bronze were the font, the seven-branched candelabrum of 1327, and the lion's head door knocker. The west front, two towers amalgamated in one vast shapeless mass of brick, still commands the ruins all around. The town hall still stands, a blocky symmetrical piece of castellated Gothic designed by Schinkel in 1826 for the old foundations, with deep windows and lots of neat relief to ease the harshness of the brick. And in 1967 a new hotel, the 'Skanpol', went up on stilts which rise through the public rooms; it sports a big aluminium entrance canopy, smart enough for a Mediterranean resort.

Szczecin (Stettin) commands one of the vital estuaries of the Baltic. It was the seat of the Slav princes of Pomerania, got a charter in 1243, joined the Hanse in 1360, was ruled by the Swedes from 1630 to 1720, and under Prussian rule grew by 1900 to be greater than Gdańsk and twice the size of Poznań. But bombing half destroyed port and city centre by 1943, and the battles of 1945 completed the ruin. Rebuilding has been rapid, but generally without much inspiration, and has shifted the centre away north-west to the huge square of Jasne Błonia. The old centre has been disregarded; the once busy grid of little streets and squares between cliff and river has vanished entirely; the restoration of ancient buildings has gone painfully slowly, and some of the fragments I have seen could only with difficulty be identified.

The oldest remaining church, the Franciscans' św. Jan down by the river, has been rebuilt. Its chancel is most odd: three cross-vaulted bays of the early fourteenth century and an apse which widens into seven sides of some irregular decagon, an imitation of the expanded apses of the 1330s at Aachen and Soest which is hardly convincing inside or out. Later in the century the nave followed, slightly askew, a decent standard hall with octagonal pillars and star vaults thrown into confusion in an attempt to match four windows on the west wall. Inside it is now very white and pure; outside it raises two richly panelled gables with turret-like buttresses. The main church, św. Jakub, may hold work of the thirteenth century, but was all rebuilt, 90 beginning in 1375 when a hall choir began to rise round the old chancel. In the 1390s Hinrich Brunsberg built at least the lower stages of the southern nave chapels; in the first quarter of the fifteenth century the nave was completely rebuilt as a hall, apparently by someone else, perhaps Nikolaus Kraft; a row of two-storeyed northern chapels followed. In 1456 the south tower fell and the whole west front was consolidated into one huge tower raised to 300 feet by the spire Hans Bönecke put on in 1503. The inside must have been imposing, with tall octagonal pillars which surprisingly carried only simple rib vaults, baroque monuments and organ and carved pews. In 1967 the chancel had been reroofed, but the whole north wall and north arcade were lost. The outside seemed grand enough – the finicky miniature gables on the south side beneath the tall main windows, the majesty of the nine-light window in the centre of the apse.

Away to the north is the one other mediaeval church, św.św. Piotr i Paweł, of ancient origin, but discouragingly much rebuilt. By the end of the fifteenth century it was an elegant little hall on slender granite pillars like those of the convents of Lübeck and Stralsund, but the seventeenth century took them out and put in a wooden ceiling with a painted centre panel, all very bright and jolly; the demonstrative outside, particularly the west front, was not only renewed but in part redesigned in about 1900. Down by the river the old town hall has been reshaped as a small, gabled brick block of the mid-fifteenth century; but its neighbours on the square, the pretty Kommandantur of 1730 and Mathias' handsome round-arched Bourse of 1834, are no more. Up the slope, the Łozice house ('Loitzenhof') has been rebuilt, an extraordinary tall towered sixteenth century survival-Gothic thing with not much conviction. Behind it lies the biggest task of all, the Castle. It covers a big irregular quadrilateral, with a subsidiary wing to the west. Of what now stands, the oldest part is the south wing east of the main gate, begun in 1503; it has towers by the gate and towards the courtyard with a staircase in, and, now on the second floor because of later adaptations, Bogusław X's hall with its round columns and rustic ceiling. By 1538 his son had completed the plain east wing. In 1575 a general rebuilding of the rest began; two long stone ranges and, at their north-western hinge, the chapel, a hall with storey on storey of galleries under round plaster arches and its own west tower. In 1967 many windows were still bricked up and trophies smashed, but the north courtyard loggia had been renewed and new scrolls and finials were reaching hopefully into the sky.

Baroque Szczecin shows up best further west. In the Plac Żołnierza Polskiego stand two decent buildings, one Walrawe's simple pedimented museum of 1725, and in the Staromłyńska there are two more of the late eighteenth century, no. 13 which is uncommonly pompous and no. 27 which is small, easy to miss, but very pretty. Best of all are Walrawe's two showpiece gates, the Brama Portowa (Berliner Tor) of 1725 which closes the Wielka with a great display of trophies and reliefs, and west of św.św. Piotr i Paweł the Brama Nakielska (or Hołdu Pruskiego), once Königstor, a massive tunnel adorned with fat children and weapons of war and smnthered in creeper. The nineteenth century expansion lacked visual amenity. The Haus Tilebein of 1809 on the outskirts used to be regarded as a model of neo-classical comfort, but how unremarkable the photographs make it. North of the old centre the huge pseudo-Renaissance government buildings of 1906, far inferior to their contemporaries

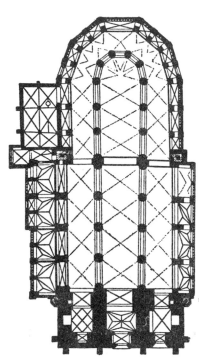

52   Szczecin: św. Jakub

in Poznań, command the wide prospect of the river and the harbour and the busy
bridge. This is as much of its old character as Szczecin has left; I may be biased, but
I would just as well have Belfast.

What Szczecin has lost Stargard has preserved. Once it must have been almost
as important a town, but its river let its trade dry up; its mediaeval monuments have
survived even the war, which laid half its houses waste. Its twelve-foot brick wall is
half preserved, with five round towers and four gates of which none is particularly
ornate, although the Mill Gate is pretty enough, with its two embattled octagonal
turrets and its arch that spans a stream. To enter this ring in 1961 was a shock. The
oval of the old town was so many heaps and waves of pink rubble, on which half-a-
dozen big buildings rode; only up in the north-east corner by św. Jan had some
plain small blocks of flats begun to infiltrate. A few gabled houses stood, the best the
former inn just north of St. Mary, with five spaces between buttresses treated with
great three-dimensional feeling as so many blind windows; and beside it rose the little
town hall, sixteenth century also, two-and-a-half storeys of sweet reason with no more
than one arty line of dripstones, which then becomes a rash of plaster curves and
circles that describe cusped and twisting patterns with a directionless enthusiasm.
And św. Jan is a decent church, a low solid hall in the Brandenburg manner; a short
nave of three star vaulted bays, a five sided chancel apse and a seven sided ambulatory
round it. The disproportionately massive tower was begun in 1408. In spite of its
confused forms this church would stand out in any meaner company than it has.

For St. Mary is the one church between the Oder and the banks of the Vistula
that challenges the great basilicas of the Hanse, of Lübeck, Wismar, Stralsund. In
origin it was a simple but large hall church of about 1300. About 1400 rebuilding
began on a visionary scale. The east end became a five-sided apse with an ambulatory
with eight unequal sides and as many chapels between the buttresses. But the
buttresses do not vanish as they did, for instance, in św. Jakub in Szczecin, for each
is picked out with two little buttress strips framing what look like very slender blocked
windows and adorned with cusped and foiled gables and circles in the richest of
moulded brick. This treatment goes on round the low, irregularly octagonal chapel
which projects to the north. Yet the nave is quite plain, and so are the southern line
of chapels built on about 1500 and, for the most part, the immense structure of the
west front. This is made of two massive towers, whose simpler panelling starts high
above the town's modest roof tops, and a six light window that fits in between them
to light the nave; the northern tower goes on, as if in Stralsund, to four pencil-like
turrets and an octagon and to a baroque double lantern. Inside, the whole central
vessel, 33 feet broad, was raised to 100 feet high. But there is the same distinction;
the chancel has octagonal pillars with gabled niches on them which recall the contemporary cathedral at Milan, a low cramped clerestory and, great surprise, a
triforium; the nave's pillars are bare, the arcade more richly moulded, the aisles
broader, and the triforium stops. The whole is vaulted with stars which have sprouted
the frills and curlicues of the town hall gable and may be a design of the 1650s.

What inspired this effort, who undertook it, and when? Other buildings of around
1400 suggest a good enough guess for the start. Hinrich Brunsberg is a possible
designer, though the only details that clearly speak for him are the little gables on
the chancel buttresses which recall the southern range of chapels at Szczecin, and
the break with the nave is clear enough. The triforium is practically unique on the
Baltic, though the now vanished contemporary Jakobikirche at Rostock had a
decorative blind one of rather different proportions, and we find painted ones of

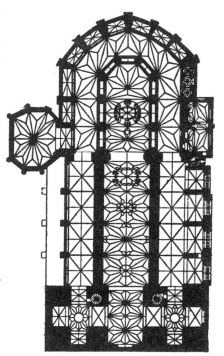

53 Stargard: St. Mary

mediaeval origin in the Cistercian abbeys of Doberan and Pelplin. The central
buttress in the ambulatory which blocks the central arch of the chancel apse is
unique in the Baltic too; it matches the east end of the great hall church of św. Jakub
at Nysa in Silesia, built between 1416 and 1431, and in the church at Kolín in
Bohemia, the rebuilding of which he began in 1360, Peter Parler had set a central
pillar in the chancel apse itself. These singular ideas give the chancel uncomfortable
proportions, but also far greater life and richness than the vast spaces of Wismar and
Stralsund. Their author must have combined much skill and daring with an attention
to ornamental detail uncommon in the brick north and with European breadth of
experience. How I wish we could see now the vaults he planned! We have to be
content with the uneven glory that remains.

6. Prussia

East of the Vistula the plain goes on. Forest succeeds forest, lake follows lake, huge fields spread in the sun between distant ranks of trees. But there are more castles, more villages with brick towered churches, more towns with busy market places, than in Pomerania. From Elbląg eighty miles eastwards to Kętrzyn the land is as rich and populous as anywhere on the shores of the Baltic, and along the Vistula towns and cities mark Poland's lifeline to the sea. A thousand years ago this land was almost empty. It became the object of one of the most determined and successful colonisations in mediaeval Europe.

In the twelfth century, indeed, much of it was still heathen. On the west bank of the Vistula a Slav dynasty ruled, and at the westernmost outlet in its marshy delta a little port had grown up at Gdańsk. To the east the Prussians lived. In 997 they had killed St. Adalbert, św. Wojciech to the Poles; they were troublesome neighbours for the Polish principalities of Mazovia and Kujavia; they resisted all efforts to control or change them. After the death of Casimir the Just in 1194 Mazovia found an energetic ruler in his son Conrad. He joined with his neighbours and the archbishop of Gniezno in expeditions aimed at conquest and conversion, with little result; the Prussians laid his capital at Płock waste in reprisal. In 1202 the Brothers of the Sword had been founded, on the lines of the crusading orders of the Levant, to Christianise Livonia. Conrad was inspired by their example to appeal to some such association which could secure his borders with a standing army.

The Teutonic Order had been created at Acre in 1198 as the German Crusade petered out. It was modelled on the Order of the Hospital of St. John, took over castles of which the greatest was Montfort, and in time came to rank next in honour after the Templars and Hospitallers. Some of its members took part in an abortive crusade in Hungary in 1210. Conrad turned to it. The Grand Master, Hermann von Salza, was cautious, imposed conditions, and, by double negotiations with prince and Emperor, secured practical ownership of all his men could conquer. The first of them arrived in 1227 and 1228. They cooperated with a few 'knights of Dobrzyń' raised by the Polish bishops and were supported by spasmodic campaigns led by Polish princes; and in 1237 they merged with the Livonian Brothers of the Sword. Their advance started at the bend of the Vistula and pushed towards the sea. In 1242 and in 1261 the Prussians rose against them, but each time outside help restored their progress; two international expeditions were led by King Otakar II of Bohemia, and after him

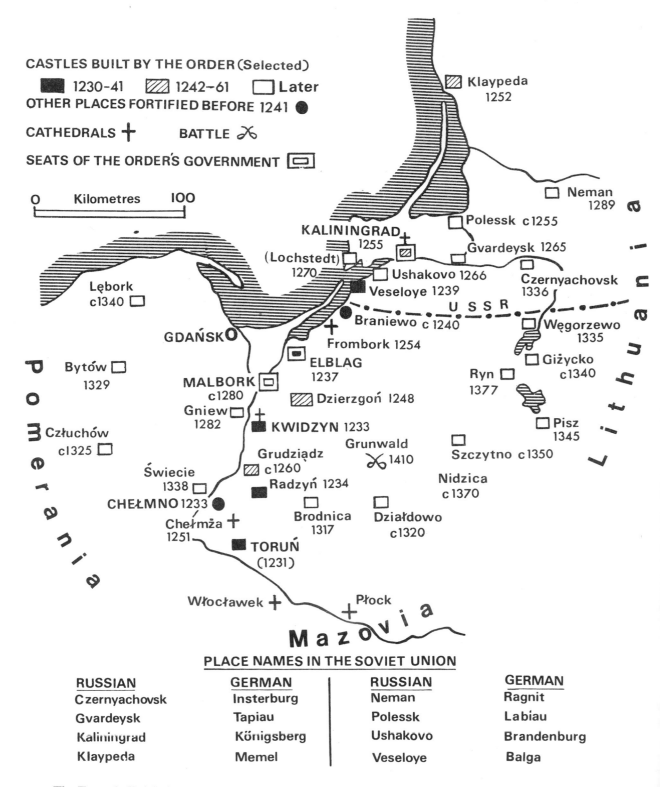

CASTLES BUILT BY THE ORDER (Selected)
1230–41   **1242–61**   Later
OTHER PLACES FORTIFIED BEFORE 1241 ●

CATHEDRALS ✝   BATTLE ✗

SEATS OF THE ORDER'S GOVERNMENT

0   Kilometres   100

Klaypeda 1252

Neman 1289

Polessk c1255

KALININGRAD 1255

(Lochstedt) 1270

Gvardeysk 1265

Ushakovo 1266

Czernyachovsk 1336

Lębork c1340

Veseloye 1239

U S S R

GDAŃSK

Braniewo c1240

Frombork 1254

Węgorzewo 1335

Bytów 1329

ELBLAG 1237

Ryn 1377

Giżycko c1340

MALBORK c1280

Dzierzgoń 1248

Gniew 1282

KWIDZYN 1233

Grunwald 1410

Pisz 1345

Człuchów c1325

Grudziądz c1260

Szczytno c1350

Świecie 1338

Radzyń 1234

Nidzica c1370

CHEŁMNO 1233

Brodnica 1317

Działdowo c1320

Chełmża 1251

TORUŃ (1231)

Włocławek

Płock

M a z o v i a

P o m e r a n i a

L i t h u a n i a

PLACE NAMES IN THE SOVIET UNION

RUSSIAN	GERMAN	RUSSIAN	GERMAN
Czernyachovsk	Insterburg	Neman	Ragnit
Gvardeysk	Tapiau	Polessk	Labiau
Kaliningrad	Königsberg	Ushakovo	Brandenburg
Klaypeda	Memel	Veseloye	Balga

54 The Teutonic Knights

Königsberg – Królewiec to the Poles and now Kaliningrad – was named in 1255. German and Polish settlers followed them and spread inland, and the original Prussians were killed or assimilated. By the end of the century the Knights' control reached up the coast to Klaypeda (Memel) and inland to places like Ostróda and Lidzbark. And then the loss of their possessions in the Levant, where Montfort fell in 1271, turned their full attention to the north, at the cost of their Christian neighbours. In 1282 they got a foothold west of the Vistula at Gniew. In 1308 the last Slav prince of Pomerelia died; in a couple of years they seized Gdańsk and the richest of his lands. In 1309 their Grand Master, who had moved to Venice after the fall of Acre, came to take up residence in the Marienburg which is now Malbork.

The next two generations saw the Order's power and wealth consolidated by a stream of German colonists and the growth of trade to its ports and along the Vistula. They also saw the appearance of new enemies. To the east a line of energetic pagan rulers created a new state, Lithuania. To the south, Władysław Łokietek recreated the authority of the Polish Crown. The Order marked its frontiers with a ring of castles; in the first quarter of the century, to west and south (Człuchów, Brodnica, Działdowo); around 1340, along the line of the Masurian Lakes to the east (Pisz, Giżycko, Węgorzewo, Czernyakhovsk); finally in the 'Wilderness' between (Olsztynek, Szczytno, Nidzica). For a time it was safe, at least from all but the Black Death. But in 1386 Poland and Lithuania were united by marriage, and on July 15, 1410, their combined forces defeated the Knights and killed their Grand Master at Grunwald or Tannenberg. The great castles held out, but the Order was no longer invincible. In 1454 the cities of the Vistula rose against it, and in favour of the Poles with whom they traded; after thirteen years of war the Order gave up half its land and the Grand Master retired as a Polish vassal to Königsberg. But he never really lost his independence. In 1525 the last Master, Albrecht of Brandenburg, made himself Duke; in 1619 his inheritance passed to the Elector of Brandenburg; in 1701 Frederick III of Brandenburg created himself King Frederick I of Prussia. The lever remained with which a much greater Prussia would in time destroy Poland.

The Order was one of the most efficient of mediaeval governments, as methodically bureaucratic as its contemporaries in Sicily and England; and this shows even now in the land it ruled, for between 1230 (Toruń) and 1389 (Biskupiec) it deliberately created almost all the towns, mostly on the usual grid plans. With the help of some rebuilding, almost all the castles and the major town churches and most of the village churches are fourteenth century. After 1500 the countryside stagnated. Under Polish rule, Warmia (Ermeland) stayed a Catholic enclave while the country round turned Protestant with the first Duke. Along the Vistula, though, the towns prospered, their Protestantism uneasily tolerated by Counter-Reformation Poland, and Gdańsk rivals Amsterdam as a sixteenth and seventeenth century city. The war struck hard, though capriciously. Toruń and Chełmno were untouched; in January 1945 the Russian drive to the sea wiped out Elbląg and Braniewo; Königsberg, which did not fall till April, is still inaccessible to the casual tourist, and said to be almost ruined. Gdańsk is being methodically rebuilt, and its riches are described with those of Toruń in a separate chapter.

Of the Knights' earliest castles little is to be seen – fragments of stone wall and a gateway with a brick tympanum in a stone arch of about 1260 at Bierzgłowo (Birgelau) north-west of Toruń, the foundations of Veseloye (Balga) on the shore just beyond the Russian border. Their first plans, such as these two, Toruń, and Grudziądz, are irregular quadrilaterals of wall adapted to readily defensible sites and crowned by one massive tower keep. But here the Order never developed this system into the sophisticated elaboration of its strongholds in the Levant; it felt too safe. It did not need the rich defences against artillery which the exactly contemporary castles of Edward I in Wales provided, but only convents protected against surprise by a lightly armed opposition. Castle after castle has a regularly rectangular courtyard, usually one dominating tower, corner turrets too small to provide the flanking fire of more than a bowman or two, sometimes no more than one wing fully built up, for there would often be only a handful of members of the Order in charge of a garrison of a few dozen. There might be outer ditches and a 'parcham' or barbican; few survive, but the outlines can be traced with ease at Radzyń. These were storehouses and centres of administration at least as much as fortresses. Their grandeur comes from the symmetry which they took from the thirteenth century High Gothic.

Of the first centre of the Order's government at Elbląg nothing remains; at Toruń and the important 'Komturei' founded in 1248 at Christburg, now Stary Dzierzgoń, no more than fragments; the largest walled space of all, Ushakovo (Brandenburg), north of the Soviet border, is only an excavation site. The earliest complete convent castles still standing are Malbork (Marienburg), begun in the 1270s but now almost all fourteenth century save the square body of the Upper Castle, and Gniew (Mewe), 98 begun around 1290, soon after this foothold beyond the river had been gained. Gniew has been little altered. It has four complete wings, over 150 feet long outside; four thin tall square corner towers, and in the north-east corner the lower parts of a once immense keep; deep red brick, punctuated on the south by the doubly tall and deep window openings of hall and chapel and decorated with a few glazed black zigzags; a severe pomp. Inside little is left beyond the southern hall's six-pointed star vaults. Along the spur spreads the little town; its square has kept a few brick arcades, and its small fourteenth century brick church has a broad three-bay hall nave, star-vaulted chancel, and the square tower with two gables and a pitched roof of which we shall see so many. The site is admirable, the neat clump of houses, the jabs of church and castle at the skyline, the water meadows around.

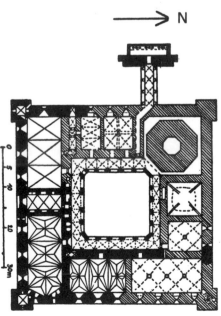

55 Radzyń: castle, 1:950

About the same time, or shortly after, the Order rebuilt the 'Komturei' at Radzyń (Rehden or Rheden) a few miles north of Toruń. The little town, a few hundred yards 9 off in the marshy land, has a church with an elaborately panelled gabled front, massive tower, and half empty flat-ceilinged interior with jolly painted stalls. The castle is larger than Gniew, though not by much; again the south wing holds the remains of hall and elaborately vaulted, finely detailed chapel, and again we find the foundations of a great tower in the north-east corner. Beside them a passage ran out on arches to the outer wall and the 'Gdanisko' or 'Dansker', the latrine perched in a tower over the moat which is the badge of the Order's care for hygiene. The grandest part of what now stands is the south entrance, a recess almost the height of the whole wall which frames gateway and windows, a portcullis housing turned to show. This monument looks lonely and alien among the dry banks and ditches. The same years saw a smaller matching castle, 130 feet square, built at Golub (Golau) on a bluff overlooking the Drwęca (Drewenz) further south. It has preserved bits of stone sculpture and a restored gallery over its cloister; the stump of a great round flanking tower stands clear of its south-west corner; along its skyline rise fragments of round turret tops and panelled battlements added around 1600 when a Vasa princess lived here. To the south, woods and marshes stretch as far as the eye can see; this is the edge of something, and out there a cloud of dust could mark the approach of Jagiełło's Tartars.

Among early fourteenth century castles many have little but a tower left. At Grudziądz (Graudenz) there is nothing but a round stump, at Rogoźno (Roggen-hausen) to the east just a square one, and at Brodnica (Strasburg) a huge solitary octagonal brick pillar; there the town is more attractive, the east gable of the other-wise standard hall church that sparkles with glazed bricks, the remains of the town hall that rise above the houses in the centre of a long market-place closed by north and south gates, one square and gabled, the other an octagon, all untouched by war. At Człuchów (Schlochau), away to the west, ditches and low walls surround a brick octagon of 1330 or so with a pretty top storey of battlements and corbels added in 1844. At Swięcie (Schwetz) on the Vistula the tower of 1338 to 1348 is much more sophisticated – round, 120 feet high, with splendid arched machicolations; there are ruins of a convent beside it, and not far off the great brick walls and gables of the fifteenth century church, ruined in the war. In the nineteenth century the town moved up out of the flood plain on to the hillside, leaving church and castle to brood solitary among the gardens and the fields. Prettiest of these castles in its situation is Przezmark (Preussisch Mark,) a tree-covered peninsula in a lake, spattered with the bases of great walls and pillars; a handsome square brick tower, where the village later used to hang its church bells, commands the east end of the landward ditch; rustling leaves and sparkling water efface plunder and ruin.

As the fourteenth century went on, plans became more and more standard, specifications which the Order used to put out to tender by competing builders. And more often the courtyards remain, often converted; three wings of the 1340s at Pasłęk (Preussisch Holland), extended in the sixteenth century as a residence and then plastered over to house local government; the courtyard with one convent wing and round corner towers built about 1400 at Bytów (Bütow), later filled with living quarters and offices by the rulers of Pomerania and of Brandenburg, and still presiding over the ruined town. On the eastern frontier little remains of once vital strongpoints like Ryn (Rhein) and Szczytno (Ortelsburg). At Giżycko (Lötzen) the small, plainly gabled fourteenth century convent became first a spartan country house and then, since the war, a simple hotel. At Barciany (Barten) a brick courtyard with sides all of 175 feet long makes a most imposing farmyard.

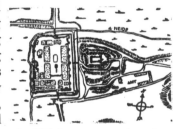

56   Nidzica: town and castle, 1:20,000

The finest example of all is Nidzica (Neidenburg) on the south frontier. It was begun about 1370 on a steep lump of land set round with lakes and marshes. The most gentle ascent, from the east, leads to a gate flanked by two square corner towers; two low hundred-foot ranges frame the narrow courtyard; at its end the convent rises, with spiked and panelled gables and rooms that have kept low star vaults. From its windows you look down on the little town so dutifully disposed on the castle's axis, town hall balancing church, rectangular market once set in a rectangle of walls. All the brute confidence of the Order's rule is there; but the battlefield of Grunwald is only a dozen miles away.

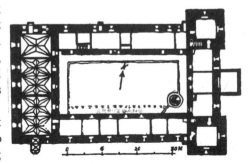

57   Nidzica: castle, 1:1,100

The only other castle builder was the Church. Hard on the Knights' heels, it set up four bishoprics, subject to the archbishop not of Gniezno but of Riga. Chełmno (Kulm) covered the bend in the Vistula and settled its cathedral at Chełmża; Pomerania centred on a cathedral built onto the castle at Kwidzyn (Marienwerder); Warmia, or Ermeland, began with its cathedral on the coast at Frombork and came to cover, and to own, the rich cornlands south and east; Samland lay beyond the Pregola with its seat at Königsberg. The bishops and chapters dug themselves in Some did not conform to the Order's models at all; the great hill-top encampment of Frombork (Frauenburg) embraces cathedral and all like a miniature Meissen or

Prague, and at Szymbark (Schönberg) the chapter of Pomesania crowned a hillock with a pure ring wall, an irregular towered rectangle more than 300 feet long. This used to hold some of the oldest half-timber building in Prussia, but it is ruined now; its situation is still beautiful, with great trees and stretching away to the south a long glittering band of water.

But after its bishop moved to Kwidzyn in 1285, the same chapter began about 1322 a castle (described later, with the Cathedral) as formal as anything the Order was ever to build, and the other clerical castles follow its example. The chapter of Warmia began theirs at Olsztyn (Allenstein) in 1348, on a spur west of the town 12 above the river. It has been much knocked about and is now a museum; over its ivied courtyard presides a Prussian idol with hollow eyes. There is a plain round tower on a square base and two parallel wings which, with one blank wall and an eighteenth century entrance block, almost describe a square. The priors lived in the north-eastern range, which has much altered arcades of about 1400 towards the courtyard and holds vaulted rooms; the best is the main hall or Remter whose great brass candelabra hangs from one of three broad, shallow, sharply-detailed cellular vaults, each planned as a star within a star, as if in a chamber cut by a lapidary out of ice. And at Reszel (Rössel) further east Heinrich von Meissen, bishop of Warmia, began in the 1350s a big rectangular group of brick blocks and towers east of the little town. In the 1370s most of it seems to have been complete, the excessively solid round keep, the fine machicolations under the corbelled passage that crowns the wall, the enormously tall and deep archway in the entrance tower. In 1505 more walls went up, and a 'Dansker' was stuck out northwards along the town wall. Interfering bishops, use as a prison, fire, and war have ruined the interiors and the timber courtyard arcade; it looks best from a distance, its towers joining the church and the house roofs around in a chorus of red brick shapes.

Warmia was by far the richest and most powerful see in the Prussian church, a Winchester of the Baltic. Its bishops' chief residence is a masterpiece, the castle of Lidzbark (Heilsberg). They moved there as early as 1300, but the present buildings were the work of the second half of the fourteenth century, conceived by Heinrich von Meissen, but completed under Heinrich Sorbom. The site is a long rectangle of ditches. You enter at the south-west corner, and find the southern half occupied by three wings, plain and partly remodelled in the eighteenth century, forming a courtyard open to the north. Beyond it rises the castle proper, a proud brick square 9 with 160-foot sides that seems exactly to follow the Order's model, with plain octagonal north-eastern tower and three tall parallel square turrets at the other corners. But the tall niche of the entrance leads to a world of preserved elaboration. The courtyard is surrounded by a two-storeyed arcade, with plain cross vaults at 1 ground level, but above them slender stone columns and steeply pointed springing vaults like those of Silesia. On the ground floor's cellars and low vaulted rooms rest the bishops' state apartments. The west wing holds the refectory, the south the summer chamber and the chapel, the east the great hall, the north the private rooms. All are profusely vaulted. Regular six-pointed stars spread canopies over hall and summer chamber; the chapel's double row of four-pointed stars on plan becomes in three-dimensional fact so many ribs radiating from three great bosses; after a fire in 1442 the refectory was given stars for its tunnel vault that are mere decoration, and the room in the centre of the north wing a dome informed by four eight-pointed stars. The hall has kept a contemporary painting on one end wall, and the chapel is full 1 of cheerful, provincial eighteenth century things – organ, gallery, paintings on the

N ←

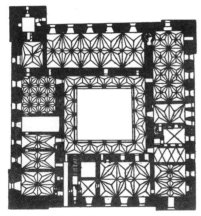

58   Lidzbark: castle, 1:800

vault. The rest houses a pleasant spacious museum. Yet its riches are only a modest imitation of the palace the Grand Master of the Order was creating at much the same time at Malbork.

97   Marienburg, now Malbork, was founded later than its neighbours along the Vistula, although it commands the vital crossing of the south end of the delta towards Tczew and Gdańsk. The first castle may already have been begun when in 1276 the town got its charter; it was a rough square with 160-foot sides on the usual scale for a 'Komturei'. The Order's conquests were still being adminstered from Elbląg. Then, in 1308, it won Pomerelia, and its drive to the west must have made Malbork seem the best residence when, in the next year, the Grand Master arrived from Venice. He lived there until 1457. The castle grew and grew until its outworks and dependencies covered an area greater than the town. Then the land passed to Poland and it was left to crumble as a barracks and a store. The nineteenth century saw it restored, first roughly under Schinkel, then from the 1880s with probably too much imagination – though helped by the drawings Gilly and Rabe had made in 1799 – to the plans of Conrad Steinbrecht. In 1945 the east side was shelled and the chapel half destroyed; I found rebuilding underway. Otherwise the greatest work of mediaeval secular architecture in Europe has come to us astonishingly complete.

Building probably began with the outer walls of the Upper Castle (Zamek Wysoki, Hochschloss), as it did at the closely contemporary Lochstedt. The original convent block, in all 4½ million bricks, must have been complete by 1309, for the Grand Master would hardly move into a half-built castle. We know that the rebuilding of the chapel began under Luther von Braunschweig, Master from 1331 to 1335; its lower part, dedicated to św. Anna, could receive the body of his successor Dietrich von Altenburg in 1341; its upper part was consecrated to St. Mary in 1344. Otherwise we have no documents. A boss in the vault of the great refectory hall in the Middle Castle (Zamek Średni, Mittelschloss) shows the Flight into Egypt. It may be there as the seal of the last 'Land Master', who resided at Malbork from 1318 to 1324; but he did so instead of the Grand Master because of divisions in the Order which are hardly likely to have encouraged such ambitious building. We do know that in 1402 a painter could start work in the Grand Master's top-floor suite in the Middle Castle. Beyond this we have no means of dating with confidence designs as rich and as original as anything built in fourteenth century Europe.

The visitor comes to the castle by travelling the length of its ravaged east side, parallel to range on range of walls, double and treble lines round its core which are probably work of the first half of the fourteenth century. Out to the north extends the Outer Castle (Przedzamcze, Vorschloss), a peninsula between river and millstream now cut by the railway viaduct, with a ramshackle collection of half-ruined buildings, storehouses, forge, chapel of św. Wawrzyniec (St. Lawrence), and trees. Here is the only addition to the enceinte the hard-pressed knights made in the fifteenth century, an L-shaped wall with round bastions that embraces its north-east corner. A covered wooden bridge leads into the north gate of the Middle Castle; its large, irregular open courtyard lives in the shadow of the mass of the Upper Castle on its hillock to the south. In shape the latter is as plain as anything the Order built. Yet it parades great blank niches towards the river, and its walls glisten with patterns of dark glazed bricks; above its eaves rises an array of square turrets and uncommonly elaborate gables, and higher still a huge rectangular tower; and to the east its chapel's apse used to display an enormous stucco relief of the Virgin covered with glass mosiac in gold and bright colours, the Italian technique used also by Venetians in 1370 on the cathedral in Prague.

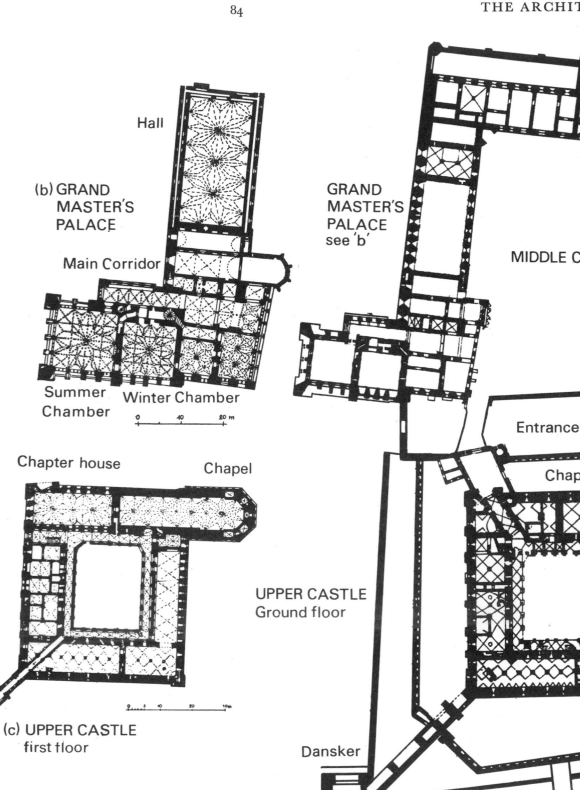

Hall

(b) GRAND MASTER'S PALACE

Main Corridor

Summer Chamber   Winter Chamber

0   10   20 m

GRAND MASTER'S PALACE see 'b'

OUTER CASTLE

MIDDLE CASTLE

Entrance

Chapel of sw Anna

Chapter house   Chapel

UPPER CASTLE Ground floor

0 5 10   20   40m

(c) UPPER CASTLE first floor

Dansker

59   Malbork: castle

(a) OVERALL PLAN Middle and Upper Castles at ground floor level

The Upper Castle's entrance is a singular device: a great niche at one end of its north wall with sides obliquely set so that the gateway in it conforms to the diagonal passage to the courtyard. This has two storeys of arcades, renewed by Steinbrecht practically from nothing, and a well under a wooden hut. The ground floor is all massively vaulted cellars, except for the undercroft chapel of św. Anna, which used to have two four-pointed star vaults and a six-pointed one fitted into its apse, and its doorway which has five columns each side, voussoirs filled with leaves, and a tympanum whose three rows of figures relate the finding of the True Cross. On the first floor, the west range has the kitchen and above it some comfortable small offices with hot-air heating and seats set in broad, light window openings. At the south-west corner the usual passage runs out on arches to a squat, undemonstrative latrine tower. The south and east ranges have long dormitories, with low semi-circular tunnel-like vaults; on the second floor of the south range is the refectory, vaulted with crosses springing from one line of seven granite columns, a room of Cistercian simplicity. At the north-east corner of the upper arcade a sort of vaulted porch in the thickness of the wall frames the chapel's Golden Door, whose colonnettes bear the Wise and Foolish Virgins, all coloured and gilt; west of it a simpler, more elegant doorway leads to the chapter house. These are late thirteenth century work, the entrances to the present rooms' predecessors; they are far richer than anything in the fine contemporary 'Komturei' at Lochstedt and suggest that the castle was perhaps already designed to be the seat of government, for the push west had started with the taking of Gniew in 1282.

The great rooms of the north range, to which these doors lead, are the products of the fourteenth century rebuilding. The chapel had fully developed eight-pointed stars that rose above statued niches, and used to be full of nineteenth-century furniture and decoration; year after year it was sad to see it open to the rain, but in 1969 the roof was on at last. In the chapter house to the west the stars run together into an interlocking system, so that the ceiling becomes so many triangular spaces, each vaulted with a triplet of ribs, all radiating from three very slender octagonal stone pillars, with the exception of those that neatly cut off the corners of the room. Compare this with the refectory; there classical repose, here endless motion. A new disturbing architecture has arrived. But it is impossible to discover when. The restorers believed that this north wing originally had hall and chapel separated by a small room like those at Lochstedt and Radzyń, and that this was later incorporated in the new chapter house; but there is no evidence for such a room in the brickwork or the wall thicknesses and no call for it, since there was no central gateway underneath. It does not help that the restorers found the chapter house vaults fallen and had to recreate them. For assistance we must go back to the Middle Castle and see where it will lead us.

50   Malbork: corridor in the Grand Master's suite

Two sides of its courtyard are of little interest. The east is a long guest house, the north one housed the vaulted offices of the Komtur to the east of the gate and the small hospital to the west. But the whole west range is given over to the Grand Master's state rooms. Its centre is his Hall. On paper its vault matches closely that of the chapter house, with three slender octagonal pillars and radiating triplets of ribs; but here there are more ribs, more corbels on the walls, a broader space, and so the impression of a series of vaulted spaces irregularly joined has been replaced by one of so many regularly spreading branches, as in an English cathedral chapter house. Since the war this grand room has lost its neo-mediaeval paintings and gained a cold, airy whiteness. The Grand Master's suite is upstairs. Towards the courtyard are his tiny chapel, which I found unvaulted, and small rooms of which one at the south-east corner has a simple cellular or diamond vault. Westwards runs the main corridor, a sort of ante-room for his visitors. It starts low and simple; then the vaults rise and on the right the wall is cut away and replaced by broad windows and detached columns before them – a marvellous effect of unexpected space, strong indirect light, and the view north along the castle walls.

The first door on the left opens into the Winter Chamber. It has one granite column and a vault of both radiating and parallel ribs which somehow resolve into so many truncated four-pointed stars round the sides of the room; the idea may come from the Václavská kaple of the cathedral at Prague. It seems chilly now, but we must imagine it hung with tapestries, and in the floor are the holes through which came hot air from the stoves beneath. To the east is the Summer Chamber. It is identical in plan, 10 but slighty larger, nearly 50 feet square. It has windows on three sides, double rows of them, groups of three below, pairs in the spaces between the arms of the vault. Through the clear glass, light splashes on the tiled floor. Outside, the buttresses have been cut away to catch more light, and, using the same trick as in the main corridor turned inside out, pairs of slender stone columns are left to support the bricky masses of the machicolation and the elaborately foiled and panelled battlements. The device is used again, more simply, on the front which faces east into the courtyard. The result is an Oriental ostentation of pattern and relief. There is an architectural revolution between the self-contained symmetry of the Upper Castle and the Middle Castle's deliberate show. In the third quarter of the fourteenth century Peter Parler had begun the south tower and porch which turned the cathedral at Prague in just this way towards the city beneath. Probably in the same generation the Grand Master's architect turned Malbork to face the river whose mouth it guards.

We do not know who he was. We have the name of one master builder to the Order, Nicolaus Fellensteyn, who had studied in the Rhineland; but we do not hear of him until the fifteenth century, and work probably started on the Grand Master's suite in the 1370s or 1380s. We have even less clue to the Hall and to its sibling, the chapter house. If we take that boss to be the Land Master's badge we must think the Hall complete about 1320. This does violence to the rest of the building. The chapel, begun as we know early in the 1330s, belongs to the last stages of the High Gothic style, in which rectangles are still rectangles and vaults go by distinct bays. Hall and chapter house are full of new spatial experiments, most conspicuously the use of diagonal arches to cut off the corners of the rectangular room, leaving little triangular spaces to be vaulted on their own. This fondness for diagonals is typical of the second quarter of the century. We find it as far away as Wells; in south German buildings that include three splendid halls in the great Swabian Cistercian houses, Salem (since destroyed), Bebenhausen, dated 1335, and Maulbronn; in the Baltic brick area, in the Briefkapelle of 1310 in the Marienkirche in Lübeck, the little Frater of the Cistercian monastery at Chorin in Brandenburg, and the castle chapels at Golub and Lochstedt; and, on the Vistula itself, in the chapter house of the great abbey of Pelplin. In architecture this is for the monks of Prussia what Malbork is for the Knights.

The Pelplin community received its first lands in 1258. But only in 1276 did the monks take on the present site, twenty-five miles south-east of Malbork, apparently from some other monastic community; in 1282 their patron Mszczuj (Mestwin) II of Pomerelia transferred it to the Order along with Gniew; they are believed to have begun their permanent buildings before his death in 1294. In 1323 enough was standing for a storm to bring a pillar down. But work on the church's nave and the big regular convent probably lasted most of the fourteenth century, and the star-vaulted north cloister walk holds a fine early fifteenth century wall painting. In 1824

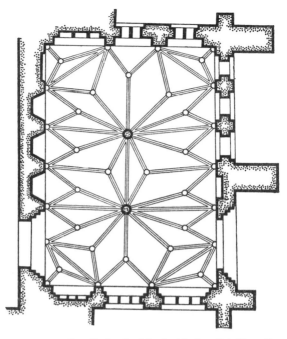

62   Lübeck: Marienkirche, Briefkapelle

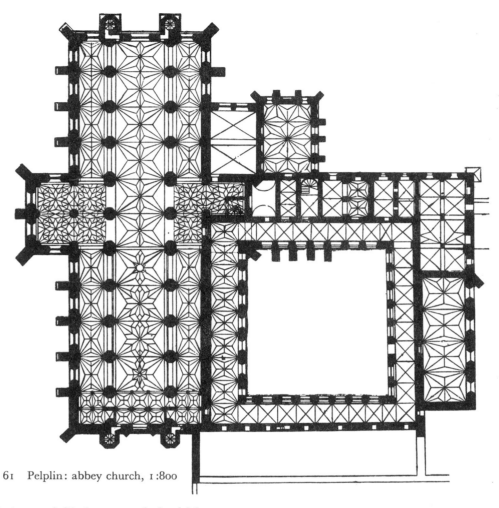

61   Pelplin: abbey church, 1:800

the church became the cathedral of the expanded see of Chełmno, and the bishops remade the west wing of the convent for their palace. This is now being made into a children's home, but the seminary round to the east provides access to the mediaeval cloisters, with a north range handsomely vaulted with great stars, and through them to the chapter house.

The church is the prince of Baltic Cistercian churches, all of brick, 260 feet long, tall as a fortress, and visible miles away over the rolling landscape. The corners of its east and west fronts are marked by massive, octagonal stair turrets; four great spiked and panelled gables face the four points of the compass. Saving the saints in little lantern niches that frame the north door, its walls are as plain as those of any castle of the Order. Inside, there is no letting up. Its length is divided into eleven bays, four for the chancel, five for the nave, two for the transept. Its main vessel rises to 85 feet; its aisles are almost exactly half as broad and half as high. The nave's vaults are elaborate stars put in after their predecessors fell in 1399. The furniture is nothing remarkable, apart from the splendid carved stalls of 1622 on the north side of the last bay.

But the transepts are a surprise, for they are great square spaces planted in the aisles, and possibly as an after-thought, for the southern one uses the north-eastern corner of

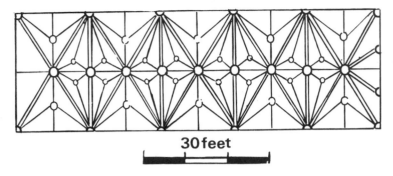

30 feet

64   Westminster: St. Stephen's Chapel, 1:280

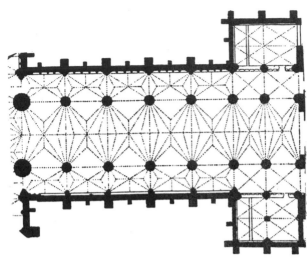

63   Lincoln: cathedral, nave

the cloister as its lowest storey and as support for an organ gallery. In each, one tall central pillar rises like a giant tree-trunk to bear the white plaster vaults, net patterns slightly scooped out into cells like those of St. Mary's in Gdańsk; how remote and brilliant they seem. Pelplin's mother church, Doberan in Mecklenburg, completed in 1368, has these oversize transepts too, but the arcade there is too solid to let them be seen. Pelplin's chancel is square-ended, unlike Doberan which has apse and ambulatory, but like the all but vanished Cistercian hall church of Neuencamp at Franzburg in in Pomerania, and also like English churches. Its aisles, like those of the nave, have four-pointed stars with extra ribs at each end, and in the north aisle a continuous ridge rib; this looks English, too, for this is the tierceron vault created as early as 1230 for the nave of Lincoln Cathedral. And its high vaults are six-pointed stars, something between those of the lower and upper chapels at Malbork, but almost identical with those of the lower chapel of St. Stephen begun in 1292 at Westminster.

So the star vault has led us back to England. There it developed differently, along the continuous horizontal lines the English loved, through the ambiguities of Lichfield to the eastward flow of Ely and Gloucester, and producing the continuous nets of Wells and Ottery St. Mary which have a good claim to have inspired German builders of a later generation in Prague. But in the east the underlying separation of spatial units persists, and the most directionless of nets are spread over so many dome-like bays. So it is after all unlikely that the halls at Malbork show the inspiration of English chapter-houses instead of the abbeys of Swabia. In central Europe the tradition of central pillared halls goes far back, and we find a radial system of branching ribs as early as 1270 or so in the crypt at Kouřim in Bohemia, and perhaps quite soon after 1300 on the Vistula in the crypt of the Franciscan church at Nowe (Neuenburg). There the builders used a couple of cut-off corners, and there are four of these in the continuous, pillarless star system of the Pelplin chapter-house. A shaky tradition makes this, too, early, but recent research has shown it to be the reshaping of a yet older building. Now its much restored but delightfully weightless vault, a big star that spreads out into two smaller ones, creates a space that is both comfortable and yet as sophisticated as any, say, of the bishops' rooms at Lidzbark.

The most we can say with certainty of the great rooms at Malbork that mark the change of style – of the Hall and the chapter house – is that they most likely belong to the same generation as Malbork's one rival among European buildings, the Palace of the Popes at Avignon; to the burst of building effort which we shall find spread through Prussia in the middle of the fourteenth century; above all, like the work of the Parlers and of the Wrocław master of the spring vaults, to the decisive shift of direction and the flowering of new ideas that mark the architecture of the century's second quarter all over central Europe.

We see what may be the influence of the Wrocław master twenty-five miles upstream from Malbork in the cathedral at Kwidzyn (Marienwerder). The bishops of Pomesania chose the place for their church in 1285. The chapter matched both its life – some of the clergy were members of the Order too – and its castle to those of the Knights. About 1322 it began to rebuild; its work is all of one piece, and in close step with mid-fourteenth century work at Malbork and Lidzbark. In form it is another closed and resolute brick square with 150-foot sides, but there is more outward show; bigger corner towers, many more whitewashed panels to show off the brick like contemporary churches do, best of all a really colossal gabled 'Dansker' tower at the end of a 200-foot passage on five bold arches. Inside the two remaining wings remains a handful of star-vaulted rooms, one of which covers a square with sixteen ribs that sprout from a central pillar in an almost English manner. The west range of the cloister has a few spring vaults. But in 1798 the south wing and most of the east were pulled down, and the gable at the south end of the west wing is modern.

Its convent begun, the chapter started in 1344 the rapid and complete rebuilding of its cathedral. Of the old parish church, built between 1264 and 1284, it kept only the fine stone south doorway. In 1355 it was able to consecrate a new brick church 250 feet long and, at any rate in plan, after Pelplin the most ambitious of its time in Prussia. It is very serious in detail; the nave arcades are six pairs of the solidest octagonal pillars with the thickest arches, and the 'clerestory' has no windows – merely two blank panels to each bay – so that over one's head the space dissolves uncomfortably into darkness. Midway in each bay two more brackets carry three ribs each, so that each eight-pointed star turns into a pair of mirrored vaults. Meanwhile, the spring vaults in the aisles capture all the light. The chancel has more star vaults, but lower, and a raised floor, so that its proportions are wholly different, a broad, light, quiet room out of tune with the strenuous march of the nave. Most of the furnishings have gone, but there are much-restored paintings, and over the south door a mosaic saint being boiled, and the bishops' inlaid wooden throne, a funny piece of sixteenth century vegetable Gothic. After the rich spring-vaulted churches of Wrocław it is all very heavy. The pretty confusion of houses round about has been destroyed, and this big earnest monument now stands alone.

Prussia is poor in abbeys. There is one Carthusian house, twenty miles west of Gdansk among the woods and lakes at Kartuzy (Karthaus). The monks arrived from Prague in 1381 and completed their church in 1403; it is big and simple, 150 feet long, no aisles, just seven bays and an apse, star vaults on the low rounded shapes of Bohemia, and a confident spaciousness worthy of the age of Charles IV. There are carved seventeenth century stalls in the nave, stamped leather hangings in the chancel, a gilt altar of 1444 in the south chapel, and fragments of the convent. But one remembers best the odd roof put on in 1731, always said to resemble a coffin lid, and indeed much like the great silver-clasped black caskets still seen in Polish country funerals. Nearer Gdańsk there is a Premonstratensian nunnery of 1209 at Żukowo

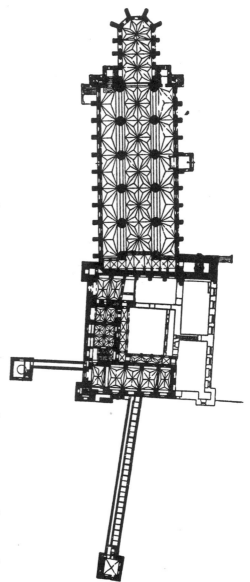

65   Kwidzyn: castle and cathedral, 1:1,300

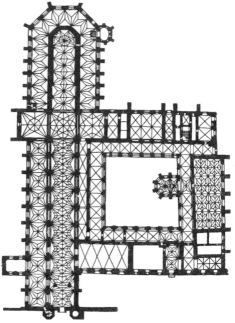

66   Oliwa: abbey, 1:1,250

(Zuckau), whose architecturally plain box of a church is full of charming and well-kept furniture, a big baroque high altar, two sixteenth century side altars, and best of all the early seventeenth century nuns' gallery, all gilt leaves, and joined by a stair to a pulpit in the same manner fenced with a grille; did it keep the nuns in or the laity out? Away to the south the Cistercian house at Koronowo (Krone an der Brahe), a community first created about 1250, moved to its present site after 1285 and there created a version of Pelplin reduced to essentials. The church has a seven-bay nave content with plaster vaults, a square-ended chancel with two big star vaults, and simple transepts; its one distinction is the three-sided, outward-facing apse of each nave chapel, a ripple of lighter spaces beyond the aisles.

Oliwa is far grander, the one Cistercian rival to Pelplin in all northern Poland. The 11 rulers of Pomerelia brought monks here before 1178. Their church has been repeatedly destroyed and rebuilt, each time a little taller. There are some thirteenth century traces, but its splendid length of 300 feet is the result of rebuilding after the fire of 1350. The west front once looked like that of Pelplin, but now there is a lively doorway of 1688, the gable is plastered over, and in 1771 the two octagonal turrets were crowned with slender copper spires. Inside, the arcade has heavy thirteenth century proportions, and the south aisle is still a narrow passage; the north aisle is broader and star-vaulted; the nave was vaultless until the restoration after 1577 gave it ten pretty plaster domes. The chancel seems all of a part with it, but its aisles run a splendid series of spring vaults all round its five-sided apse. The space is ruled by its furnishings, Michael Wulff's 5,000-pipe organ of the 1760s which fills the west end with dark clouds and mechanical angels, the burst of fleecy white clouds in the east. There is a pretty monument of 1760 by the Gdańsk sculptor Meissner. The convent has kept its Cistercian plan – the cloister, the tall apsed and vaulted fountain building on its south side, the chapter house vaulted from two elaborate granite columns. But its refectory is a little classic of the latest Gothic, a fiddly rib vault set on Tuscan columns in 1594 by Bartholomaus Piper, who may well have vaulted the nave too. And some of the park remains, part formal, part picturesque, part suburban, preserving a long watery vista between ill-tended avenues towards the sea.

VISTULA TOWNS AND VILLAGES

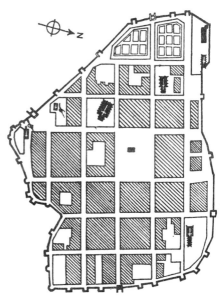

67   Chełmno: town plan, 1:10,000

Toruń was the first town to be incorporated under the Order, Chełmno (Kulm) the second. It seems that the original settlement, which got a charter in 1233, lay in the Vistula flood plain, and that the grandiose plan on the edge of the bluff above was made a generation later. It is a chequer of streets half a mile long and a third broad. It was too ambitious; Toruń and Gdańsk soon passed it and by the middle of the fourteenth century, the heyday of other Vistula towns, its bloom had gone. Only one important building went up after 1400, its unlikely town hall.

The parish church lies south of the market place and at an angle, designed or not, to the street grid, so that as you approach it it displays to you its full 160-foot length, its majestic north tower, solid and well-proportioned and yet oddly rough, and the martial array of gables and pinnacled buttresses that crowns its aisles. It was begun about 1300, and in 1333 the north tower was complete; yet its south companion never got beyond a stump lower than the nave's end gable. Inside it is a five-bay hall, with an aisleless rectangular chancel of singular clarity and grace. There are no fantasies over our heads, only cross vaults, but the octagonal pillars are slenderer than usual, slenderer even than in the great sophisticated churches of Toruń; everything is held together by a system of thin shafts that climb the walls of the chancel and the corners of the pillars of the nave. This is almost the only survivor of the first generation of brick hall churches in Prussia.

113   The town has five other churches, not one to be ignored. The Dominicans settled in its northern corner about 1240; their church has been much altered inside but has kept an admirable fifteenth century face, a big gable which is just row upon row of panels set in a wavy motion by shallow canted buttress-like pilasters, and on the porch in front a smaller fellow to it. In the north-west corner on the bluff's edge an alarmingly gabled nineteenth century hospital conceals an aisleless Cistercian nuns' church of the early fourteenth century which is as full of baroque furniture as the parish church. In the southern salient, where the road leads out to Toruń, lie the hospital church of św. Duch (the Holy Spirit), six aisleless bays of about 1300 with a tall plain tower of the best proportions, and the tiny chapel of św. Marcin with two lively gables on its simple box. The best is the church of the now vanished Franciscan convent founded west of the square in 1255. It seems it went up as the fourteenth century went on; first the simple three bay chancel, then a three bay hall nave whose centre vessel and centre bay are wider than the rest while the centre vessel is also higher – a delicate exercise in centralisation. Walls and windows are all bare, but the rectangular pillars have shafts in the centres of their sides and above there is a surprising elaboration of ribs. Outside it is plainer still, with but one friendly turret; do not let that put you off the search for somebody to let you in.

Secular buildings of value are few. The walls are almost complete, but very plain, and only one unambitious north-eastern gate remains. In 1772 Frederick the Great found only an eighth of the houses occupied, and everywhere vacant lots and the cellars of vanished buildings; it is not surprising that the streets are dull and even the square simply framed in decent eighteenth and nineteenth century façades. But in the sixteenth century Chełmno had prospered under Polish rule, and its monument

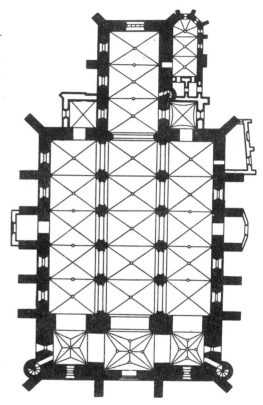

68   Chełmno: St. Mary, 1:625

28 is the extraordinary town hall begun in 1567. It is a miniature of that begun at Poznań in 1550, a simple block with a tall square tower. For two storeys it sports no more than tricky heads to doors and windows, but the third has a playfully ill-conceived Ionic order, and the roofline is all scrolls and finials and little flags, and in 1721 the tower got a double lantern. It is as bright as an iced cake and quite as unsuitable for this sober town.

4 The cathedral of the Chełmno diocese lies out in the country half-way to Toruń at Chełmża (Kulmsee). The first church was begun here in 1251, and by 1263 its transepts stood with their odd little corner towers. But after a fire in 1286 the work slowed down, and what we see was not complete until about 1350, and much adapted in the fifteenth century. It is a typical large Prussian town church; the plan built up out of rectangles, octagonal pillars with corner shafts and half-hexagonal ones on nave and aisle sides, star vaults, more elaborate in the chancel which has liernes like Pelplin. Much of the furniture is lost, most recently in a fire in 1951, and including, alas, a pretty rood arch with angels climbing its double curves; but some monuments remain, in red marble for bishop Kostka who died in 1595, and, high on the chancel wall, a tablet of 1661 from which a disdainful clerical face complains, the inscription says, of 'hostilitas indigena'. The surroundings are peaceful enough now, and the elaborate but modernised panelling of the east gable faces a reedy lake where people row and swim.

The other towns along the river are remarkable if anything for their situations. I have described what is to be found at Gniew and Świecie. Bydgoszcz (Bromberg) conceals two ordinary fifteenth century brick churches in miles of industrial sprawl. Grudziądz (Graudenz) is a smaller version of Chełmno, with even duller houses and 115 a rough, squat fourteenth century hall church; but it confronts the river with a splendid rampart made spontaneously of tall fortified warehouses, buttress on buttress. On the opposite bank, Nowe (Neuenburg) did not get its charter till 1350. The Order built a small house at its north-east corner; its parish church is solid and conventional, the hall nave vaulted only in 1911, the chancel's tunnel roof a maze of ribs. The Franciscan convent to the south is the first in the area, founded in 1282, and probably built in the first half of the fourteenth century. Its surprising crypt supports the apsed chancel on a complete eight-pointed star spreading from one granite column, and the octagon the brick ribs describe adapts to the nave foundations with the cut-off vaulted corners that appear at Malbork. Most of what stands above was rebuilt in 1902 after a fire – vaults and all – and it is hard to believe that before that the chancel had a wooden roof of 1658, so convincing is its present elegance.

The road north along the river passes some handsome fourteenth century churches. That of Piaseczno (Pehsken) has a star-vaulted chancel dated 1348, a nave later widened to a six-pillared hall and ceiled in plaster, and a lively eastern gable; and its country rococo furniture – green and gold high altar, pulpit and font to match in white and gold, organ, side altars, carved benches – is all as fresh and delicious as two hundred years ago. Beyond Gniew, Lignowy (Adlig-Liebenau) has more white and gold furnishings, though not so good, and here the chancel has cellular vaults, and the outside is singularly imposing, with a tall gabled and buttressed tower and the whole on a mound ringed by a great ditch. The last town on the main stream is Tczew (Dirschau), an ugly place well by-passed. It had taken shape before the Order seized it in 1309. The Dominicans came in 1289, and built a church which is plain enough inside but admonishes the town with a strange bell turret placed off-centre above a huge west porch like a deep archway. The parish church is better, simple outside save for gables ranked above the aisles but with a fourteenth century nave which is a crisp consistent model of the type. In 1961 I thought the town's most impressive monument the wreck of the truss girder bridge, built by Lentze in 1850, and then one of the largest in Europe.

West of the river there is little to see that I have not already described, the castles far out at Bytów and Człuchów, the convents of Kartuzy and Żukowo. The undistinguished town of Starogard (Preussisch Stargard) has a much restored church which has kept east and west gabled fronts of a pomp quite unrelated to its size. Just south of Wejherowo (Neustadt) a rustic Calvary has pink painted chapels disposed on a beech clad hill, like the Kalwarya Zebrzydowska near Cracow. For the rest, Kasubia is woods and lakes and stony fields. But on the main road south of Gdańsk can be found, all but swallowed up in the suburban sprawl of Pruszcz (Praust), the best village church west of the river. It is a solid late mediaeval hall, fat tower with octagonal spire; its joy is its Lutheran furniture, which starts with the pulpit of 1578, goes on to the font of 1635, galleries adorned with grotesque creatures, stalls painted with scenes and rhyming captions, and finishes with the organ of 1728; and, outside, its churchyard gate is carved with skulls. It is all much earlier than the Romish glitter of Piaseczno and Żukowo.

Malbork matches Tczew, twelve miles away over the flat meadows that separate the main stream of the Vistula and its largest branch the Nogat. The town got its charter in 1276; its long oblong beside the river repeats the gigantic castle's shape, and takes less space. The ruins of its houses have been replaced by well-designed, four-storey flats in long staggered rows, and among them some monuments still stand: two gates, the southern battlemented, the western gabled; the delightful town hall, probably of about 1370, windows in big arched recesses, a frieze above them, battlements above it and on the saucy corner turrets, a handsome south gable with tall recessed panels crowned by arches, a perfect expression of the confidence of these small towns when the Order's rule was undisturbed; the church of św. Jan, rebuilt completely after the siege of 1457, a hall almost broad enough to have been built for Protestant sermons, almost all net-vaulted but with three cellular vaults and one that can't make up its mind, well-restored and surprisingly well-furnished with old altars and a carved archangel hung from the ceiling.

In antiquity and riches Elbląg (Elbing) used to rank with Toruń and Gdańsk; half-a-dozen churches, streets of houses in the Dutch fashion. The castle was founded in 1237, and settlers came from Lübeck to build the new port for the Order's conquests; from 1251 to 1309 the Order made its headquarters here; in 1347 it had grown enough to need a 'new town' added to the east. But as time went on it yielded more and more to Gdańsk, and profited only from Gdańsk's quarrels; from 1579 to 1628, for instance, the English timber buyers settled here. Their monuments survive in the battered cloister of the Dominican church, which I found in 1961 fenced off behind a notice that said BEWARE! EVIL DOG. The friars came in 1246, and their chancel, low, bare, with cross vaults rising from wall shafts, was one of the oldest surviving church buildings in Prussia, but had been gutted. Beside it stood the big simple north gate, the Brama Targowa. To the south the old town lay in rubble, all the way to the skeleton of the hospital chapel of św. Duch and the site of the Knights' castle which the citizens destroyed in 1454. The fragments of old houses were too sad to be described. In the centre of it all św. Mikołaj still rose, newly rebuilt, gaunt and grand. Most of it is unvaulted, as it has been since the fire of 1777, but there are rich vaults in side chapels, two of 1403 above the sacristy south of the chancel and north of it one most elaborately starred, with three big windows and uncommon outward show, built on in 1494 for the town council. A fine set of late mediaeval altars has been installed, and above the high altar hangs again the crucifix of 1410, a long exhausted gentle figure. Around the church new blocks of flats are rising, and shops, and a modern street system for pedestrians; sensible, but the end of the parallel streets running down to the riverside which once made Elbląg so handsome a miniature of Lübeck and Gdańsk.

South of Elbląg the delightful lake country begins again, a consolation for the ruin of towns like Susz (Rosenberg) and Dzierzgoń (Christburg) and the salvation of others like Ostróda (Osterode) and Pasym (Passenheim) whose buildings do not bear much inspection but whose situations charm. The best church exterior is that of Iława (Deutsch-Eylau): east gable, gabled north tower, all the detail very three-dimensional, fourteenth century work rich and harmonious enough for one of the churches in Toruń. At Nowe Miasto Lubawskie (Neumarkt) nearby the church is odd and solid, very low chancel and aisles and tall nave, but full of seventeenth century Catholic clutter, many altars, pulpit, font dated 1652; the nave's almost blind walls display huge rustic frescoes of the Old and New Testaments, dated in one place 1625; and nave and aisles are spanned by carpenters' arches, that of 1713 which carries the Rood, solid enough for all its jerks, those in the aisles quite innocent of structure and seeming only to bear little pictures in gilt frames, pretty travesties of great rood arches like that of św. Jakub in Toruń. For a mediaeval church interior one must seek Morąg (Mohrungen), a low early star-vaulted chancel and aisles with fan-shaped cellular vaults put in in 1503 by Matz, who was recommended by Hetzel the master of St. Mary in Gdańsk. The church is full of furniture and monuments still, and the war spared the handsome gabled brick block of the town hall. The most ambitious of these town halls, though, is that of Pasłęk (Preussich Holland), extended on arches over the street; its front is fifteenth century and in 1650 it was given a pilastered gable. I have mentioned its plain castle; it has a big plain church too, and an imposing south gate; but the war has removed the old gabled houses the guidebooks list.

I have not visited all the village churches, and fear to list too many when the enthusiast can find them catalogued elsewhere, and war and time may have done their worst. There should be more cellular vaults, very possibly also by Matz, at Marianka (Marienfelde) north-west of Pasłęk. Pretty sixteenth and seventeenth century interiors should survive in the neglected and overgrown church at Stare Miasto (Altstadt) further west where one Haarhausen painted pews, gallery, and ceiling in the 1690s, and at Młynary (Mühlhausen) east of Elbląg where the chancel ceiling was painted, and everything else, from pulpit of 1654 to two-decker stalls of 1739, most elaborately carved. In the forest country of southern Pomesania wooden churches are still in use; the best is south-east of Ostróda at Rychnowo (Reichenau) where the tower is an irregular octagon, apparently of 1707, and the nave has painted ceiling, gallery, pulpit, and doors. Outside Olsztynek (Hohenstein) some typical wooden buildings of the 'Wilderness' have been collected, the start of an open-air museum on Scandinavian lines; scattered about a big, bare area are a windmill, thatched cottages, a timber-framed 'bolt' house whose upper storey projects on an arcade, and a pretty thatched church with more painted furniture.

North of Tczew and Malbork extend the Vistula fens, the Żuławy. A hundred-foot wall of dunes from Gdańsk to the lagoon entrance at Baltijsk shuts them in; here the north-east gales throw up amber from its deep and secret mines off the Soviet coast. In the early Middle Ages much that is now land was swamp, with inhabited islands now just visible as contours on the map; in the thirteenth century cultivation extended only so far as the road that twists from Cedry through Lubieszewo to Marynowy, and a belt of marsh ran from the present river mouth to the lake south of Elbląg. Drainage went on piecemeal for centuries, but the greatest effort was made in the sixteenth and seventeenth centuries, as in England under Dutch direction. Much was flooded once more in 1945 as the Germans retreated, but now it is back to polder country, innumerable ditches and willows, a grey-green vastness, grim in winter but exhilarating under driven cloud and splashes of sunlight. Here the standard farmhouse is the 'bolt' type, with a half-timber gable carried forward on a row of wooden posts. The oldest known is 'Gute Herberge', which sharp eyes will spot amid the suburban sprawl of Lipce, by the main road about four miles south of the centre of Gdansk. In some of those built around 1800 the posts have become rustic columns with Ionic capitals, as in one beside the road south-west from Nowy Dwór through Orłowo. More survive in villages like Stalewo (Stalle) and Marynowy (Marienau), solid memorials of the work of generations on this prosperous earth.

Old churches are many but, with soft foundations, seldom massive. The largest is at Nowy Staw (Neuteich), begun about 1400; two unfinished western towers, a nave with low aisles, flat ceiling, a great blank arcade that reaches up its walls to the clerestory, and a low, well-proportioned chancel star-vaulted in the 1570s. Most of them advertise themselves with timber tower tops, often huge and hardly related at all to the brick structures beneath. At one time or another, for these timber things are practically dateless, octagonal belfries were set down plump on square bases at Kończewice (Kunzendorf) near Tczew and Kmiecin (Fürstenau) and Lubieszewo (Ladekopp) near Nowy Dwor; at Fiszewo (Fischau) between Malbork and Elbląg the wooden stage stayed square, but tapered, expanded, and tapered again; and at Tuja (Tiege) the brick tower is an octagon with buttresses of astonishing mass that carries its bells in an anticlimactic wooden shed. There are pretty, rustic seventeenth and eighteenth century interiors. At Cyganek (Tiegenhagen) the half-timber nave of about 1640 has battered but still lively painted gallery and ceilings. Near Malbork, the church at Kacynos (Katznase) still has a complete set of carved and painted pews, gallery, and pulpit, but in 1967 it served only to house chickens. And at Stegna (Steegen), on the edge of the dunes, pulpit and font are elaborately carved and a model ship hangs from the painted ceiling among the brass chandeliers.

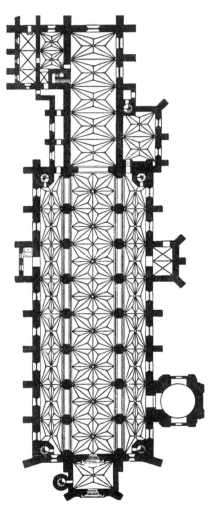

WARMIA AND MASURIA

The success of fourteenth century colonisation inland made Warmia the largest and the richest of the bishoprics founded under the protection of the Order. When the clergy took a third of its land they marked out a compact triangle with its apex at Braniewo, divided in turn between bishop and cathedral chapter; in 1466 they came under Polish rule, joined to Poland by a narrow coastal strip at Frombork; this area is the Ermeland of the historical atlases, and it corresponds roughly to the present powiaty of Braniewo, Lidzbark, Biskupiec and Olsztyn. For three centuries it remained a Catholic peninsula in Lutheran Prussia. It has not only a charming countryside, lakes, woods, red-brick village churches standing in clumps of trees, but also a distinct architecture, created in part by its bishops' fourteenth century builders and in part by generations of Catholic devotion.

Frombork (Frauenburg) is the cathedral town, small, now largely ruined, its ambitious hall church of św. Mikołaj in 1961 still a shell. On the hill above, the cathedral and its surroundings suffered too. But the wealth of the place is clear enough. A massive brick wall, solid west and south gates, a huge south-western keep on a fifteenth century octagonal base protect an ample cathedral close. Another fifteenth and sixteenth century building, the bishops' palace, filled in the south-eastern side, later buildings include a museum to Copernicus who was a canon here, and above them all rise the branches of great trees.

The cathedral was begun in 1329. The chancel was consecrated in 1342; there may have been a pause before work started on the nave, but the whole was complete in 1388. On plan it is most ambitious, a hall nave of eight bays, an aisleless chancel of five shorter ones, in length – 300 feet – among the three or four largest churches of Prussia. But its first master set the chancel vaults surprisingly low for his generation, keeping to the old classical height no more than double width. This Cistercian self-denial cramped the whole building under vaults no more than 55 feet high, and the first glimpse of the interior is a disappointment. The chancel best repays examination; dark, heavy, but handsome stalls of the 1730s, sedilia of about 1500, and above this

69   Frombork: cathedral

clusters of shafts that climb the walls to spray into steep and elegantly drawn four-pointed stars. Beside it the nave seems crude, for the six-and-eight-pointed stars rise from nineteenth century cardboard crowns on the octagonal pillars and the eighteenth and nineteenth century furniture is mediocre. But to the south projects the chapel bishop Szembek built in 1732 to house his collection of relics. Its grille, all curling leaves of iron, is our introduction to East Prussian metalwork, made by the Schwarz brothers from Reszel who also worked at św. Lipka. Behind it rises a painted cupola, and the altar's frame is set with silver-mounted boxes that hold tiny bones, at least thirty-three different, like so many postage stamps.

There are the same contrasts outside. The east gable is well proportioned and as simple as they come. But within the big, closed rectangle of the nave rise four showy octagonal corner turrets crowned by long thin spikes, an uncommon device, and on the west front they frame a gable with a procession of blank niches, each with a tiny finial, up one slope and down the other. Beneath it a big west porch was put on, probably when all else was finished. Its gables seek by ingenious double-talk to repeat the angle of the gable above while screening a horizontal roofline. Its outer door is framed in stone carved with beasts, vines, and geometrical patterns, and the main door within is richer still, its jambs a shallow pattern of blind tracery with incised heads in a row where there should be capitals, its voussoirs little canopied figures ranged in a schematic Last Judgment, and stone beasts climbing up its outermost edge to be silhouetted against the dark pressed-clay patterns of the wall. The very ribs of the vault are carved into a choir of angels. Rude in detail, the work perhaps of Gotland craftsmen, it is a most festive whole. And so is the silhouette of the whole church, its turrets and attendant towers, a flurry of spires you can see far away across the shallow sandy sea.

The bishops resided chiefly in the splendid castle I have described at Lidzbark and in the much larger coastal town of Braniewo (Braunsberg). It got a charter about 1250 and in 1345 sprouted a New Town, like those of Elbląg and Toruń, on the right bank of the river. Here in 1565 Cardinal Stanisław Hosius, the leader of the Polish Counter-Reformation, founded the first Jesuit college in Poland. But in 1945 it was laid waste, and in 1961 I found little sign of any effort to pick up the pieces. The great parish church of św. Katarzyna was begun in 1343 and vaulted, it seems, in the 1440s. It is a six-bay hall given a liveliness of plan unusual in Warmia by attaching a five-sided central apse and by chamfering off the eastern corners of the aisles. From its great octagonal pillars used to rise the richest of star vaults, four four-pointed stars to each nave or aisle bay. I found it a shell open to the air, and the mass of the square tower that aimed to rival the towers of Gdańsk was reduced to one vertiginous finger of brick accusing heaven. There were fragments of the half-baroque town hall, of the bishops' castle, and of the four-storey block of the 'Stone House' remodelled for the Jesuits in the 1690s. I stood in the dust and puzzled over the seven close-printed pages in Dehio, and a cadet band came past leading what could well have been the whole adult male population of the place.

The typical Warmian town church is simply a great box, a brick hall with octagonal pillars, star vaults, tall gables at each end of one huge roof, no separate chancel and one massive square west tower. The classic example is Dobre Miasto (Guttstadt), built for a college of priests whose simple brick convent still stands to the south. Its body went up between 1376 and 1396, seven bays long, bigger than the nave at Frombork; its tower was begun a century later and got its present gables in 1895. Inside, it has very marked arcades between nave and aisles and relatively steep and three-dimensional eight-pointed star vaults. Its furniture is mediocre, except for the mediaeval lions built into the choir stalls. Much more imposing is the view from south of the town of church and convent established with such solid authority in the green water-meadows. And on the way we passed the Storks' Tower, a plain round brick thing, and there upon it perched a great storks' nest.

With one exception the main town churches follow this pattern. At Reszel (Rössel) the church was begun about 1350, like the castle already described which stands beside it, and finally vaulted in the 1470s with the crowded Braniewo system of four stars to a bay. After a fire in 1806 it was rebuilt with oppressively repetitive detail, and of its furniture only a big baldacchino over the font looks good. But the town is pretty, little injured, crowded with old houses, irregular in feeling despite its apparently regular plan, displaying well clumped gables and towers above its trees. Barczewo (Wartenberg) has suffered much more; its market-square has been extended northwards by a whole razed block. Its main church has a solid tower, all white plastered panels, and a box nave of five bays covered after a fire in 1544 with the latest types of vault; in the centre, domes covered in stars developed into net-like directionlessness, in the aisles a cellular bay or two. East of the square rises the Franciscan church originally built in the 1380s, of which only the east gable is evidence, and revaulted around 1600, inside still impressively tall if bare of detail. In its south chapel stands a big expensive-looking black and white marble monument to Cardinal Andrzej Batory, King Stefan's nephew, who kneels at a carved altar and on a tomb, and his brother Baltazar who sleeps under it; it was commissioned in 1598, probably from the Gdańsk workshop of Willem van den Block – good Netherlandish work, nothing original, but a surprise.

At Lidzbark (Heilsberg) the church was begun before 1350, and as a basilica; only after a fire brought down the vaults in 1498 did it become a hall, with more elaborate star vaults; the nineteenth century added a chancel and most of the furniture. But its tower is a fit foil to the superb castle I have already described, with two finely detailed stages with flanking chapel gables that must be fourteenth century and then a huge mass of plain brick topped by a triple baroque lantern. The town has kept one brick gate between two fat round towers. And south of the church across the river rises the simple orangery created by the Polish noblemen who came here as bishops, Potocki who began it in the 1710s, and Ignacy Krasiński who inspired the conservative patriots of the Confederation of Bar and chaired the committee which drafted the 1791 Constitution.

Grandest of all these churches is that of Olsztyn (Allenstein), now the duchy capital, with a new hotel, and a thumpingly emphatic department store by Ihnatowicz and Sołtan, and the pretty canons' castle, and fake gabled fronts going up round its ruined square. Św. Jakub was begun in the 1370s. Its plan is a big six-bay box, which sports a proud east gable with nine sharply-detailed panels. Its west tower is a stupendous mass of brick, specked with yellow and green glazed bits and pieces, panelled with irritating iteration, the deep passages cut through its base well showing how solid it is. Inside, the eye rises quickly from the octagonal piers and the tall moulded wall arcades to the fascinating sixteenth century vaults, nets that progress from what might almost have been stars to a jabber of tiny parallelograms, and in the aisles pretty almost weightless crinkly paper patterns of cells.

Among Warmian town churches the one exception to the rule of the hall is at Orneta (Wormditt). The little town stands, almost undamaged, on a wooded hill above a tributary of the Pasłęka. Its square has a few respectable eighteenth century houses on lumpish arcades and in its centre the brick mass of the town hall begun in

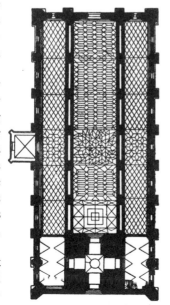

70 Olsztyn: parish church, 1:800

1373. The church lies to the south-west, on the edge of the bluff. As originally built between the 1340s and the 1370s it was modest and plain, five bays of nave and of aisles no more than half its height, no chancel. But between 1422 and 1494 it was wholly reshaped. The nave was revaulted, and ranks of disproportionately broad chapels added to north and south. Inside it became alarmingly restless, with huge baroque altars, four stars to each steeply arched nave bay that to the eye persist in spelling out great eight-pointed ones that overlap and interlock, and the great bare spread of wall above the arcades grudgingly contradicting this elaboration. This is nothing to what goes on outside. Aisles and chapels together got new transverse roofs, and to leave the clerestory windows clear their gables were set, not over each bay, but over each division, so that at each end half a gable rises and is cut off by the sheer wall of the east or west façade. Everything but the solid tower, left flush with the west front, is broken up by buttresses and finials and panels into a complete set of *chevaux de frise*. Above and below the chapel windows run horizontal bands, now broken, of bricks moulded into faces and vegetable spirals, and there are vertical strips of them on the north side too. This odd inspiration combined the spiked buttresses of św. Jakub at Toruń and the multiple gables of Gdańsk churches to create one of the showpieces of mediaeval brick architecture.

Warmia proper is poor in old village churches; the best, on its northern edge, belong to the rich group around Bartoszyce and Barciany. There are some wooden towers like that of Radostowo (Freudenberg) east of Dobre Miasto, and this church and that of Szalnia (Schalmey) south of Braniewo have excellent baroque interiors, the former all done between 1752 and 1783, the latter late seventeenth century with pulpit and altars and painted panelled ceiling and the Last Judgment on the east wall. In 1639 a Franciscan convent was founded at Stoczek (Springborn), a couple of miles north of the Lidzbark-Bisztynek road; later rebuilding, particularly between 1708 and 1741, turned it into a splendid sculptural pilgrimage church group – the convent of several different heights, the church with a chancel tied into the convent by an eastern tower and a rather gloomy circular domed nave, and round this dome a three-sided cloister with two jolly turreted corner chapels. It had become one of the Warmian succession of baroque pilgrimage churches, which would seem commonplace enough perhaps in Bohemia or Bavaria but appear most exotic in these Protestant forests.

Św. Lipka (Heiligelinde) is the earliest and the finest. It lies out in the country 12 two miles east of Reszel; coming down the shady road you catch a glimpse of pink and white plaster, and suddenly the whole iced cake stands there in front of the trees' intense green, sprouting two copper spires, framed in a high wall with towered corner chapels all as brightly painted, preceded by a balustrade of saints. In its elements this is a standard east European pilgrimage place, and the church interior conforms to Counter-Reformation rules, with galleries in its aisles and colossal fluted pilasters and heavy dark altars; across its nave, though, a carved lime-tree with a silver Madonna faces the pulpit. It was begun in 1687, the builder Josef Ertly from Wilno, whom some historians seem to think unqualified to design it, and completed about 1730. The cloister that surrounds it was not begun until 1704 and finished even later, but it was the first of its kind in Warmia and looks much like the seventeenth century hill-top sanctuaries of Bohemia. Its glory is the iron gates Johann 1͏ and Christoph Schwarz of Reszel made in 1734, a confident and unsparingly rich display of three-dimensional foliage in solid metal, nothing wiry or tinny. And the whole group is audaciously pretty, the otiose architecture, the Madonna high on the façade in a deep niche full of leaves and branches, a pointless delight.

Prussia did not escape the great plague which ravaged eastern and central Europe in 1709 and 1710; it checked building at św. Lipka, but encouraged it elsewhere as vows were carried out. Three more pilgrimage churches went up, all by the Orneta builder Johann Christoph Reimers. In 1715 he began the first, at Krosno (Krossen), down two miles of rough cobble track north-east from Orneta, hemmed in by splendid chestnuts and sycamores. Here everything is broad, fat, earthbound, the squashed domes of the cloister's corner chapels, the fussy façade; but there is more decent wrought iron, and inside it is a big light hall, white, pink, and gold, with side chapels, a hideously blue organ, and pretty rococo stalls. In 1720 followed Chwalęcin (Stegmannsdorf), north-west of Orneta across a military area, which I have not seen; it should be a three-naved church, its ceiling richly frescoed in 1748, its cloister not complete till 1836. Międzylesie (Schönwiese) east of Dobre Miasto is even simpler, a mere chapel of 1722 rebuilt in the 1750s, containing more white and gold rococo furniture, and surrounded by no more than a churchyard wall that merges with the west façade. But, for their unexpectedness, these pretty churches can be forgiven much.

Outside Warmia the mediaeval hall church becomes rare again. Only one south of the Soviet border is as old as the fourteenth century, the solid little church in the ruined and disregarded town of Sępopol (Schippenbeil); outside it is all tall proportions and brandishes a huge tower, but inside it is low and broad under fifteenth century star vaults and has some admirably lively seventeenth century furniture. The church at Kętrzyn (Rastenburg) began in the 1360s as a basilica, and only after 1470 turned into a Warmian sort of hall, with a chancel, block-like octagonal pillars, and cellular vaults by Matz whose shallow relief stars hardly crinkle the underlying domes. Its effect has been sadly blunted by plastering. The rest of the town has been much damaged; pieces of the fortifications remain around the church, and there is a fragment of a fragment of the castle.

Most attractive by far of these towns is Bartoszyce (Bartenstein). In the last century its market-place was extended into a broad street, so that one end is now closed by the brick panels and gables of the Lidzbarska Brama, and along its north side extends the church, plainly made of the most ingratiating brick. Inside it is all white, two-bay apsed chancel, very low aisles, and a tall nave with blank wall arcades that reach short of the clerestory. This is the result of enlarging a church of the 1330s in 1370 or so; in the 1480s it got new vaults, four stars each to bays that nonchalantly do not quite conform to the ground plan. Whatever their elaborations, these Prussian churches are country buildings, and their vaults are the ideas of men who have lain in the fields and watched the patterns twigs and branches make against the sky.

Between Bartoszyce and Kętrzyn the country is uncommonly open, ploughed acres roll away to distant dark margins of forest, and every few miles another village clusters in the trees about its church. These are just clumps of houses, and almost never planned; an exception is Wojciechy (Albrechtsdorf) west of Bartoszyce, a rectangular 'green' framed by two rows of cottages and on which church, inn, and smithy stand. But the variety of church towers and gables makes this a sort of Somerset in brick. I can hardly do more than list them and suggest to the enthusiast a day in a car on the country roads. The most classic is Sątopy (Santoppen) between Reszel and Bisztynek, founded in 1337, a long building with a distinguished east gable of pinnacles diagonally set, corner buttresses with lantern tops, and a tall gabled tower with a carefully proportioned succession of panels, all on a steep hillock among grand trees. West of Bisztynek Kiwity (Kiwitten) displays the same proportions and decoration, much restored, and should preserve a set of rococo furniture; north of it, Paluzy (Plausen) has another big tower with slenderer panels, and the date 1400 on the weathercock; Łabędnik (Schwansfeld) sports one imposing east gable, and Sokolica (Falkenau), though small, another that would not disgrace an abbey. Łankiejmy (Langheim) got its tower as late as 1500, and is more elaborate, the brick twisted into curved shapes and arcades, and at Kraskowo (Schönfliess), further towards Kętrzyn, the tower's sides have three tall panels only, one of which reaches up into a small gable recently altered. At Sątoczno (Leunenburg) and Parys (Paaris) 12 two-layered panels frame the bell storey's deep windows so that the tower loses mass as it goes up. Further north, Mołtajny (Molteinen) faces the village with the grand but rather rough gables of chancel and sacristy side by side, and Srokowo (Drengfurth) has a big tower with three storeys of panels. There are other churches notable for furniture, baroque at Wozławki (Wuslack), a very grand object on a lump with a domed south chapel of 1727, rococo at Grzęda (Sturmhübel) where the whole building was remodelled between 1755 and 1783, at Galiny (Gallingen) almost neo-classical in simplicity. But the whole group's charm is in their red, red brick against the infinite green distance and the limitless sky.

Further east you are in Masuria, and the wilderness closes round again. In spite of the Order's fourteenth century outposts, settlement reached here only in the sixteenth century. At Węgorzowo (Angerburg) the church begun in 1605 still has big ribby star vaults over the nave, but its superb furniture is properly seventeenth century, all gold and dark blue – pulpit of 1610, organ of 1647, prayer seats of about 1700 with twisted columns. At Olecko (Treuburg) still farther east the town was not laid out until 1560, almost contemporary with Zamość, and then on a parody of a mediaeval plan with one of the largest market places in all Central Europe. Out here the churches are of timber, simple belfried wooden boxes like Ostrykół (Scharfenrade) begun in 1667 and Wieliczki (Wallenrode) begun in 1693, and the scattered villages often wooden too; an exception is the brick octagon of 1826 at Radzieje (Rosengarten), said to have been designed by Schinkel's patron and pupil Frederick William IV of Prussia. Much odder is the Greek Orthodox settlement at Wojnowo (Eckertsdorf). Members of a sect expelled by the Russians were given land here by Frederick William III about 1840. They built wooden cottages with bath-sheds behind them on the edge of the slow river, and a wooden box of a church – the second on its site – which sports a silvered spire on its bell turret and a silvered onion dome. An old true believer let us in to see its valueless possessions, a strange empty experience.

In mediaeval Prussia secular landowners were insignificant. Though the Order handed out great blocks of land to speculators, it usually recovered the greater part of them when the immigration quotas went unfilled and the land unploughed. But under the Protestant dukes great estates were formed, though hardly a country house that stands now was begun before 1600; an exception is Galiny (Gallingen), where most of the plain ranges round the courtyard were built by 1589, and have some still Gothic rooms. An example of the early seventeenth century house, a plain block with a big hipped roof, survives at Nakomiady (Eichmedien) south-east of Kętrzyn. Greater ostentation awaited the example of the showiest of Prussian rulers, Kurfürst Frederick William III who, in 1701, had himself crowned Frederick William I at Königsberg. In 1693 his builder Nering, who had introduced the colossal order into the architecture of Berlin, began for him a small but imposing hunting-lodge called Friedrichshoff at what used to be Gross-Holstein west of Königsberg in the Pregola marches. In 1696 he created the Berlin Academy, and one of its first professors was Jean Baptiste Broebe, a Frenchman who had been city architect at Bremen. In the same year this man produced plans for the remodelling and extension of the big plain house of the 1620s at Słobity (Schlobitten) near Pasłęk; work went on there until 1721 under a local builder, Johann Caspar Hindersin, who also reshaped the big half-courtyard house at Markowo (Reichertswalde) in 1721 and in 1717 the 'Schlösschen' at Morąg. Słobity is not a very strenuous effort. The shape of the old house is clear enough in the long simple fronts with two or three projecting bays at each end; there is no centre-piece, no colossal order, just panel strips marking the corners and arms and trophies framing three dormers on the entrance side. It seems the interior was more ambitious, but all that stands now is a roofless shell.

In the end, the type of the big Prussian house was created by another Frenchman, Jean de Bodt, possibly of German descent, who when young had served in William of Orange's siege train in Ireland, drawn plans for Greenwich, and perhaps designed Stainborough (or 'Wentworth Castle') in Yorkshire. He came to Berlin about 1699 and in 1701 began the great Dohna house at Gładysze (Schlodien) a few miles east of Słobity. It is a long white and yellow pilastered block of thirteen bays with three of them advancing on each flank, a pedimented and columned three-bay centre, and a two-pitched roof. It used to hold painted ceilings, portraits, and tapestries, but now it is a barn. In 1709 Christoph Dohna's friend, Otto Magnus Dönhoff, gave Bodt his grandest job, Friedrichstein, south-east of Königsberg, with fronts of nineteen bays organised in the same manner, burnt out in 1945. In 1713 he planned the rebuilding of the now almost obliterated Dohna house at Karwiny (Karwinden) close to Słobity. His influence, and possibly his hand, can be seen in the original thirteen-bay centre of the house Otto Magnus' brother Bogislav Friedrich began in 1710 at Drogosze (Gross-Wolfsdorf) north-west of Kętrzyn and called Dönhoffstädt. Later, perhaps in the 1760s, a five-bay wing was added at each end, crude pilastered things, but the garden side has kept its original proportions well. It is a farm school now; I found a solitary man peeling potatoes in one of the less huge rooms, and he took me to the big plain staircase and to a pleasant enough salon upstairs. All these houses quite lack the richness of Bodt's French models, and are very far from the exuberance of Stainborough, but their English and French roots are plain enough.

Perhaps the prettiest Prussian house was Kamieniec (Finkenstein) near Susz in Pomesania, begun in 1716 possibly by John Collas, a military surveyor born in London of a Lorraine family, who had supervised the work at Friedrichstein and Dönhoffstädt. It was quite simple, with two big three-bay wings framing its entrance side and a carved pediment towards its formal garden. The local story is that the Russians burned it in 1946 out of vandalism. It makes a grand plastered ruin, with chimneys and their linking arches rising like a skeleton where the roof should be. Some smaller houses do not follow the norm; Lipowina (Lindenau), south-east of Braniewo, is of Danish neatness, only one main storey save for the pedimented centre, a three-sided projection towards the garden; it holds a school and a cinema now, and there is a ticket office in the hall. At the end of the century the Bodt tradition was still very much alive in places like Arklitten at Mołtajny, begun in 1782, now shabby but little damaged, fifteen bays with two projecting at each end and a self-consciously Doric columned centre with no pediment looking down an avenue of beeches. But by then the big building effort was over. Polish neo-classical intruded in the Vistula valley at Nawra, north-west of Toruń, a crisp little block of 1804 by Hilary Szpilowski with an inset portico, pilastered end bays like those of Zawadzki's Śmiełów and detached and set back flanking pavilions. More mild neo-classical designs went up north of the Soviet border; and there were attempts at sub-English neo-gothic like Sorkwity (Sorquitten) near Biskupiec with its 'Tudor' battlements.

The plain Prussian tradition is epitomised in Sztynort (Gross-Steinort) which stands on a long peninsula in Lake Mamry. From 1400 or so it was the home of the Lehndorffs. As it is now, it is mostly work of about 1690; the garden side is unaltered, a blank two-storey range whose height is doubled by a huge single-pitch hipped roof; its simple outward appearances give little help with dates. On the spit of land that encloses a lagoon-like part of the lake beside it a pretty little octagonal neo-gothic brick chapel stands among the trees, surrounded by the family's graves. Its last owner is not there; he was hanged in 1944 for his part in the plot against Hitler, whose headquarters, the 'Wolfschanze' or Wilcza Jama, are now a cyclopean mess of upheaved concrete, full of tiny frogs, in the woods east of Kętrzyn. Sztynort today is the grubby centre of a very ineffective looking state farm. Like its fellows it reminded me of great ruined or neglected houses in Ireland. And the 'Prussians' whose uncritical sense of duty served the Berlin monarchy and who so often symbolise German militarism had something in common with the Anglo-Irish gentry – the hard life in big plain houses, the military virtues, if not so many eccentricities.

The charm of Masuria is not architecture or anything man-made. It is the great meandering expanses of water, the long lines of trees, the light rippling away into a silent distance. It is hardly touched; the boats that cluster in the harbour at Mikołajki are insignificant spread upon the lake. One may come here in autumn, when the green is lightened everywhere by russet flames, and walk or ride or swim or sail, and forget the world.

7. Torun and Gdansk

The Order made its first settlement at Toruń (Thorn). It was a key ford and ferry point on the Vistula, and the garrison they set up in 1231 four miles downstream was soon transplanted to it; in December 1233 the town was given its charter. Its oldest part is only roughly regular, probably adapted to existing tracks, perhaps begun with the area around św. Jan between the main east-west street and the river; to the east the castle was fitted without symmetry into the angle made by a stream. The first market hall was built in 1259 on the present town hall site, and in 1264 the Order laid out the New Town to the east, along the castle stream and askew to the Old, but more regularly planned. In the fourteenth century Toruń was the leading city of Prussia and the focus of resistance to the Order, but she increasingly lost ground to Gdańsk and in 1900 her population of 30,000 was only a quarter of her rival's. Now there are big new factories and schools outside and bustling nineteenth century streets within her ancient centre. But she has preserved rows of old houses and warehouses and three churches which are the most expressive that the fourteenth century built anywhere in brick.

Most of the castle was ruined by the citizens in 1454; there remain only lumps of wall and the low solid 'Dansker' tower pushed eastwards astride the stream. From it a complete brick city wall runs west, and from this rise both a pert glass and concrete café and all sorts of ancient things, best seen from the imposing modern bridge. First come the pretty gables and little square tower of the Fraternity of St. George, built about 1490 and much renewed; then the Mostowa Brama (Fährtor), a massive rounded square reshaped in 1432 by Hans Gotland, marks the end of the immense mediaeval bridge demolished in 1877; a small tower sports a hoist; the Żeglarska Brama is just three openings in the wall; the Brama św. Ducha (Nonnentor), a broad chunk of brick, is the oldest of all; finally, at the south-west corner, the Krzywa Wieża (Schiefe Turm) is made of two great slabs that lean together. All this faces the broad river and beyond it nothing but a rough beach and scrubby trees.

Św. Jan itself, though begun about 1250, is now most of all a fifteenth century building, and the Dominican church founded in the 1260s has vanished. So Toruń's monument to the generation of Malbork and the parish church at Chełmno is the New Town's church of św. Jakub. It was begun in 1309 on quite a modest plan, first a long rectangular chancel, then a nave of three bays whose aisles embrace a massive square west tower. This starts plain, but the corners of its belfry stage are stepped out slightly; in photographs and drawings this looks alarming, but from ground level it satisfies the eye. The nave is a basilica, extended after 1359 by spring-vaulted chapels ranged between the buttresses; as a result it is very broad at ground level, and the

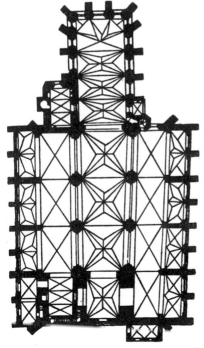

71   Toruń: św. Jakub, 1:650

72 Toruń: St. Mary, section, 1:500

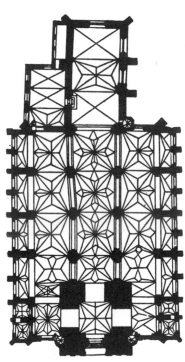

73 Toruń: św. Jan, 1:800

bare, dark height of the central vessel does not connect with the low, richly-shaped arcades, the wide aisles, the chapels' brightly lit elaborate furniture. A coarse, lively three-curved baroque rood arch leads to the chancel. Its star vaults are shorter and steeper, and half an eight-pointed star is accommodated in its square end by cutting off its corners with the rib triplets which at the same time were filling corners at Malbork and Pelpin. Its rich internal elegance is nothing to the frenzy of brick without. It has a superfluity of buttresses, every one crowned by a great panelled pinnacle; the east gable raises blank tracery and more pinnacles behind those the buttresses carry; there are a glazed inscription frieze, and deep splayed windows, and, in the angle of the north aisle, a stair turret is crowned by a pepper-pot of ingeniously moulded brick. If this marvellous *chevaux-de-frise* was all designed in 1309 it marks the enrichment of Prussian architecture as decisively and as proudly as anything the Order or the Cistercians built.

The Franciscans came, it is said, in 1239 and settled north-west of the main square. In the middle of the fourteenth century they built St. Mary, a prouder church still, 13 which they were using by 1371 and which has a bell in its east gable dated 1386. Outwardly it is just two great brick boxes. The nave is absolutely unadorned, for the wall conceals its buttresses and one huge roof has replaced the three which used to end in three fussy western gables. Height is the only target. You come from the square; the pretty jagged battlements and gables on the churchyard wall and gates are a last reminder of a human scale; above them sheer brick – plain shallow buttresses, tall untransomed windows – rises for ninety feet to the chancel gable's three octagonal turrets. The inside is almost as single-minded. The narrowness of the aisles enormously emphasises the nave's height. Triple shafts on each cardinal face give its octagonal pillars a delicate verticality. The vaults are rather depressed, and the scissor movement of their six-pointed stars puts us back in the Prussian forest. In św. Dorota at Wrocław, so similar in technique and scale, space was far more clearly articulated; in Toruń we see the directionless way architecture was to go. The church continued in Protestant use until 1724, and has the town's best furniture: a rood, carved stalls, gallery fronts, monuments like that of 1637 to Princess Anna Vasa behind rococo gates in the chancel, above all the superb organ of 1602 and pulpit of 1616 which would overbear a church of lesser volume, but in this huge space seem modest and refined.

Św. Jan was begun as the Old Town's parish church about 1250. Its present 1 chancel, a modest rectangle, by Toruń standards, of classical proportions with a 1 couple of blank roses in its gable, wall half-columns, and one of its three bays vaulted 1 with a plain star, must date from about 1300. About 1340 a sacristy was built on to the north, and one of its bays covered with an early example of a 'Piast' spring vault. In 1407 one Jakob began the present west tower, and various builders, of whom Hans Gotland was the last, carried on with it until 1433. It has elaborate north and south porches, and a deep recess divides its whole west side into two colossal buttresses; 130 feet from the ground they stop abruptly under a mean brick hat; in the conception this should have matched the brick skyscrapers of Stralsund. The nave was at first a low hall. In the fourteenth century shallow spring-vaulted chapels like those of św. Jakub were set between its buttresses. Finally, between 1468 and 1473, it was practically doubled in height; 90 feet up, its vaults stand higher than those of St. Mary in Gdańsk, and its three roofs dominate the view of the town across the river. Inside it is a big self-contained white room, lit high up by tall clerestory windows of plain glass, closed on the east by a blank wall with two windows in which the chancel arch seems very small, vaulted with all sorts of stars adapted to their positions

and carried on pillars whose sections compromise oddly between octagon and cross.
All this dwarfs the numbered pews and the baroque altars. A fourteenth century
relief shows the Magdalen ascending, swathed in black hair, attended by grinning
angels; I cannot believe the same master carved the serious, finicky Madonna by the
north chancel wall. There are more mediaeval works there, the best of them the
gentle Christ above the altar, and white and gold rococo stalls. But I found this great
church restless and unsatisfying.

Toruń built its first market hall in 1259. Over the next century it spread, like that
of Wrocław, to fill much of the square with stalls and galleries; in 1309 a start was
made on a big square tower, and in 1385 this reached its present four storeys and
gained corner turrets. In 1393 the citizens undertook completely to rebuild the rest
40 as the largest of all mediaeval town halls, a rectangle 175 feet by nearly 150. At first
it was only two storeys high; its walls were informed by uniform ranges of simple
deep blank arcades like those of the Order's castles, a far cry from the Flemish cloth
halls which may have inspired its builders. In 1602 a third storey was put on all
round, and the arcades extended upwards to embrace it, probably by the Fleming
Antonius van Opbergen who had been working for Gdańsk; either he or Wilhelm
Merten of Elbląg added the gables and corner turrets that look so frivolously small.
Inside, the museum has set out some excellent sculpture in the long, spring-vaulted
galleries which occupy the whole ground floor of the east and west ranges; the northern
corners hold elegant 'Piast' vaulted rooms, and upstairs the whole west side used to
be one vast, flat-ceilinged hall, which even as it is cut up now makes most imposing
rooms.

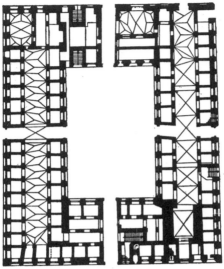

74   Toruń: town hall, 1:800

The square around has some good buildings; no.9 is a mediaeval house of two
bays framed in tall pointed arches like the town hall; on the east side nos. 29 to 35
put up a great show that culminates in the 'Star', once Haus Wendisch, of 1697,
sparkling with plaster relief and holding a newel stair carved with Minerva and a
lion. And to the west lies the Protestant church which Ephraim Schröger put up in
1753, a simple hall with some ornate furniture spoilt by a depressing tower of the 1890s.
39 Two more houses have stucco like that of the 'Star': Piekary 37 which raises above
the gateway at the end of the Rożana three storeys of delicate undisciplined archi-
38 tecture and vegetation, and the house the bishops of Włocławek built in 1693 at
Żeglarska 8 with a rusticated base and plenty of garlands unordered by so much as
a pilaster. This was a rich street; a proud gable survives at no.6 and a show attic at
no.7, and I found other houses being restored. North of the square, the Dzierżyńskiego
has delicate early eighteenth century fronts at nos. 26 and 28. The Nowy Rynek, the
New Town market which is a sea of multicoloured stalls, has plain Renaissance
houses and one inn heavily restored as a pleasant coffee-shop. But, as at King's Lynn,
Toruń's greatest private buildings are the merchants' houses and stores between the
main square and the water. The Kopernika has kept two big mediaeval houses, much
restored, at nos. 15 and 17. The Piekary (Bäckergasse), which I found the best kept
street, leads past the pretty gables of nos. 23 to 27 to no. 9 with its brick front of about
1350 and to the great brick mass of no. 14 punched with five rows of stone-framed,
round-headed windows. Beside it no. 21 in the Rabiańska (Arabergasse) has two
huge storeys framed in tall mediaeval blank arches again, and no. 8 has a mediaeval
show gable, eight bays, no less, framed as five. East of św. Jan, no. 16 in the Łazienna
(Badergasse) is a mediaeval mass with a Renaissance portal, and there is more still
in the Mostowa and in the Podmurna at the back of the castle. Walk these streets,
where men trundle barrels and hump sacks in and out of the best monuments to

Toruń's riches and her decline.

Gdańsk (Danzig) was at one time the greatest city both of the Baltic and of the Hanse, overshadowing even its mother Lübeck. The settlement at the mouth of the Motława, an arm of the Vistula, can be traced back to 997. A document of 1148 mentions the castle of the rulers of Pomerelia which stood in the north-east of the later city where the Radunia (Radaune) joins the Motława; the first town seems to have lain west of it along the banks of this creek. Its parish church was św. Katarzyna, perhaps founded in the 1180s, probably first given a solid brick or stone building by Świętopelk. In 1227 he installed Dominicans from Cracow in the existing chapel of św. Mikołaj, he may have given the town a charter in 1238, and he was the first ruler of Pomerelia to call himself 'duke'. When his house died out, leaving their inheritance to Poland, the Order moved in briskly. In 1308 they seized Gdańsk, destroyed much of the place – though św. Katarzyna certainly survived – and replaced the dukes' castle with their own. Further south, on firm ground fronting the broad Motława, they enclosed the Rechtstadt or Główne Miasto, with the same system of streets at right angles to the water as at Lübeck and Elbląg. Brick walls were begun in 1343, and in the next decade the Nowe Miasto was laid out on a completely regular plan – the only part of Gdańsk to have one – in the swampy ground between the new settlement and the old. In 1393 the city embraced also the suburb of Przedmieście to the south. The walls of 1400 enclosed an area almost a mile long and held some 20,000 people, as many as London.

With Toruń, Gdańsk led the revolt against the Order; in 1454 the castle was razed to the ground. The city knew its greatest prosperity in the next two centuries, in alliance with, rather than under the rule of Poland. It controlled the bulk traffic of the Baltic and the Vistula – grain, fish, timber. It spread beyond the Motława, digging a second river channel, filling the island with storehouses and the land beyond with houses and gardens. Between the fifteenth century and their peak in 1618 its grain exports seem to have multiplied ten times; its population reached 70,000, and its merchants took to putting gold leaf in their after-dinner drinks. But it suffered in the wars of Sweden and Poland and of Russia and Prussia. In 1659 no grain went out at all, and even by 1700 exports had recovered to only a third of what they had once been. The plague of 1709 is said to have killed 20,000, and by 1800 the population was half its peak. Instead of massive brick gates and elaborate houses this declining age created only rococo furniture and sculpture.

In 1793 Gdańsk passed to Prussia. It rose again as a German city, with a population that included many of Slav descent, and in 1900 was up to 130,000. Yet this did little violence to the character of the inner city; its streets kept their gables and the *'przedproży'* or *'Beischläge'*, the raised platforms with low carved stone parapets between the houses and the street which appear also at Lübeck and Elbląg but are the badge of Gdańsk. The Great War was followed by the uneasy truce of the Free City, the defence in 1939 of the Polish fort on the Westerplatte and the Polish Post Office, and the catastrophe of 1945, when the Russians battered down almost anything that looked German.

Much is irretrievably lost, including virtually all the rich furnishings of a dozen churches. But two-thirds of Główne Miasto, a great block at the city's heart, is being rebuilt as the proud Gdańsk of 1450 to 1650, without thought for time and money– or fear to invent what should have been there but was not. The rebuilding of Warsaw seems mere mechanics beside this prodigal passion. At the same time, Gdańsk and Sopot and Gdynia are being deliberately moulded into one vast conurbation. Its

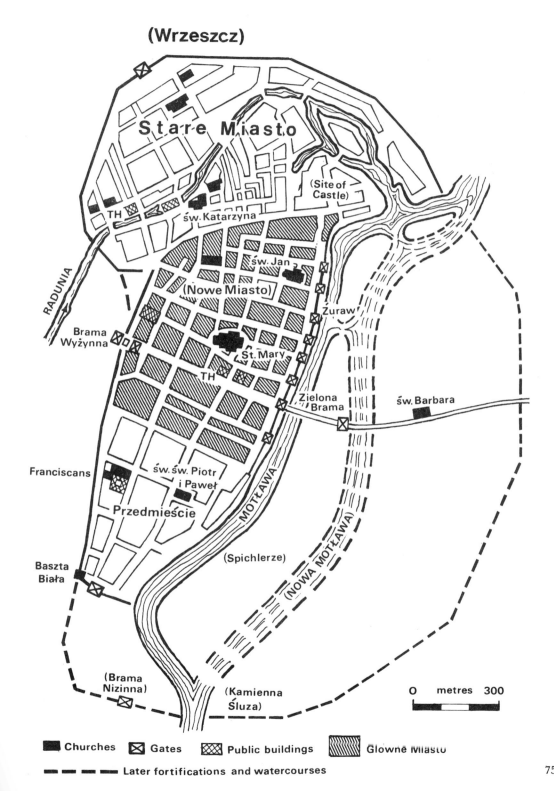

(Wrzeszcz)

Stare Miasto

(Site of Castle)

TH
św. Katarzyna

RADUNIA

św. Jan

(Nowe Miasto)

Żuraw

Brama
Wyżynna

St. Mary

TH

Zielona
Brama

św. Barbara

Franciscans

św. św. Piotr
i Paweł

Przedmieście

MOTŁAWA

(NOWA MOTŁAWA)

Baszta
Biała

(Spichlerze)

O   metres   300

(Brama
Nizinna)

(Kamienna
Śluza)

■ Churches   ⊠ Gates   ▦ Public buildings   ▨ Glowne Miasto

– – – – Later fortifications and watercourses

75 Gdańsk: the mediaeval city

stuff as always is huge blocks of flats, some well shaped like the 'Osiedle Młodych' of 1963 whose eight-storey egg-crates rise north of the abbey of Oliwa, some just inhuman like the 'H.L.M.' type fortresses of the Przymorze development north of Wrzeszcz (Langfuhr), designed by Tadeusz Rożański to house 50,000 people in ten endless walls each made of 2,000 flats. The one relief is the light-hearted holiday architecture of Sopot, the Opera in the Woods with its ingenious suspended roof, and the flimsy looking pavilions by the beach where summer visitors dance and drink. And out on the open shore, Władysławowo boasts a church of 1961 by Szczepan Baum and Andrzej Kulesza which in photographs appears as an intriguing group of triangular tent shapes.

The original shape of św. Katarzyna, the oldest church, is little more than a guess; it was most likely a dark little basilica in the area of the present nave; a wall-painting probably done about 1330, before the rebuilding, has been found in its south-east corner. In 1326 a single narrow chancel was added, but it was not until 1400 or so that the rise of younger churches probably provoked a general rebuilding, and then work went slowly, the west tower completed in the 1480s, the new east front in 1515, the vaults perhaps in 1526. And the result is hardly imposing. The interior should be a big spreading space, nowhere over 45 feet high, with nave and chancel a long tunnel vaulted with a maze of little stars, aisles of equal height in all directions under star and very pretty cellular vaults, and a flood of light from broad eastern windows; I found it all shut up, the vaults intact but most of the early seventeenth century furniture seemingly lost. The tower is grander, with a main storey of tall and deep blank arches, though it has lost its jolly lantern of 1634. The east front makes the greatest effort, three gables all different, the central one the best with three turrets and many blank ogee shapes. Św. Brygida next door was nothing but a shell. Originally it housed Oratorians; in 1374 it received for a time the body of St. Birgitta on its journey from Rome to her daughter's convent at Vadstena in her native Sweden; it became the church of one of her Order's double convents. Over two centuries it was extended piecemeal into a three-naved hall, with cellular vaults over east and west choirs, but nothing of the marvellous space and proportion of the stone churches which the Order's founder wanted and which at Vadstena it achieved.

Stare Miasto has four more little churches, totalling half the mediaeval churches in the city. Round behind the town hall the Carmelite church of św. Józef has a star vaulted chancel of 1482, now all white. To the west of it the hospital chapel of św. Elżbieta, founded in 1394, is a single line of four low star vaults and a deep open porch with a turret above it like that of the Dominicans at Tczew. A few cell and star vaults remain in the minor parish church of św. Bartłomiej, begun in 1482, and the chapel of św. Jakub built in the 1430s to the north of it. A couple of secular buildings have been restored; the Town Hall which van Opbergen may have rebuilt in 1587 with two small turrets and a big one and odd flags and gables, and west of it, in the Elżbietańska, the town house of the abbots of Pelplin, one of the best detailed of the brick and stone Dutch houses, just three bays, neat and busy, plausibly the work in 1612 of Willem van den Block. But the old houses of the Korzenna (Pfefferstadt) are gone, and the brick block of the Order's mill on the Radunia beside św. Katarzyna is a shell. Now the unrelated looking blocks of flats and shops run on into those of Wrzeszcz beyond, and the coarse and jolly brick-Gothic railway station to the west confronts the post-war Hotel Monopol, a papier-mâché edifice designed by Kuczowski, Listowski, and Tomaszewski.

There are few old houses left in the 'Nowe Miasto' to the south either. Its parish church, św. Jan, was first mentioned in 1358. We have no early building history;

one guess is that the first church, just a chapel subordinate to św. Katarzyna, was followed about 1400 by an imitation of the new St. Mary's, with four-bay basilican nave, transept five bays across, and three-bay hall chancel; then the nave was converted in the 1460s into a hall vaulted with eight-pointed stars. Shaky foundations caused endless trouble, and in the war the whole church was gutted. It used to boast admirable furniture, including a whole set of guilds' chapels and pews and organ and glazed stalls in the excellent local rococo of J. H. Meissner, which was amply housed in a nave 60 feet high and overall 65 broad. But I could admire only the chequer bands of green and yellow brick on the fifteenth century tower and the transept gables, sophisticatedly fitted with finials set diagonally by turns in front of and behind the edge of the actual roof. Św. Mikolaj to the west was the only church in Gdańsk not burnt out. Of the original building of 1200 or so there is hardly a trace; in the 1380s, most likely, the Dominicans began a big hall church, its nave buttressed inside like that of the Franciscans in Toruń and vaulted in the 1480s with simple stars, its chancel long and square ended. From outside it seems imposing enough, the octagonal turret which may be as old as 1350 against the nave's east wall, the battle-mented sacristy, the alternation of tall windows and blank panels, the three rough west gables. But inside it is disappointingly ordinary, for the pillars and vaults are standard Prussian and the precious furniture the most elaborate baroque routine.

Św.św. Piotr i Paweł in the 'Przedmieście' is the most modest of the four parish churches. It was begun in the 1390s, burnt in 1425, completed as a five-bay hall with an aisleless chancel, vaulted in 1514; its joy was the elaborate net vaults in the nave and cellular ones in the south aisle. In 1967 it was still a grand ruin surrounded by crisp new blocks of flats. But to the west the Franciscan convent survives. Its fifteenth century cloister was rebuilt about 1870 to house the Muzeum Pomorskie, and the star vaults of its chapter house and the simple cellular vaults of its passages are now white caskets for its treasures. Here are things saved from the holocaust – Lauenstein's paintings of 1534 from the Lübische Bank in the Dwór Artusa; Möller's 'Tribute Money' of 1601 which used to hang in the Town Hall and has Gdańsk for background; but above all the 'Last Judgment' which Hans Memling painted in Bruges about 1470, and a Gdańsk boat captured in 1473 on its way to Florence.

Though the friars arrived here in 1419, they do not seem to have undertaken a serious church, św. Trójca, till 1481; the nave they began in 1496 fell in 1503; the chancel was vaulted in 1495, the new nave in 1514. I found the chancel still ruined, but the nave seemed the second grandest church interior in Gdańsk and perhaps the best – all white, pillars slender and octagonal, delicately vaulted, sparsely furnished with little beyond an ornate pulpit of 1541 and a grand organ of 1648. From its south-west corner sticks out the chapel of św. Anna which is older than its seeming parent, a delightful room vaulted with five stars all fused together which holds a pulpit of 1721 that almost contrives to merge Renaissance and rococo in its twirly, twiddly detail. The west view of the group is magical. A little courtyard is framed by a half-timbered house with a first-floor gallery and by the chapel whose gable has tall pinnacles joined by ogee arches above the roofline; the big plain wall of the main church is crowned by three of the most fastidiously fantastic gables on the Baltic, a hierarchy of pinnacles and arches in warm red brick.

So we come at last to St. Mary. Its tower and gables rise clear above all the roofs around, its colossal red brick walls stop every street that touches it, and its place in the city is more like that of its castle than of its chief church. Its foundation stone was laid on March 28, 1343. The first design was a basilica, perhaps much like Pelplin,

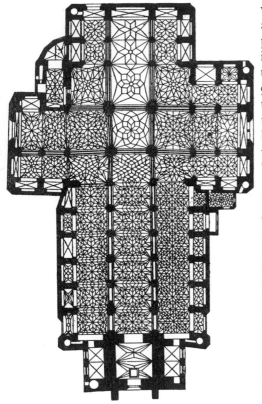

76 Gdańsk: St. Mary's, 1:1,000

with a nave that reached to the vaults' present 90 feet, much lower aisles only as wide as the present tower chapels, and a square east end near the eastern piers of the present crossing. The tower followed, and by 1373 it had reached nearly 150 feet and its bells were being cast. In 1379 a builder of genius, Hinrich Ungeradin, contracted to begin the new east end. Round the old one he raised a three-armed circuit of walls 90 feet high with cross-vaulted chapels between deep internal buttresses. They seem to be the first example of this device on such a scale anywhere; more than anything they decided the building's shape today. But he had built only the two easternmost bays of the chancel, with aisles conforming in breadth to those of the nave, when work stopped, it seems about 1410 at the time of the Order's first war with Poland. The old east end must have been left surrounded by a gigantic roofless courtyard.

From about 1425 Claus Sweder was in charge. He knocked down the three end bays of the old church and filled the space between the nave and Ungeradin's stump of a chancel with something not in the plans, three bays instead of four, broader aisles, a crossing borne by four great four-armed piers. The roof went on in the late 1430s, and between 1442 and 1446 Master Steffen put up the gables on the chancel and transept fronts. Victory in the second struggle against the Order, though desperately costly, only increased the city's pride. Between 1456 and 1466 the tower rose to its present 230 feet. In 1484 Master Michael, followed by Hans Brandt, began to rebuild the nave as a hall as broad as the crossing, hacking away its walls to make pillars for the new arcade, and framing its new aisles in two more ranges of tall chapels. In 1496 Hinrich Hetzel took over the work on the south aisle, and in July 1502 he completed its last vaults. Half of them fell in 1945, and in 1961 some were still being rebuilt, and revealed the intricate brick substance of their cells.

The feeling outside is indeed nearer to one of the Order's castles than to any other church, even the sheer brick walls of St. Mary in Toruń. Inside, the first effect is one of enormous breadth, for its great uniform height and its extension in all directions by aisles and transepts and chapels gives this space a volume of some five million cubic feet, as much as St. Paul's or Westminster Abbey, though it is only two-thirds as long as they. The chancel seems truncated, as if the plan were only a T, and the vaults an endless empyrean of crinkled paper, the cells of the south aisle hardly to be distinguished from the nearby nets from which they are derived. Everything is white, the chancel's forms elegant, slender, and considered, those of the nave rude, with dust caught on the irregularities in the carved out brick. And the whiteness makes the church very empty. It used to be full of the trophies of centuries – banners, candelabra, epitaphs. A little has survived; they have reconstructed the immense Rood of 1517; the base of the octagonal grille of 1554 still surrounds the font; in the north transept rises the wooden tabernacle of about 1480, as huge and elaborate as anything in Nuremberg; there are a handful of monuments and the remains of a few rococo chapel grilles. Old photographs, and the sight of unhurt churches like those of Stralsund, show how much is lost. You are left with the building's space, that would swallow the whole city's population with much ease.

Gdańsk never built a town hall to rival that of Toruń. The citizens felt that a great market hall would only encourage foreigners to come and trade among themselves and that the 'Dwór Artusa' served well enough for their entertainments. So they needed only to house the city's administration, and in about 1380 Hinrich Ungeradin began its first permanent home, a small two-storey block at the head of the Długi Targ. Even by 1465 its tower was only four storeys high. But it shared in the enthusiasm that raised St. Mary's nave, and between 1486 and 1492 its plain and modest block was suddenly made huge and showy. Its tower rose to its brickwork's present height and sprouted corner turrets, and towards the market a show wall went up, with two turrets and four big blank arches, on the model of Bruges and Lübeck and Stralsund. Embellishment went on with the tower's timber lanterns, all columns and cupolas and little metal weathercocks with a figure of Zygmunt August for the topmost, thought up about 1560 by the Dutchman Dirk Daniels; two lanterns and a pretty stone balustrade for the east front; big rectangular windows and the northern courtyard wings added in the 1590s; the handsome baroque south doorway Daniel Eggert made in 1766. And the same centuries created an interior furnished and decorated with a stifling richness, which is practically all lost.

The 'Dwór Artusa', 'Artushof', or 'Arthur's Court' which I have mentioned is first heard of about 1350. The present building on the north side of the Długi Targ is a complete recreation of that built between 1477 and 1481; a neat hall whose four slender granite columns, apparently taken from the Order's destroyed castle, carry nine delicately ribbed and unusually three-dimensional star vaults, the central one dominating by its breadth; the end of the tradition of late Gothic castle and convent rooms. There are fifteenth century buttresses on the north front towards the Chlebnicka, but in 1616 the south front was plastered over by Abraham van den Block, marked out as masonry, crowned with a pilastered attic and speckled with statues in the Antwerp fashion. Inside it used to be rich with hanging ships and the carved benches of the merchants' companies; but now there remains, beside the fragments in the Museum Pomorskie, only a grey 'Last Judgment' on the eastern wall.

77   Gdańsk: Dwór Artusa, 1 :800

The chief monuments of Gdańsk's rise to power – most typically, the vaulting of her churches – seem to have been designed by native or, at least, east Baltic masters. But in her greatest wealth and glory the city turned for architects to the Netherlands. One Regnier of Amsterdam led the way, followed by the tribe of van den Blocks – the almost unknown Egidius who appears in 1573, Willem who settled at Königsberg in 1576, and his son Abraham who produced a mass of furniture for Gdańsk churches before his death in 1628. Hans Vredeman de Vries, born in 1527 at Leeuwarden, a pupil of Cornelis Floris at Antwerp and the author of the books of Renaissance detail that so well satisfied ostentatious tastes all over northern Europe, came here in vain pursuit of work in 1592. And Antonius van Opbergen, born in 1543 at Malines, who had completed Steenwinckel's castle at Kronborg (Elsinore), was the city's Master Builder from 1592 to this death in 1611. It found its first native master in Jan Strakowski (Hans Strakofski), born at Gdańsk in 1567 and Master Mason for forty-five years to his death in 1640. But even he was content to adapt, with skill and enthusiasm, the vocabulary the Flemish builders had created. Gdańsk's old streets are picturesque and lively, but they do not boast the assertions of individual personality that mark the prodigy houses of Elizabethan England and the castles of the Scandinavian kings.

This predictability has been the restorers' opportunity. Pattern-books and photographs in hand, they have gone out to create the city's centre as they think it should have been. They have designed whole five-storeyed houses, complete with pilasters, strapwork, gables, finials, and statues, from the ground up. And they have gone on to treat their surviving stock of old doorways and figures and, above all, of the carved panels for the 'przedproży' or 'Beischläge' as so much icing to be applied to the cake where it will make the best show. In 1961 I could walk down the Mariacka and look up at great gabled houses still in unplastered and roughly mortared brick. Every principle is defied in the belief that this is how Gdańsk should be. The end has justified it.

Its showpiece is the Długi Targ (Lange Markt). Monuments mark its ends; to the east the Zielona Brama (Grüne Tor) begun in 1563 by Regnier and used by the Kings of Poland on state visits spreads a broad curtain of Dutch brick and stone between it and the river; to the west the Town Hall is partnered at the opening of the Długa by the 'Dom Krolów Polskich', a great Antwerpish job of the 1550s, rows of fluted pilasters, a gable to the street, three dormers to the market. In its centre a bronze Neptune cast in 1612 by Peter Husen is surrounded by a grille of 1634 and a pretty rococo basin. The house numbers start by the Town Hall and go down the south side to the river; no. 3 has a shot at a colossal order, rococo doorways follow, and at no. 20 by the gate a colossal order of 1680 and much decoration culminate in a phoenix. This faces some very tall and deep gabled houses only two bays wide, caricatures of the Baltic conventions. The remaining houses around the Dwór Artusa make the greatest display of all. No. 43 was the warehouse attached to it, has the richest of civic entrances, and now shows its mediaeval brick; no. 42 has a handsome columned doorway once in the Długa and an entrance platform from the Piwna, and no. 45 likewise another from the Korzenna in Stare Miasto. Their crown is no. 41, the Złota Kamienica, built between 1609 and 1617 for one Speimann, the last word in the Antwerp taste, four storeys of decorated pilasters and herms, biblical and antique scenes in the entablature panels, four big antique figures on the balustrade, everything carved by a Rostock craftsman called Voigt from the workshop of Abraham van den Block. You must imagine these broad 200 yards of street as a Jacobean gallery, open to the sky, panelled and carved on a scale for heroes.

The streets to north and south are more modest. Indeed, to the south only the Ogarna (Hundegasse) has been rebuilt, and that all in pastel plaster, too even in effect, saving the tall gable at no. 54. In 1967 the northernmost to rise again, the Szeroka (Breitgasse), was only partly done, but the św. Ducha (Heiliggeistgasse) was complete, and next to it the short Mariacka (Frauengasse) east of the church had recaptured some of its atmosphere; the splendid rows of platforms were half remade, half still Cyclopean ruins, and down at the river end a seven-storey house of 1598, perhaps by Opbergen, still showed off its turrets and gables. The Chlebnicka (Brotbänkengasse) south of it I found still partly under scaffolding; its jewel used to be the superbly elegant Schlieff house of about 1520, which Schinkel incorporated in 1824 in a house that still stands on the Pfaueninsel in the west Berlin part of the Havel near Potsdam; but at no. 16 much still stands of the massive and – with such correct orders – quite exotic 'Englisches Haus' Hans Kramer from Dresden built in 1570. This street bends past St. Mary's to become the Piwna (Jopengasse). Here everything is now in place: rococo doors of which one at no. 47 leads to a night club, and a row of platforms like so many church pews, some like that at no. 54 with reliefs carved by Meissner. At the street's end a corner house of 1640 by one of the Schlüters, now adorned with wrought iron signs, faces the festive brick and stone of the Arsenal.

The Długa (Langgasse) is shops and offices, busiest of the restored streets. Its south side has the better houses. No. 12 is the Uphagenhaus, which once had a splendid rococo interior and is still obviously enough work of 1776. A good sequence runs from nos. 27 to 29, the first with five storeys of banded pilasters and an attic of 1560, the second with medallions, the third with a gable and a pretty door of 1619. No. 35 is the 'Lwi Zamek' of 1569, all lions, heads, and gargoyles, but the hall, stair, and vaulted passage gone. And no. 37 puts on a stunning show of 1563, all that is not window covered in figures and someone declaiming from the peak of the gable; next to it no. 38, four years younger, is almost modest to have no more than friezes and medallions.

Most of what one sees opposite has been invented or improved to match, but at no. 47 next to the Town Hall they have reconstructed a handsome late mediaeval house with a gable over four bays of tall and deep blank arches.

48   At the Długa's west end, the city's chief landward entrance, the years from 1500 to 1650 created a splendid bunch of buildings. The first west gate stood where the Złota Brama now is, and beside it something of the mediaeval walls shows in the plain low octagon of the Baszta Słomiana (Strohturm). When the walls were reshaped to withstand artillery their line went forward about a hundred yards, and in 1576 Willem van den Block faced the new Brama Wyżynna (Hohes Tor, but the English should be 'Height' or 'Hill Gate') with a rusticated mass of stone on the model Sanmicheli had created two generations before at Verona, with coats-of-arms and lions. It stands in front of the mediaeval outwork or barbican, which holds a galleried courtyard and was reshaped in 1593 as the Katownia (Peinkammer, torture chamber), a plain and solid shape with a gable or two. Behind that rises the Wieza Więzienna (Stockturm, prison tower), the late mediaeval outer gate, which the sixteenth century raised by two storeys with odd sharp pointed windows. And in the end, in 1612, Abraham van den Block and Jan Strakowski turned the old Złota Brama (Langgasser Tor) into a ceremonial entrance with two orders of projecting columns, broken entablatures, balustrade, and statues.

   North of this parade of gateways the advance of the wall created a triangular open space, the Targ Węglowy (Kohlenmarkt). It has rather lost its character. On the west there is a sharp furniture store of 1961, and in the middle a neat glassy bus station. Next to the Baszta Słomiana, the Dwór Bractwa św. Jerzego (St. Georgshalle, like that in Toruń, the meeting-place of the city militia), a square two-storeyed brick box of about 1490, windows framed in deep arches, turrets at its angles, now makes a handsome clubhouse for the Association of Architects. On the north a standard stone-faced box which could be anywhere has, alas, replaced the old Theatre, a severe Doric job of 1799 by K. S. Held with pedimented portico and low dome. On 9 the east the Arsenal presides. It was begun in 1600, while both Opbergen and the elder Strakowski were in the city's service; in 1643 Strakowski's son Jerzy (Georg) flanked it with the simple 'small arsenal' on the north; gutted in the war, it has become a shopping arcade. To the west it presents stone-framed windows and four Netherlandish gables with the usual spikes. Its big show is the east front which closes the Piwna; two gables, two big octagonal turrets, odd half gables at the corners, statues on the skyline, two doorways with blocky frames and fierce, fierce lions, and a pretty little well house on the street.

5   There are fragments of the mediaeval walls scattered southwards from the Brama Wyżynna, but their most imposing remains are the water gates turned storehouses along the Motława. The broad asymmetrical masses of the Brama Chlebnicka and the Brama Mariacka still close the streets they are named after, and they have rebuilt the Brama Straganiarska (Häkertor) of 1482 close to św. Jan; with walls informed by enormously tall blank panels, of double depth on the Straganiarska, and octagonal corner turrets, these look like miniature castles for the Order. The second bridge on the road east is guarded by a gate of 1517 with two plain towers, and on the island between it and the Motława survive great gabled warehouses like those of Toruń, some more or less opposite św.św. Piotr i Paweł, others grouped north of the Zielona Brama bridge. They face the gate everyone knows best, the Żuraw (Krantor) of 1444, which once more sports a projecting hoist under a great wooden shed where men worked on treadmills to step the masts of the city's ships.

The Renaissance fortifications survive best in the south. In 1534 the citizens began progressively to replace the mediaeval walls, and in 1554 they constructed the first low diagonal bastion on the Italian model, an exact contemporary of the similar work at Berwick. The old line stopped at the Baszta Biała of 1460 and the Baszta pod Zrębem of a generation later; it gave the thriving commercial harbour no protection, and after 1600 the whole enceinte was pushed out southwards. In 1626 Jan Strakowski set the Brama Nizinna (Leege-Tor) between two of the new bastions; it was a bizarre artistic compromise, which intimidated the enemy outside in a massive Italian shape like that of the Brama Wyżynna and tried with gables, brick, and strapwork to comfort the citizens within. He also took part in the engineering of the Kamienna Śluza (Steinschleuse) to the east, which controlled the levels of the harbour and the ring of moats. Its stone breakwaters are still there, and the crumbling grassy banks of the bastions, and the marshy ditches, a mouldering desert of once proud military architecture.

Gdańsk, that gave the Schlüter family to the north European baroque, was to receive just one baroque building of a quality to celebrate beyond its walls. In 1572 its Catholic population was excluded from St. Mary; on the orders of King Jan Sobieski a new chapel, the Kaplica Królewska, was built for them between 1678 and 1681 north of St. Mary in the św. Ducha. The contractor was Bartel Ranisch, but his other work does little to suggest that he could have designed it. It is a rectangular room at first-floor level, covered by a dome on a central square and so many small groin-vaulted spaces, empty of decoration but full of light; over the corners of its street front pretty open lanterns rise, and an octagonal drum carries the dome; its doorways are low, severe, but admirably carved. We can be sure the sculptor was Andreas Schlüter the Younger, whom Sobieski called in 1681 to work at Wilanów; the architect must be Tylman van Gameren, the Dutchman who built for Sobieski in Warsaw and later collaborated with Schlüter on the Krasiński palace there. Between 1687 and 1695 he was to build three churches there, each with a central dome, a scheme taken from van Campen's work in Holland, and a drawing in his hand that still survives seems from the flanking symmetrical houses to be a sketch for the site in Gdańsk. This little building is altogether less provincial than anything the city had put up in the previous century. But its author, Netherlandish though he was like so many Gdańsk architects, came there as the representative of Warsaw. The city's independent glory was over, and with Poland it now stood or fell.

8. Great Poland

The first Polish state, such as it was, was ruled from Great Poland; its capital was Poznań, Gniezno the seat of its first independent archbishop; its kings were Mieszko Stary and Bolesław Chrobry, its aint św. Wojciech (Adalbert). At Gniezno settlement has been traced back to the eight century, and in the lake at Biskupin, fifteen miles to the north, are excellent remains and reconstructions of an island settlement of the Iron Age. There are traces of tenth century stone building, a round church on the site of the present Gniezno cathedral, a castle chapel on an island in Lake Lednickie to the west. Just before or about 1000 the first Benedictine abbeys were founded at Tum and Trzemeszno. Yet in Polish history Great Poland never played its expected part. The leadership passed to Cracow and Warsaw; of the nobility of Poznania only Stanisław Leszczyński ever grasped the crown; from 1793 to 1918 Prussia ruled practically the whole rich province. German and Pole fought bitterly to control education and the land, and the Poles' fidelity to the Roman Church sharpened Bismarck's 'Kulturkampf'. So to make old maps and records more easily used I shall occasionally quote the German alternative names for very Polish places. The architecture matches the history; the best Romanesque left in Poland, a modest enough inheritance from Gothic and Renaissance, a flowering early in the eighteenth century when the Leszczyńskis' architect Ferrari designed some of the few original buildings of the Polish Baroque, then the growing power of German neo-classic and neo-gothic.

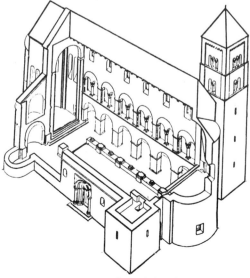

78 Tum: reconstruction of the church

Of the Romanesque churches, Tum is the easternmost and the most attractive, grandly set on a rise above the broad river plain across from Łęczyca. The ancient abbey here passed in the eleventh century to a college of priests, and between 1141 and 1161 a big new basilica was built for them in pink and grey granite. Inside it is all very rough, the original arcades replaced by pointed ones partly in brick, so that only the fine tall proportions are left; and even this is the work of a complete reconstruction since the war, which has removed the octagonal tops of the west towers, raised the eastern ones a storey, replaced big single clerestory windows with pairs of little ones, and partly rebuilt the grand north door with its smooth columns alternating with plain jambs, voussoirs carved with birds and leaves, and battered Madonna. But it still has a castle air, two square towers to the west, and to the east the splendid sculptural elaboration of two round towers flanking three apses.

Hands just as ruthless have restored the churches along the 'Piast road' from Poznań towards Włocławek. At Inowrocław (Hohensalza) St. Mary is just a thirteenth century apsed stone box, bare and very dark inside, out of which two disproportionately massive square west towers swell. Kruszwica received the first

Cluniac settlement in Poland, and was the seat of the bishops of Cujavia until they moved to Włocławek in 1159. In 1930 its church was put back into twelfth century granite, basilican nave of three broad bays, transept with two small apses, one bay apsed chancel, square piers and round arches and flat roofs, unusably grim but for the pinks and pale browns that flicker in the stone. At Mogilno further west the abbey church was completely reshaped in a plain country baroque, and now it is a funny little building, with cell-vaulted aisles, no transept, and a tiny apse, perched on a mound-like hill above a long narrow lake. But from the anteroom to the sacristy you can descend to the crypt, a tunnel-vaulted stone cellar divided by two arches and one pier, which should be that of Bolesław Śmiały's foundation in 1065.

79   Strzelno: św. Prokop, 1:800

The most interesting churches of the group are at Strzelno. Św. Prokop was built about 1160, of granite blocks varied with brick, barely 60 feet long; its round nave has an opening high up into a round tower, a dome with eight flat stone 'ribs', and two miniature northern apses, and its square chancel a cross vault and blank-arcaded sides. A bigger brick tower has been built on, and the nave's apses replaced, but it is still dark and simple. Beside it a Premonstratensian convent was founded in the 1170s; and in its big churchyard there rose a gaggle of unrelated buildings, their inconsequence capped by the characterless baroque front of the convent church of św. Trojca. Inside, this is still a tiny Romanesque basilica – three bays, transept 152 which has lost its apses, long apsed chancel, revaulted clumsily throughout with late gothic stars which do not fit. Its arcade has jolly columns, one carved with a barley-sugar twist, one plain, and then a pair covered in rude figures under arcades separated by bands of vegetation. South of the chancel, the chapel of św. Barbara's simple gothic rib vault is borne by one central shaft of granite rudely carved with more plants; its broad, light elegance contrasts with the nave's dark ancient fuss.

Of the second cathedral at Gniezno (Gnesen), an eleventh century basilica, there is nothing but foundations. The present church was begun about 1350; under bishop Skotnicki, who died in 1374, the east end rose as a seven-sided apse with a ring of seven chapels; above them, a great skirt of roof hides the arches that relieve the clerestory buttresses and allow them to dwindle to mere shafts in the ambulatory; the chapels' own buttresses in turn are crowned with saints, and the whole view from the steep street to the east is most picturesque, the tall narrow clerestory rising from this comfortable breadth like a bony woman in a crinoline. In the last quarter of the fourteenth century the nave continued the system, slightly at an angle, to make the whole 200 feet and eight bays long. The two square-buttressed west towers have tops of 1779 that look as solid as if carved from mahogany.

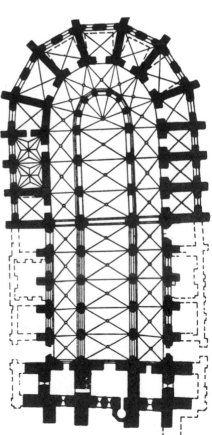

80   Gniezno: cathedral, 1:800

Inside, it has been restored yet again since the war, and the experts' rib vaults 15 have replaced those of the 1760s. The broad apse reads as half a circle, its ring of thick piers and narrow arches as a wall, plain, cautious, but delicate in the frieze above the main arcade and the finely moulded chancel arch. The nave looks provincial, solid piers, an emphatic string course; too much effort to express mass and space by insufficient means. The whole scheme is a pale reflection of French ideas and their embodiment in the cathedral begun at Prague in 1341, Poland aping Bohemia again. But it gains life from the strange tiny figures of men and animals who swarm up the artificial stone ribs of the south aisle vault, and have been imitated by the restorers in the nave; rustling streams of sculpture that spread above one's head. The aisles are dominated by rows of baroque chapel doorways, pedimented and heavily grilled; in one are to be seen the cathedral's great treasures, the bronze doors whose scrolly vegetation frames eighteen scenes of the life of św. Wojciech, work of the late twelfth century which has too much of the busyness of manuscript illumination, but at its best matches the finest to be seen in Germany. The experts think they have found on one edge the battered words '*me fecit Petrus*'.

Better are the late mediaeval monuments. Two great slabs stand against the west wall of the nave; in bronze, archbishop Jakub of Sienno, dead in 1480, the artist unknown; in marble, archbishop Zbigniew Oleśnicki, made in 1496 by Veit Stoss. He is a broad man, fat faced, fully vestured, filling all the three-arched panel the inscription frames. His face is not a study in psychology or pathos like those we see on the pillars of Würzburg and Mainz; its sad expression dissolves in the colours and glints of the stone. What imposes is the authority of his stance, the authority of the artist's whole conception, its feeling for volume bodied in the shallowest relief. Stoss had already made, in 1493, a monument to archbishop Piotr Bnin which lies now in a dark northern chapel of the nave of the cathedral of Włocławek (Leslau). There the marble is orange-brown, the figure lies in high relief on an awkwardly tilted slab, and its face is again sad, plump, and beardless. The town, I may add, is grim; the great church was fifteenth century once, but rebuilt in the nineteenth century and betowered in the shiniest brick; the streets without character of any sort.

But at Gniezno there is plenty of the Renaissance. In 1516 archbishop Łaski commissioned four monuments at once from one Giovanni of Florence who worked at Esztergom in Hungary, and stationed these red marble slabs along the north aisle. And one can go round all the chapels, collecting. In the south aisle the easternmost ones have the red marble slab with a Cracovian surround, attributed by some to Padovano, that commemorates archbishop Dziergowski who died in 1554, and archbishop Baranowski, dead in 1615, fills a whole wall with undisciplined architecture; further west, the Lubieński chapel holds a splendid fifteenth century bronze font. The apse chapels have seventeenth century efforts in black and white like those to archbishops Olszowski and Gębicki. The north aisle is dominated by the huge Potocki chapel built between 1727 and 1730 by the leading architect of the province, Pompeo Ferrari; red and grey, three sizes of orders, an oval dome, competent controlled elaboration. And behind the altar polished steel girders carry the elaborate silver sarcophagus and the jolly recumbent św. Wojciech on it which Peter von der Rennen of Gdańsk made in 1662.

The town of Gniezno is a bright little place on a hill. Its buildings are modest and its churches small. The Franciscans arrived in the middle of the thirteenth century and built just north of the square the usual long narrow church, its elegant proportions now plastered over. And further north the Holy Sepulchre Canons' odd fourteenth century church of św. Jan has an apse which is four sides of a none too regular hexagon and a nave vault with cast stone rosettes and grotesque hanging bosses.

Throughout the province the churches of these two centuries are modest too. The Cistercian houses are all baroque; though at Łekno, which they occupied in 1143 and left for Wągrowiec in 1383, the brick hall church incorporates the torso of a west front whose doorway, great blocked window, and half-octagon turrets remind one sharply of Oliwa and Pelplin. On the endless main road from Poznań to Warsaw, Koło has a parish church, with low star-vaulted chancel, solid, simple hall nave of about 1400, and fine brick gables, that despite clumsy decoration can claim judgment by Prussian standards. A pretty Bernardine church of the 1770s, country baroque with a succession of domes inside, is well set by the bridge; and from the plain porticoed Doric of the nineteenth century town hall a brick tower of 1390 incongruously protrudes. Konin has another such town hall, a pink and white block topped by an

odd wooden belfry. Its church is a fourteenth century brick basilica with elaborate
star vaults, an older stone sacristy, and a domed south chapel, pale echo of Cracow;
in the churchyard a 'mile post' supposed twelfth century stands, a rough grey phallus
of satisfying mass.

Fifteenth century builders were more ambitious and more original. Their grandest
effort is the parish church at Gostyń. The apsed chancel is older; the big hall nave
was built in the second half of the century, followed by a tall tower expressively
windowed, buttressed, and, after a fire in 1682, battlemented. Along the south front
the gables of the porch and the chapel of 1529 put up a show; star vaults remain in
the aisles, and the chapel is covered with a broad domed net which resolves into
endless stars within stars; the rococo furniture is more or less complete. Further north
at Środa the church was begun in 1423. At first it was only a long narrow chancel
and a broad nave vaulted with stars and buttressed so emphatically within that it
appears so many compartments between deep arches. It got aisles about 1500, and
in 1598 Christof Oldendorf from Gdańsk built the Gostowski chapel, the usual
domed octagon, on to the chancel. Its plaster is provincial enough, but the monuments
look metropolitan, all coloured marbles, an effigy of Anna z Ostrorogów Sieniawska,
and between the windows a fine small figure of a child, Zygmunt Stadnicki.

At Szamotuły, north-west of Poznań, the big basilican church was apparently
built in the second quarter of the century, and rebuilt a hundred years later. It is a
severe brick mass, dignified among tall chestnut trees, and inside it star vaults combine
with the classical proportions – nave twice the height of aisles – of the Cistercian
churches of Silesia and the Neumark, a surprising conservatism. By the chancel arch
stands the red marble monument of Jakub Rokossowski who died in 1580 at Cracow,
work worthy of a Cracow sculptor such as Canavesi. There are some surprises among
village churches too. Murek near Leszno has a two-naved one, with two columns
and six star vaults. And north of the huge Konin power station Gosławice has a tiny
brick octagon, consecrated in 1444. It has been through all sorts of trials and looks
spikily neo-gothic outside. But inside it is a delight; one slender stone pillar, a
spreading pattern of brick stars, space that flows into star-vaulted chancel and north
and south chapels. How the idea came here is a puzzle, whether from the Karlov
octagon in Prague or the many-sided cemetery chapels of Pomerania or the single
pillared square naves of Little Poland. It is singular and beautiful.

At Poznań (Posen) the first fortified town lay round a stone cathedral like that of
the same time at Gniezno. Like Cracow and Wrocław the city grew up as a chain
of settlements astride the many channels of a wandering river, and again the Mongol
invasion was followed by the creation of a new town, laid out regularly on the right
river bank and protected by a small and perhaps older castle, which got a charter
in 1253. Its limits were always too small; in the Middle Ages they contained only
three churches, of which the great parish church of św. Marie Magdalena, founded
in 1263, was ruined by fire in 1773 and 1780 and never rebuilt; only the ample lines
of the seventeenth and eighteenth century fortifications began to acknowledge the
city's prosperous sprawl. Now its population is as great as that of Wrocław, greater
than that of long superior Gdańsk, and the baroque city's limits are in their turn
dwarfed by interminable suburbs.

The cathedral has a rough history. After it was burnt in 1772, Schroeger gave it
a complete new west front with stumpy half-classical obelisks for spires, and sixty
years ago Baedeker thought it 'architecturally interesting'. Since 1945 the restorers
have tried to create a building externally of the mid-eighteenth century, with ogee

81   Gosławice: church, 1:500

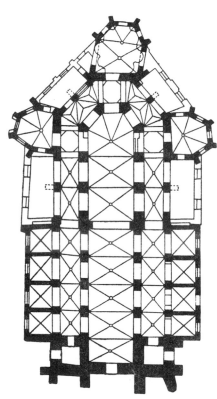

82   Poznań: cathedral, 1:800

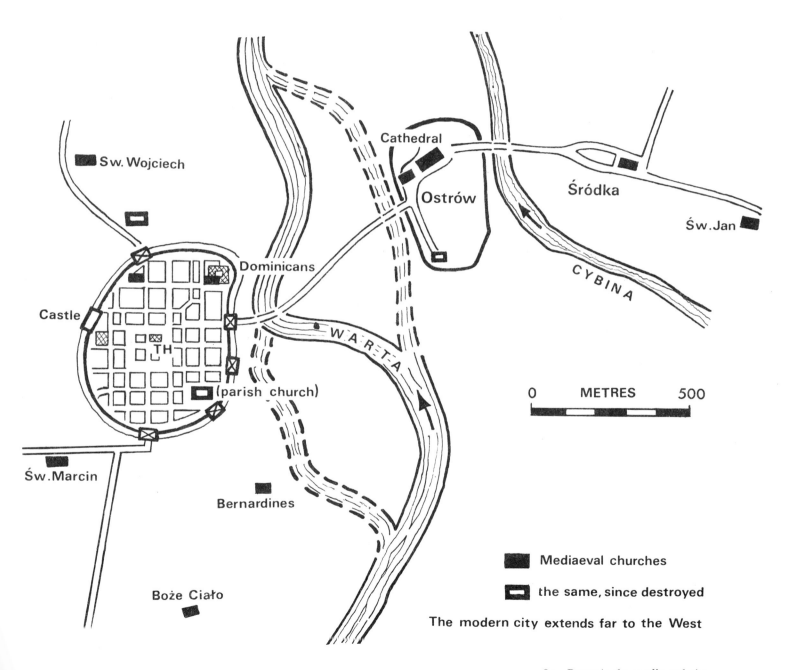

Św. Wojciech

Cathedral

Ostrów

Śródka

Św.Jan

Castle

Dominicans

C Y B I N A

TH

W · A · R · T · A

(parish church)

Św. Marcin

Bernardines

0   METRES   500

Boże Ciało

■ Mediaeval churches

▭ the same, since destroyed

The modern city extends far to the West

83   Poznań: the mediaeval city

domed lanterns in unexpected places and two plain brick west towers crowned by square early baroque ones, and internally of the fourteenth and fifteenth, all brick ruthlessly bared. It seems that in the fourteenth century the romanesque cathedral, a stone basilica like its contemporary at Gniezno, had become a ruin. In the 1340s and 1350s money was raised to build the present nave, extremely severe, the arcades to its low aisles simply cut from its walls and vaulted by the restorers with straightforward stars. The chancel and the ambulatory round its five-sided apse followed between 1403 and 1410. In its two rectangular bays a gallery is set over arcades as high as in the nave; in the apse the arcade is lower, and the gallery awkwardly taller. But the north, south, and east bays of the ambulatory rise to the full height of the main vessel, and squinches turn them into irregularly five-sided apses, that open surprising views and shed unexpected beams of light. Still further east, F. M. Lanci built the Złota Kaplica in 1836 in a brassy 'Byzantine' style to house monuments to the first kings of Poland.

In all the furniture the one good piece is an almost rococo pulpit of 1720. But, as at Gniezno, aisles and chapels hold monuments from the workshops of Renaissance Cracow. That of bishop Branicki, dead in 1544, in a north chapel is a very proud piece of red marble for its early date; in the ambulatory bishop Idzbieński, dead in 1553, appears in a shape full of authority from the hand of Jan Michałowicz; and Canavesi is twice represented, in the basic sausage figure of bishop Konarski and in the whole wall of the Górka chapel north of the chancel that is filled by two figures lying, two standing, and the blatant inscription 'opus Hieronimi Canevexi qui manet Cracovia in Platea S. Floriani A.D. 1574', so that you know where to go if you want one like it. Another north chapel, further west, has the well placed and tranquilly sleeping figure of Cardinal Ledochowski which Marcinkowski made in 1903.

Just west of the cathedral the little brick church of St. Mary stands, perhaps where the chapel of the earliest castle stood. It was built between 1442 and 1448 by Jan Prusz for a college of priests, and in plan is a truncated hall church, two bays and aisles that run on round a three-sided apse. Outside its proportions look preposterous, in spite of its pinnacled west gable and the glazed brick of its pilasters; it has lost the elaborate cresting above the eaves which made it seem the work of the school of Hinrich Brunsberg. But inside it is a delight. Apse and ambulatory vaults are lost, but the nave's octagonal pillars carry two eight-pointed stars; the ceilings are painted, the rest whitewashed, the modern windows not too assertive; this compact but spacious room shows how well some Poles can restore churches. Its west wall faces the gabled brick 'psalteria' built in 1512 by bishop Lubrański, who also began the priests' college in 1519 and rewalled the whole island.

Further east, the ancient settlement of Śródka has a pretty single nave brick church, św. Małgorzata (Margaret), vaulted with canopy-like stars of which the last fits into the five-sided apse; to the north are bits of a small baroque convent of the Philippines. And out on the main Warsaw road lies the city's oldest church. About 1170 a hospital already founded here was taken over by the Knights of St. John, and in the next century they built the tiny brick church of św. Jan Jerozolimski. It is an early use of the material, a rectangular box with a square chancel and still Romanesque west door and east window. In the sixteenth century it got two star vaults which seem like one big tent inside, and all sorts of bits – an aisle, a tower, a chapel – have been stuck on, making it inconsiderably picturesque. In spite of its age, in spite of the main road traffic, this is an odd villagey corner of the city.

With one exception, the Gothic churches west of the Warta are hardly more

imposing. Only one remains within the walled town, and it is tiny – św. Katarzyna
in the Wroniecka, built about 1400 for Dominican nuns; outside it, neither św.
Wojciech nor św. Marcin is more than 100 feet long. Św. Marcin started as a three
bay hall; in the sixteenth century its aisles were extended eastwards, and whitewash
and abstract glass have made it a standard looking star-vaulted north Polish job.
Św. Wojciech was rebuilt in the fifteenth century as a long, narrow single nave, and
in the sixteenth century aisles were added, more elaborately vaulted and running so
far east that the chancel apse is hidden in a rectangle. It is much restored, rather
dark, and in a south chapel heroes of the Napoleonic wars are commemorated,
among them the author of '*Jeszcze Polska nie zginęla*'. The hill commands a fine view
of cathedral, river, and power station.

When their convent was founded in 1406 the Carmelites, it is said, chose its site
far south of the town because there three consecrated hosts had been miraculously
6 found. In the second half of the century they began their brick church of Boże Ciało
(Corpus Christi). From the by-pass road it seems just a tall, unbroken roof and a
regiment of fat stepped buttresses. Its nave has aisles almost of hall height, but cut
off by a solid arcade, and it has lost its old vaults. The chancel is very simple, four
bays, apse, tall slender windows with details in artificial stone, cross vaults, but the
most satisfying proportions. There is a west doorway built of bricks glazed in
incongruous colours; the west front, the small tower, and some furniture are baroque;
Pompeo Ferrari built on a north chapel with a ribbed dome and many fake marble
columns of ill-calculated shapes and sizes. This is the best surviving mediaeval church
in Poznań, but dim enough by the standards of the Carmelites in Wrocław and in
Prague.

7 We first hear of the town hall in 1310, but it was completely rebuilt between 1550
and 1561 by Giovanni Battista Quadro from Lugano, and it is the chief monument
to Poznań's Renaissance. It is a rectangular block, about 100 feet by 50, its parapet
80 feet up; its main front is the short east one, informed by three storeys of arcades,
the topmost doubled, all made rather heavy by the imposition of the main orders on
arches carried by pilasters; inside there is a first-floor hall whose two columns bear
a stuccoed and painted ceiling. Its tower rises to 275 feet, but it was taller still before
the wind blew its top off in 1725. In old prints it and the equally tall tower of the
vanished parish church dominate the town, and still the building's jolly silhouette,
the turrets and fidgety palmetted parapet, make it serve well enough for a mascot.
Yet architecture of this period is rare all over Great Poland. One can think only of
the jolly cresting of the castle the Cracow chapter built in 1567 at Pabianice and of
the house of 1610 at Poddębice which has two arcades, the lower rusticated and the
upper of plain deep arches with half columns tucked into their sides. In Poznań even
the Górka house of 1548, at the corner of the Klasztorna and the Wodna, is
distinguished by little beyond a broad doorway decked in vegetation. But the
restorers have given the main square something of an air, and created the pretty
arcaded row south of the town hall from the ground up.

The Baroque had far more effect. In 1571 the Jesuits arrived, taking over a little
chapel of św. Stanisław south-west of the parish church. In 1651 they began work
there on a huge new church of their own, and it went on for most of a century. Its
builders are a roll-call of the Italian Master Masons who were as much in charge
here as at Cracow. First was Tommaso Poncino from Gorizia, who had made his
name with the bishops' palace at Kielce and worked at Cracow and Warsaw before
his death in 1659. He was followed by Cristoforo Bonadura, who had been at work

on Great Polish country churches, like Grodzisk and Sieraków, for some forty years. Then came the Catenacci family; Giorgio, who had come around 1660 from Como with his little-known brother Andrea, and his son Giovanni who may have been born in Poznań and was still employed by the Jesuits well into the eighteenth century, above all to plan their grandiose north façade. In 1727 they completed the succession by commissioning Pompeo Ferrari, the Leszczyńskis' architect and author of the best Great Polish country churches, to design the main doorway and the high altar. What their efforts produced was in most respects a typical big Jesuit church; Latin cross plan, side chapels here run together into aisles with galleries above them; the nave piers push forward detached fluted columns of imitation red marble, colossal and oppressive. The north front is blackened and unprepossessing, the convent to the east with its pilastered tower has been much altered for offices. But on the north side of the street an arch leads to the Jesuits' schools of about 1700, a handsome long courtyard with arcades, rounded corners, and at its end a big archway leading to the staircase. The Society was driven out in 1773; when the parish church was ruined their great church stood empty and inviting.

The Bernardines had built outside the walls as long ago as 1456, and the Discalced Carmelites had settled on the hill beside św. Wojciech in 1618; both convents were ruined in the wars of the 1650s, and both rebuilt by Bonadura and the Catenaccis. Yet they appear quite different. The Carmelites' św. Józef was consecrated in 1667; it is straightforward to bluntness, an elementary Latin cross inside, and a boring front of Renaissance shape which rises from the ground with eight pilasters, has six on the next storey, and then four on the gable. The Bernardines' św. Franciszek was further damaged by fire and storm, and had to be reshaped between 1730 and 1750. It is very broad inside, a succession of side chapels as tall as the nave, separated by buttress-like piers whose white pilasters carry an excessive entablature, the brightest of Poznań's church interiors. And its two towers and their bronze lanterns preside over a noisy and colourful market place piled with the plums and radishes the Polish peasant brings to town.

The most ornate of these baroque churches is the tiny one some Franciscans built on the hill beside the few walls of the Castle that remain. But the most interesting is that of the Dominicans. They came here in 1231, settled on the west river bank in 1244, and the city wall later bulged to compass them. Of their thirteenth century church, enough has been found to make up one geometrically-decorated brick doorway now in the crypt. All else you see was reshaped after a storm in 1698 by Giovanni Catenacci, plain outside, and inside broad and light, much like św. Franciszek, though the long narrow chancel preserves its mediaeval lines. But the north cloister still has some expressive star vaults, and beside it, at right-angles to the church, the Rosary Chapel remains a complete late gothic church, five aisleless bays, star vaults, wall shafts and internal buttresses, all most distinct and elegant.

In 1775 the Lutherans began, on the site of an abandoned convent by the river, the city's last eighteenth century church, św. Krzyż na Grobli, later rededicated to All Saints. Its designer was, it seems, a Prague builder called Antoni Hoene. It is a circular preaching hall fitted into a rectangle of walls, pilastered piers that bear a broad ribbed dome, behind them two storeys of galleries, the pulpit beside the altar; it takes after the baroque Protestant churches of Saxony, whose greatest example is the Frauenkirche Bähr begun in Dresden fifty years before, and it seems conservative indeed beside the neo-classical drum Zug was building at the same time in Warsaw. Even the façade of the palace the Działyńskis built in the 1780s on the west side of

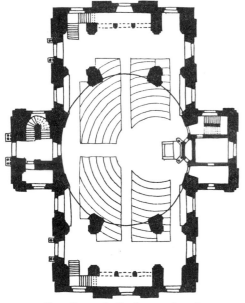

84   Poznań: Lutheran church, 1:500

the Rynek, with help from the same Hoene, is still baroque in the ordering of its great Composite pilasters, and its solid attic and great skyline trophies look like afterthoughts. But it faces Kamsetzer's Watch ('Odwach') of 1787, wholly classical, a deep five-bay Roman Doric portico in antis, pilastered and banded corner blocks, a triglyph frieze, more trophies; a cool and charming echo of west European taste.

Under the Prussians the most conspicuous buildings at first went up in a watery classicism like that of Nash; examples run from the Raczyński Library of 1829 in the Płac Wolności, a long run of fluted columns set too close, to the Teatr Polski of 1875 at the top of the same square with heavily-banded masonry at odds with a discreet big order. The Prussians built a big mediaeval looking fortress on a hill to the north; in 1900 Baedeker thought it the only building worth a star; it is now a ruin. The first appearance of 'Rundbogenstil' was a piece of native Polish self-assertion, the building about 1840 of the north front of the 'Bazar' building along the Paderewskiego. But it reached a late flowering in the granite masses of the University and the Castle (now the town hall) that face one another across the Fredry; the latter was built in 1905 by Franz Schwechten, and the contrast of its solid corner tower with the bits that are gabled and all cut up with arches and little windows is a fascinating exhibition of Wilhelmine temper.

Then in 1910 Hans Poelzig, the leader of the Wrocław school, designed the famous water tower, the 'Wieża Wodna górnosląska', now destroyed; and in the next year a chemical works at Luboń (Luban) to the south, wholly plain blocks with half-circle windows punched in them, now hidden in a sprawl of dusty plant. Between the wars public building was not impressive. Since 1945 it has got slowly better; livelier pavilions in the exhibition grounds; Marek Leykam's Powszechny Dom Towarowy of 1952 in the 27 Grudnia, a department store in a towering ten-storey cylinder made of deep concrete framed window units round a hollow core that holds three spiral staircases; a pyrites store of 1954 out at Luboń, by Sawicki and Tetzlaff, whose tent-like shapes have the bounce peculiar to Polish industrial architecture; conventional but grand, the three smooth glass blocks built by Liśniewicz along the north side of the Armii Czerwonej between 1967 and 1969.

Of the early baroque masters, Christoforo Bonadura left his mark best outside Poznań. He lived at Grodzisk, and there between 1628 and 1648 he rebuilt the parish church. Outside it seems massive, with a plain single west tower, and on each flank a pair of domed side chapels as tall as the nave and punched with deep unadorned niches and windows like so much Swiss cheese. Inside, the piers with their strange tapered pilasters are just as solid, and the detail all oddly tense; yet there is a feeling of great breadth and airiness, for everywhere one can see fresh spaces through other spaces, up into the chapel domes and into the octagonal dome over the chancel. Between 1627 and 1639 he built the Bernardines a striking church at Sieraków (Zirke), down the Warta. In plan it is a straightforward Latin cross, and outside it merely seems unusually tall and plain. But the dome over its crossing rises from an octagon most oddly created; its diagonal sides start as little corner clumps of stepped pilasters, and then shunt inwards and broaden while their capitals sprout not only leaves but faces in an outburst of Gothic conceit. Of his contemporaries, Giorgio Catenacci worked all over Great Poland, but his largest contract seems to have been the Cistercian church at Przemęt (Priment), where work from 1651 to 1690 produced a big standard brick basilica, well furnished with soundly carved stalls and grand enough, its two towers seen far away over the marshy plain, to make Dehio think it the best convent church in the province. Of the other Cistercian houses,

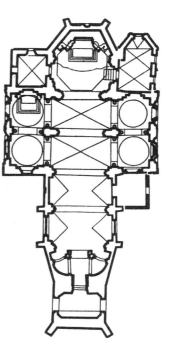

85   Grodzisk: church, 1:750

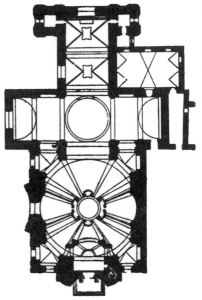

86   Ląd: abbey church, 1 :800

its neighbour at Obra was content in 1722 with two plain towers, a line of rococo domes over a broad nave, and very pretty late eighteenth century stalls bathed in plenty of light.

But at Ląd, on the Warta forty miles above Poznań, the Cistercians' achievement was far more impressive. The rebuilding of their mediaeval church started in 1651 under Poncino and gathered pace between 1679 and 1685, mainly under Giorgio Catenacci, though at one point plans were obtained from Bellotti, Sobieski's architect in Warsaw. The original orientation was reversed, and on the old nave's foundations rose a rectangular chancel flanked by two tall square methodically pilastered towers; transepts with pedimented gables followed, a small dome was set on the crossing, and thus far all passed conventionally. Then in 1728 Pompeo Ferrari took over work on the new nave. Rather like the builders of the octagon at Ely he cleared the whole i rectangle laid out for nave and aisles, turned it into an irregular octagon with north and south sides pushed inwards, and covered it with one huge frescoed dome whose ribs rise to a pretty lantern. No photograph can do justice to its unobstructed space and the movement those concave projecting sides give to it. Outside, some of the late fourteenth century convent survives, the simple vaulted cloister and, off its eastern range, an excellent small chapter house whose rectangle is converted with Prussian sophistication into an octagon by cutting off the corners, and vaulted with ribs branching from a central pillar. And from the high wooden bridge over the Warta the whole group can still be seen, unruined and grand among tall trees.

Pompeo Ferrari, for lack of competition the most interesting church builder in this chapter, was born about 1660. At the end of the century he came to Poland to work for Stanisław Leszczyński, the Great Polish magnate who in 1704 was proclaimed king in opposition to August II, the Strong, of Saxony. In 1735 Stanisław exchanged his glimpses of a crown for the comforts of the Duchy of Lorraine; Ferrari hardly survived his patron's fall, and died in 1736 at his old seat af Rydzyna; the great house he had hoped to finish passed to Aleksander Sułkowski, the first of August III's drinking companions. Yet of the few baroque church builders in Poland with any imagination he alone got opportunities to match. He is usually described as a follower of Borromini, which sounds reasonable since he studied in Rome; but his detail has far less of Borromini's sharpness and tension than much Little Polish work, and his planning has more in common with Longhena in Venice and even with Guarini in Turin. Most of his work is so conservative it could have gone up in Bohemia a generation earlier, but it is interrupted by strokes of spatial invention which are not always successful but do seem to be his own.

The palace he built for Stanisław in Warsaw was burnt by the rival prince's mob in 1707, and his earliest surviving works of substance are at Leszno (Lissa), a little town near Rydzyna which was also almost destroyed by fire in the same year. He helped Giovanni Catenacci reshape the plain block of the town hall, giving it huge corner columns and framing its tower in pilasters. Catenacci had begun in 1685 to rebuild the parish church of św. Mikołaj, near the square, as so many compartments between great pilastered buttresses like some of the big Poznan churches; Ferrari set a dome on its chancel and designed the monuments to Rafał and Bogusław Leszczyński, father and uncle to the would-be king. In 1707 he began the Lutheran church of św. Krzyż in the south-west part of the town. Outwardly it is just a rectangle that pushes outwards a bit to north and south and has a western tower. But inside it eight pillars describe a long octagon, and this is vaulted with a central barrel separated by sketched arches from two odd apses; the plan is that which Paolo

Antonio Fontana was to use in the country towns around Lublin a generation later. Now it is neglected, as Protestant churches are, the windows broken, leaves carpeting the grass of the churchyard where niches in the wall still hold the respectable memorials of the vanished German community.

Ferrari made a botch of his next independent job, the little church of św.św. Piotr i Paweł which he began in 1714 on the western outskirts of Obrzycko (Obersitzko) on the Warta. He stuck a tower on the end of the chancel, crowned the crossing with a squared-off dome, and flanked the nave with two big chapels; its uniform plainness, inside and out, cannot make this very bitty plan cohere. But in 1720, in the church for the Cistercian nunnery at Owińska north of Poznań, he went back to his Leszno plan, a rectangle that contains an octagon here covered with a low dome. A bell turret had to do for the two-towered front he never built. He was probably the author of the nave of the parish church at Wschowa (Fraustadt), built on the same plan at the same time. And in 1729 he started the big Franciscan church of św. Walenta at Osieczna (Storchnest) north-east of Leszno. The pilastered blandness of its huge towerless façade is interrupted by a central niche and doorway framed in broken projecting pieces of wall. Inside it is like Catenacci's churches – broad, a series of domes, niche-like chapels between the tall pilasters. Beside it extends the plain convent of 1680, and in front of that rises a jolly columnar structure bearing St. John Nepomuk. But its façade overbears everything with its great voids and solids.

Meanwhile, from at least 1726 onwards, he was completing the pilgrimage church of the Philippines or Oratorians at Gostyń. The Catenaccis had begun it in 1679 on a hill a mile east of the town and part had been consecrated in 1698; the work then lapsed for twenty years, and was not ended until after Ferrari's death, in 1756. In spite of the break, there is little to distinguish his work; some think Giorgio Catenacci was responsible for the whole plan, which owes a lot to the Salute in Venice. But it is tempting to see here a transformation like that Ferrari set in motion at Ląd in 1728; Catenacci should have built the small dark chancel with its flanking apses and good plaster decoration, and Ferrari have created the dome from the ground up. Its grandiose form and sparse decoration seem characteristic; the frieze and spandrels of the massive base arcade are content with painted imitation of stucco, and the tall drum is oddly reduced in scale by the plain pilasters which mark each corner and the centre of each side with equal emphasis. What looks like an ambulatory on the plan is no more than a succession of tall square chapels linked by low passages, pleasant to walk round. The sheer volume of the central space fails to connect with it, and makes its statement alone.

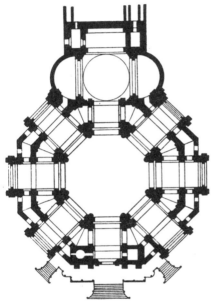

87   Gostyń: Oratorian church, 1:800

Great Poland has plenty more baroque churches, but few were distinguished. The ancient town of Kalisz alone runs to three proud but dull convents, the grandest the huge still Mannerist box Bernardoni began for the Jesuits in 1587; at Buk there is even a dome in timber, with a tall lantern, set on eight great posts inside a sort of Greek cross plan. At Lubiń, north-west of Gostyń, the mediaeval nave of a little abbey church was vaulted in 1739 with a low, uneasy dome, and it holds splendid stalls of the 1730s carved with angels and Fathers by a Silesian workshop such as furnished richer houses like Lubiąż and Krzeszów. The last and grandest abbey rebuilding was near Gniezno at Trzemeszno. The Benedictines came about 1000, and fragments of their earlier buildings survive in foundations and in the buttressed and towered west front. But between 1760 and 1791 the church became a great elongated basilica, with two east towers to command the little town and a dome which blocks off the aisles to make the most of the crossing space, as if this were St.

Paul's in London, and which is really far too large. The most convincing design of these years is much smaller, the pilgrimage church built between 1746 and 1756 at Rokitno on the borders of Brandenburg. Outside it is just a white box, two towers with lead spikes; but inside the square centre is chamfered to an octagon, a dome fitted on, small domes set on entrance and chancel, and domelets put over the galleries to north-east and south-east; the pews curve to match the shape of the broad central space. The architect was Ferrari's successor at Rydzyna, K. M. Frantz, the son of the author of the best Silesian Protestant churches and of the church at Siciny which is only ten miles from the Leszczyńskis' and Sułkowskis' seat.

Rydzyna (Reisen) is the ideal of a Polish magnate's residence, and for that reason exceptional in Greater Poland, where beside the Leszczyńskis there were almost no 'magnates' to grow fat on the spread of serfdom and the bribery and intrigue of the succession wars. The estate is also the town; to north and west spread out-buildings on the scale at least of Stupinigi, whole avenues of stables, and the pretty eighteenth century square with its statues and its church simply occurs where the axis of the house and the high road meet. The layout was decided by Rafał Leszczyński, probably with Ferrari's help, between 1696 and 1704, but work went slowly under Stanisław, and even between buying the place in 1737 and dying in 1762 Sułkowski, with Frantz as his architect, could not complete it. Anyway, the house is no more than a square mass with corner towers and the vertical banding Austria and Bohemia had used in the 1680s; the northern entrance and staircase block has big pilasters, a balustrade, and lively frames to door and window above that suggest Ferrari. Inside one ought to find early rococo plaster and grand rooms that culminate in the pomp

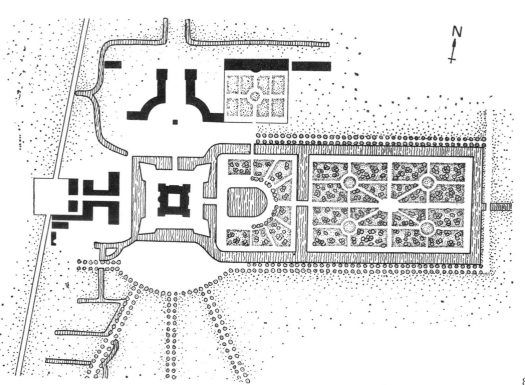

88 Rydzyna: house and park, 1:6,250

of an apsed ballroom with immense fluted pillars installed in the west wing in the 1760s by Ignacy Graff. But it suffered in the war, and I found the windows still blind and young trees sprouting in the moat.

In 1731 Augustus the Strong, Stanisław Leszczyński's rival, began to build a residence to Knöffel's plans on the western edge of the province at Kargowa (or, appropriately, Unruhstadt). Like so many other Saxon projects this got nowhere, and all that stands now is an odd little house on a sort of E plan whose central bay has an apse crowned by a pediment that follows the angles of its three sides. At Ciążeń near Ląd we find a stylistic intruder, a big block of a house built in the 1760s whose interiors seek to be French in planning and decoration. But the weakness of the province under its enemies the Saxon kings is reflected in the lack of baroque houses. Only in the last third of the century did the middling gentry retrieve their fortunes; and improve their agriculture; and turn to Western Europe not only for new crops but also for new tastes – the neo-classical and the picturesque.

The gradual shift in taste shows up well at Rogalin, south of Poznań. The first plans, made in 1762, were still in essentials Viennese baroque. When Ignacy Graff carried them out in 1770 the rococo decoration gave way to a much severer manner, and only six plain Ionic pilasters were left on the front that commands the magnificent avenue of trees down to the village. 1782 saw the first undoubted importation from the England of Adam, the curved orderless wings that run round to join flanking pavilions. Inside, where the young Dresden architect Kamsetzer was at work from 1788, fresh from travels in the West, we find a single flight of stairs that rises parallel to the façade, a parti very popular a generation later; the authorities have furnished the rooms around with tapestries, gilt chairs, and Meissen china taken from other houses. By 1820, we have reached the Romantic sort of picturesque neo-classicism, with a tiny Roman chapel, a 'Maison Carrée', that stands hidden among trees on a hillock by the road.

In fact the first man to introduce English ideas to Great Poland was the Silesian architect Karl Gotthard Langhans. Between 1779 and 1783 he built at Pawłowice, east of Leszno, a house far more satisfying than his ruined Wrocław palace and harsh Silesian churches. Like his patron Maksymilian Mielżyński, he had travelled in France and England; his big Ionic columns above the entrance and under a straight architrave recall Heveningham, his pilastered quarter-circle flanking galleries, Kedleston; the side pavilions they lead to are sharper and cooler still. Inside, his plan for a circular saloon was altered in 1789 by Kamsetzer, who enlarged its centre, added a rectangular bay at each side, and informed the space he had almost trebled in size with twenty-four huge free-standing Corinthian columns that also echo Syon and Kedleston. This room was far grander even than the columned hall Merlini had built in the Royal Palace in Warsaw ten years before.

Though I have not seen it, I can believe that the paradigm of Kamsetzer's art is the relatively modest house he began in 1786 at Sierniki. It is compact, modelled on the 'pavillons' of France a generation earlier; on one side an Ionic portico, with steps and pediment, its space half inside and half outside the block; on the other a three-sided bay that accommodates a circular saloon; no flanking pavilions, the simplest detail. It was much praised, and imitated too; a good example by some local builder is that of 1788 at Lewków, the plan copied with the greatest care, but the classical spirit half smothered under scrappy but enthusiastic plaster decoration. Closer still to France is the simplicity of Racot, built in the late 1780s possibly by Merlini himself, with no great saloon, only a plain Doric portico and a flash of white and

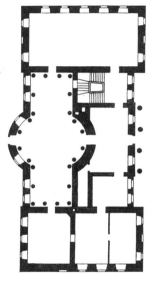

89 Pawłowice: first floor, 1:625

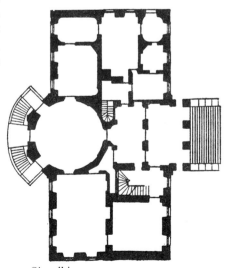

90 Sierniki, 1:500

orange paint through the big trees of the State stud farm; and that of Walewice, 163
begun in 1783 by Hilary Szpilowski, with Ionic portico, and side pavilions, but
simple straight galleries to lead to them. There are grander undertakings that follow
Rogalin, like Czerniejewo (Schwarzenau), begun in the early 1770s, its Ionic portico
stuck on about 1790; a long deferential approach up the village street, outer and
inner courtyards, and, inside, two circular halls one above the other; fluted Doric
columns round that on the ground floor and pilasters round that on the first.

Most distinguished of all this family of buildings are those of Stanisław Zawadzki.
Born in 1743, he made his career at first by designing barracks now long vanished;
his opportunity came only late in the 1780s, when one of Stanisław August's family
commissioned from him the now lost 'Ustronie' palace in Warsaw. In 1797 he began
the splendid house at Śmiełów that you see from miles to the south as you drive over 16ᵗ
the flat fields. The plan and the garden front are nothing remarkable, but the main 16ᵗ
elevation has found a new richness in the combination of Ionic columned portico
with Ionic pilasters and trophies on the end bays; the flanking pavilions are more
subtly sculptural, entrances framed by sunk Doric columns, triglyph friezes, and
ingenious two-stage roofs; inside, the projecting saloon and a room beside it still have
Smugłewicz' paintings of trophies and ruins. In 1798 he planned the bizarre house
at Dobrzyca in the shape of a set-square with the entrance in the re-entrant angle.

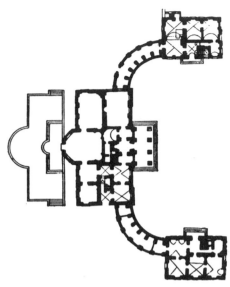

91   Śmiełów, 1:750

It is possible, of course, that he knew Rinaldi's little house of 1758 for Peter III of
Russia at Lomonosov (Oranienbaum), but the essential reason was that his client
was a leading Freemason. In its position, little wonder that the portico is both
compressed and attenuated, with tall Doric columns on detached plinths. But some
of Smugłewicz' most characteristic painted views survive inside; and the best thing
about the place is its small neglected informal park, which holds a 'Gardener's House'
on the model of the pavilions at Śmiełów and a 'Masonic Lodge' which is a round
temple with portico and dome, windows and doors framed inside by half round
columns.

Meanwhile his handsomest project was taking shape, the Palladian cube villa at
Lubostroń away to the north towards Bydgoszcz, planned in 1787, though building 1ᵗ
did not begin till 1795. It follows English adaptations of the Villa Rotonda, such as
Mereworth, and only one portico stands free to mark the entrance. It became a
political gesture, for its great central hall was designed to hold the columns made for
a projected Temple of Providence in Warsaw which should have commemorated the
independence which the Partitions scotched. It is a rich space now: red walls, ochre
scagliola columns, white plaster friezes and trophies and historical reliefs, the inlaid
floor and the bronze chandelier; other rooms have stucco decoration and, on the

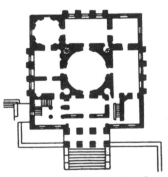

92   Lubostroń, 1:800

south side, walls with more painted views. The park, planned for romantic eyes, drops
suddenly away to the valley beyond. And the entrance quotes Virgil: '*hic secura quies
et nescia fallere vita*'.

After Napoleon, not all the province came under Prussian rule. Kalisz became one
of the chief towns of the Congress Kingdom, and Sylwester Szpilowski, the son of
the architect of Nawra and Walewice, put up big, cold public buildings in imitation
of Warsaw, the Tribunal in 1820 and the north wing of the archbishop's palace in
1824. Few of the textile mills which made the town's fortune survive, and those are
hardly so interesting as the ironworks of Little Poland further east. But Ciechocinek,
the scruffy spa down the Vistula, preserves not only the neat swimming baths and
post office built in the 1930s by Romuald Gutt, but also one splendid industrial
monument, the salt-works Jakub Graff built between 1824 and 1833; two apparently

endless timber frames on which brushwood still drips with trickling brine.

    Under German rule, some of the gentry turned to Berlin for new ideas. In 1822 Schinkel designed for Antoni Radziwiłł the strange hunting lodge by the lake at 71 Antonin south of Kalisz. Four three-storeyed wings with steep gables radiate from an octagon which turns out to be one huge space surrounded by galleries and centred on a gigantic stove. The chimney apart, everything is timber, now a dirty ochre colour, the hideous but pregnant conception of a great mind. And it was to Schinkel's designs 69 of 1834 that Tytus Działyński remodelled his moated house at Kórnik. Over the years it turned into a Gothic castle, arcaded, embattled, machicolated, turreted; a great blunt pointed arch informs the garden side; inside, the entrance hall is star-vaulted, and on the first floor one room is ludicrously Moorish while another sports carefully three-dimensional rib vaults on elaborate capitals. To remodel the fifteenth century church on the edge of the park they employed, alas, the egregious Lanci and the reddest and hardest brick. And the slippery slope led on to Gołuchów, where in 1872 a team of Frenchmen full of the ideas of Viollet-le-Duc took in hand the Leszczyńskis' Renaissance house, of whose courtyard loggia an elegant fragment remains, and tried to make it seem to stand upon the Loire. There is a happy antidote in the melancholy charm of the park around it; but the history of the 'English garden' in Poland is best studied on the plains of Mazovia.

9.　Mazovia

East of Poznań on the great road the land becomes ever more monotonous. Setts succeed asphalt, the rows of trees go past, small grey towns like Kutno and Sochaczew guard the river crossings. There is not much forest, and every slight hill is like the last. Mazovia is the most negative of Polish provinces. It is also one of the poorest, and in the Middle Ages its greatest place was Płock – which even now has barely passed a population of 40,000 – and tiny Drohiczyn served as capital for the expanse of Podlasie astride the Bug. Warsaw was a small fortified town that commanded yet another river crossing, and beyond it stretched a waste of sand and gravel which even now is as much a desert as the outskirts of any city can be. It became the capital because of the union with Lithuania and because Cracow was too far south for kings who hunted endlessly in the forests of Augustów and Grodno and Białowieza. And beyond the Vistula these forests take over as the distances increase. On a rise on the way to Brześć I stopped; a deer came from the scrubby pines, stood in the centre of the international highway, and considered me; the endless grey-green horizon beyond was Russia.

Płock, the old capital, sits on a scarp beside the Vistula. War and time have not left it much. The cathedral is still Romanesque in structure, and a very grand structure: nave of three big square bays, aisles each of six, apses in the transepts and a lost eastern apse. Under all the tepid sixteenth and seventeenth century plaster, the proportions are clear enough. The west front with its two odd, slightly tapering octagonal towers is work of the late Middle Ages. There is nothing else interesting to report except Kubicki's pretty toll gates, Ionic columns in antis of the 1820s. The town's best building is Marek Leykam's P.T.T.K. hostel, the Dom Turysty planned 1 in 1957 and actually begun in 1959. It stands east of the cathedral in the Piekarska, on one of the most commanding points on the edge of the hill; its low, recessed ground-floor carries what seems one long slab six-sided in section, a mass as powerful as a fist. Further upstream and still on the northern bluff, the abbey of Czerwińsk was founded in 1148 beside a castle of the duke's, and can show more of its Romanesque church than Płock – two slender square towers, the carved capitals of the thirteenth century west doorway. There are remains of old wall paintings, but here again the impression is of a skimpy baroque. The lonely stone buildings house a handful of hospitable Salesian fathers, and the windows of their vaulted rooms command the broad shallow river and the wooded heath of the Kampinos beyond.

The greatest of Mazovian castles stands at Czersk on a spur which dominates mile 1 upon mile of the Vistula valley as though it were the very edge of Europe. Though rebuilt about 1500 with brick walls on stone foundations, this has the form of a prehistoric fortress, an irregular enceinte 200 feet across designed to shelter a whole tribe, with two valiant round towers and one square one over the gate. In the province it has only one rival, away to the north at Ciechanów, a fifteenth century attempt to emulate the Teutonic Order's symmetry; its plan is a rectangle, now large and empty; two great round towers decorated with glazed bricks look south over the water-meadows at the town's ancient, smelly brewery.

Parish churches begin by trying to follow the brick gothic of Prussia, and run on without any stylistic break into a provincial Renaissance. A chain of them lies eastwards along the line of the Narew; some are low halls with narrow aisles and elaborate net vaults, like that of 1526 at Wizna; Szczepankowo has a shot of 1547 at a basilica, rude, massive, innocent of buttressing, its decoration one awkward gable, its vessels unvaulted. At Łomża in 1520 the builders seem to have started on another basilica, and then lowered the nave and raised the aisles enough to exclude a clerestory without getting the vaults in line; inside it is broad, roughly handsome, but dark, with rich star vaults and, in the aisles, cellular ones, on star plans like those of Olsztyn and Kętrzyn; of the many monuments, one in the south aisle is of capital quality. Even the church the Bernardines began in 1585 at Przasnysz is still straight gothic outside, its broad panelled gable high above the little town, and smaller gables over chapels that are baroque inside.

At Pułtusk the brick collegiate church begun in 1443 was drastically reshaped in 1560, by one Giovanni Battista who had worked on the cathedral at Płock. A fussy but flat kind of Renaissance decoration covers the long tunnel vault with coffering and the upper part of the nave with innumerable blank arches; the aisles have got gothic stars back; yet its proportions and its tall arcade of square white piers make the interior quite grand. There are Renaissance monuments and stalls, the churchyard holds big trees and a bell tower of startling neo-classicism, and a long dusty market place leads past plain old houses to the bishop's palace on the castle mound. At 76 Brochów, west of Warsaw, the church begun in the 1550s looks fortress-like outside, with two round western towers and a third over its apse; but the remodelling of 1665 made the interior white, light, and peaceful, with plaster patterns, new arcades, and the odd effect of looking up through the chancel into the eastern tower. The sixteenth century church at Węgrów was yet more thoroughly rebuilt in 1703, by Carlo Carlone. Its old walls are still there, its low aisles oddly screened on the west by blank walls that end in cone-topped turrets, its churchyard set with square corner pavilions with steep triangular roofs, like models from a lesson in solid geometry.

A similar church at Łowicz, twice rebuilt in the seventeenth century, is more distinguished by its contents. Its aisles sprout elaborate domed chapels, of 1580 to the south, of 1718 to the north; one archbishop, Przerębski, is commemorated by Canavesi, another, Uchański, by Jan Michałowicz, and Willem van den Block of Gdańsk appears as the author of a Tarnowski tomb; there are black and white baroque marble bishops in the chancel and many tablets to lesser clergy of the see of Gniezno. The little town has pleasant, cottagey streets and squares, above all the treed space of the Płac Kilińskiego; and a Piarist church of 1672 with a solidly expressive concave-convex front, remarkably up-to-date; and a neo-classical town hall of 1825 with swags and banding and two huge columns in antis, and a post office of 1829; and out to the south-west bizarre fragments of the freely mediaeval tower and gatehouse which survive from General Klicki's romantic garden of 1809

Mazovia lacks the romantic extravagance of the Wilno baroque, the freedom in planning and plasticity in decoration – all those broken-off ends of gables made into commas and exclamations – that alone produced a Polish style of interest outside Poland. The nearest we can get to this is the north-east corner of her present frontiers, a wilder Masuria amid whose lonely lakes and forests Zygmunt August founded Augustów in 1561; here Sejny's big church was built for the Dominicans in the seventeenth century and reshaped in the eighteenth, splendidly dominating on its embattled looking hill but hardly worth the journey; and on Lake Wigry near 17 Suwałki the Camaldulensians began in 1704 a great white church on a fortified peninsula, gates and ramps and walls and more gates, amid the endless trees and water. Nearer Białystok, at Tykocin, a surprisingly large church was built in the 1740s for a college of priests, fronted by two storeys of pilasters, flanked by two towers attached by covered wings as if they were part of some great house, and in 1771 the whole small town was replanned to centre on it. I have not seen it, nor other churches further south-east like that of the Benedictine nuns at Drohiczyn, begun in 1744, with what seems an admirably plastic concave front that uses columns only for the centre bay.

But the grandest Mazovian baroque church is that built for the Jesuits between 1740 and 1763 in the pilgrimage spot of Kobyłka near Warsaw. Its west front is enormously broad, two serious flanking towers and between them architecture poured like chocolate over some underlying system of bulges and indentations. Its nave's tunnel vault leads to a short chancel with a low dome and a wall painted up to seem an apse; but its low and very broad aisles run three bays further on, and embrace the sacristy and a Calvary under a painted dome and open to the east. Some detail is handsome, like the freehand shapes of the blank windows above the nave arcade; the colours are all pale – grey, blue, pink, ochre; provincial indeed, but all of a piece. The architects were Guido Longhi and Jacopo Fontana.

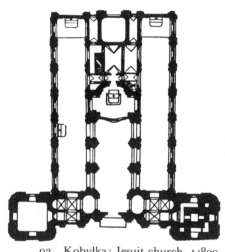

93   Kobyłka: Jesuit church, 1:800

The move of the capital to Warsaw made residences in the nearby country more desirable. The best architect of the age of Sobieski, the Dutchman Tylman van Gameren, built several, for the most part since altered. In 1690 he began one for the Radziejowskis at Nieborów near Łowicz. It is a long, low block of two storeys and, 1 originally, just twelve bays; a pediment over the four-bay centre, hardly a pilaster, surprisingly tentative beside the brisk assertion of his Warsaw palaces. The insertion of three tall windows over the entrance and the addition of extra storeys to the square towers which flank it have spoilt its scale, and inside I found it disappointing – bits of plasterwork, mediocre furniture and pictures. Tylman's small formal garden has given way to a grand avenue and an L of water framed in hedges, and there are the hothouses Zug built for the Radziwiłłs, Doric, rough, still full of trees in pots. The smell of lilac hangs around the great trees of this oasis in the dusty plain.

In 1681 Tylman probably designed the very pretty little house – hardly more than a farm – at Obory a few miles south of Warsaw beyond Wilanów; one storey, a big 1 roof, just broken pediments over the windows. And between 1693 and 1703 he built an admirable house for the Bielińskis on the other side of the Vistula at Otwock Stary (not the modern suburb on the railway, but the old village south of Karczew). It is just a seven-bay block; its south entrance side has two flanking turrets and a projecting five-sided centre; the north side towards the lake was adorned with delicious plaster relief, urns and trophies in broken pediments over the windows, a garlanded Bacchanal in the steep central pediment. But in the eighteenth century the entrance side was crowded up by adding wings, and in the war the plaster decoration was all lost. Bare as it is now, under its steep roof it looks more Dutch than ever.

Tylman's larger houses were less fortunate. He built two for Marshal Stanisław Lubomirski; that on the river bluff at Puławy passed in 1731 to the Czartoryskis, who went on and on adapting it so that it is now but an adjunct to their great romantic garden; that of the 1690s at Łubnice, south of Staszów in Little Poland, was the grandest of all, with an entrance courtyard and pilastered halls, but it has been totally destroyed. In 1697 he designed the central block of the Branickis' palace at Białystok. In the eighteenth century it was progressively expanded, mainly by Deibel, into a parade of inexpressive pilastered masses round a vast square courtyard. They call it 'Wersal Podlaski'. It is a fit butt for Marta Bibescu's taunt at the residences of Polish magnates – 'C'était Versailles sans la Révolution française; mais aussi Versailles sans génie'.

It was left to one of the Fontanas to build the Mazovian palace which has best survived. They came from Castello in Valsolda on Lake Lugano and became the leading Italian builders in Warsaw, in the manner of the Catenaccis in Poznań or the Luragos in Prague. The first to make a real name was Giuseppe, who worked mostly in Warsaw itself; I have already described Paolo Antonio's churches round Lublin. Giuseppe's elder son Jacopo studied in Italy and at Paris and became one of the most accomplished architects of the Polish baroque. When still in his twenties he built the pretty little church at Karczew; in the 1740s, the church I have described at Kobyłka; in 1755, the church and Bernardine convent of the increasingly popular pilgrimage spot of Góra Kalwaria.

He was apparently using a plan by the Saxon court architect J. F. Knöbel, then working on the Brühl palace in Warsaw, when in 1750 he began the reconstruction of the Potockis' house at Radzyń Podlaski, whose church I have described among its Lublin Renaissance fellows. It frames a square courtyard 250 feet across; its two low office wings have centre gateways with pilastered concave recesses outside, banded masonry within, and obelisked towers on top; between them lies the main house, two tall storeys high, most unemphatically panelled, with three bays at each end pushed undemonstratively forward and a centre, only half a storey taller, which has three sides of which two are slightly curved. Inside, some rococo decoration remains, and a neat staircase climbs on a couple of muscular statues through 180 degrees into the light. The Orangery to the east is hardly more emphatic, with nine big windows, pilasters framing those at the ends and pairs of plain Ionic columns that in the centre. It is all very formal and French, and when Fontana was in Paris he seems to have taken most note of the courtly architecture of Hardouin-Mansart. I found it still much battered, walls pocked by shots, a bright red new tiled roof, and new planting on the old avenues to the south-east. But it still had its brilliantly conceived sculptural ornament; and the figures that perched on the gateways' skyline, the rococo shields and garlands cresting the main house, the chariot and horses that rose from the centre of the orangery, gave it the ample pomp of a magnate's residence.

The greatest of all these magnate families was that of the Czartoryskis, whose ideas and plots are almost the only continuous thread in the miserable tangle of Polish eighteenth century politics. Adam Kazimierz Czartoryski married the brilliant Izabella Flemming and made Puławy a second court for artists as well as magnates; his cousin Stanisław Poniatowski was made King Stanisław August in 1764; his son Adam Jerzy Czartoryski became Alexander of Russia's confidant and minister and shaped the Polish settlement at the Congress of Vienna. But in 1830 Adam Jerzy emerged at the head of the Polish revolt, and in 1831 the Russians confiscated the family's chief estate, at Puławy on the bend in the Vistula west of Lublin; the collections went to Cracow to become the Czartoryski Museum, and the house Tylman began became an Agricultural Institute. It is a pretty characterless pile today. Its best side, the work of Deibel and Mayer in the 1720s, faces the river with Doric pilasters that advance and recede above a massive battered basement; inside it has a still rococo pillared entrance hall, the romantics' obligatory Gothic Room in plaster, and a riotous cast-iron staircase. But the beauty of the place is its park and the buildings in it, the grandest of Polish landscape gardens.

The idea of the English – or, as it was often thought to be, Anglo-Chinese – landscape garden came to Poland about 1770, partly directly through the writings of Chambers and the example of Capability Brown's plans for Catherine of Russia, partly through the visits which patrons – rather than architects – made themselves to England. The first attempt at one on Polish soil was made by the Izabella Czartoryska I have mentioned, with the help of the painter J. P. Norblin, at Powązki on the outskirts of Warsaw. She was followed in 1776 at Siedlce, east of Warsaw, by Aleksandra Ogińska, who brought Zawadzki in to reshape her simple house and add a portico, and behind it laid out a crowded and tortuous little park which still remains. But the most characteristic Polish gardens are the work of the best romantic classical architects, Zug at Arkadia and Aigner at Puławy.

Zug's first garden was also in the Warsaw outskirts, begun about 1775 for Elżbieta Lubomirska at Mokotów ('Mon Coteau') and now practically obliterated. In 1778 he started work near Łowicz on Helena Radziwiłł's 'Arkadia'. Here there was no large house, but, as in many Continental landscape gardens, just water, trees, and pavilions. You enter from the north by a Swiss Cottage. To the left a path leads to Gothick objects, a chapel, a line of ruined arches, a tower, a priest's house; to the right are traces of an amphitheatre by the lake, whose outlet is closed by a big ruined aqueduct. There are odd fragments of building everywhere; the water ripples, birches and chestnuts rustle and shiver in the light; across the Ionic portico of the Temple of Diana Zug built in 1783 is written DOVE PACE TROVAI D'OGNI MIA GUERRA. [18]

Zug's first work for the Czartoryskis was the very pretty house at Natolin, just [18] south of Warsaw beyond Wilanów. It was begun in 1780 as the 'Bazantarnia' [18] (Pheasantry), and decorated by Brenna, the Florentine we have met at Łańcut. It has an oval room on the garden side, but this is wholly open to the air through its six Ionic columns; there is no portico over the entrance, and there the one-storey-high order was changed to Doric by Aigner and Potocki when in 1808 they turned this summer retreat into a year-round residence. It is a refuge for Government now, and heavily guarded; I cannot report on the Dutch Farm of 1814 or on Marconi's grandiose Doric Temple of 1834; still, the glimpse one can catch from the lane is worth having.

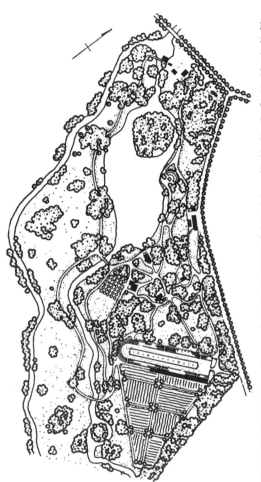

94   Arkadia: garden, 1:1,400

Piotr Aigner was to become one of the leading Polish neo-classicists – though his career was sadly interrupted by war – and the chief designer of the Czartoryskis' buildings on their greatest estate, all through the inspiration and tutelage of a great dilettante, Stanisław Kostka Potocki, who had travelled in western Europe and visited the great Whig palaces and in Rome had been made by David the subject of one of the best of all equestrian portraits. The Puławy which Aigner tackled was already on the move; in the 1770s a 'wild promenade' had been planted beyond the large formal garden, and in the 1790s the whole park was turned into a garden half-a-mile long. Experts came from Germany, Ireland, and England, the last James Savage who was also to lay out the Saxon Garden in Warsaw, and 260 varieties of trees were planted, half of them foreign. In 1798 Aigner began to put up the

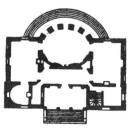

95   Natolin, 1:800

fashionable buildings; a tiny Chinese pavilion, white and undecorated, at the bottom of the slope below the house; a Gothic House with bits of sculpture built in; west of that, on the edge of the bluff towards the river, the peripteral Temple of the Sibyl with a high plinth, Composite columns, a shallow dome, and steps guarded by two lions. At the park's southern end a massive bridge leads to the 'Marynka Palace' of 1790, a nine-bay block informed by a colossal pilaster order which turns into columns to make a shallow portico with no pediment, a perfect expression of Stanislavian classicism. As usual, the park is over-planted, and one can never get a fair idea of its extent; but now and then the trees part and open a vista over the poplars and orchards of the water meadows that stretch to the Vistula.

Away to the north, where the main road leaves the town to cross the river, Aigner built a church in 1803. It is a miniature Pantheon raised on steps, with a charming interior where Ionic columns carry a gallery, a forerunner of his św. Aleksander in Warsaw. Unfortunately, the satellite house he built in 1800 at Góra Puławska is no more; it was the first of his essays in asymmetrical villas with corner towers, in the manner of Nash's Cronkhill, which culminated at Zarzecze in Little Poland.

Other classicists worked all over Mazovia. In 1781 Schröger built a round church at Skierniewice, almost contemporary with Zug's more radical Protestant one in Warsaw, fussy inside but outside admirably plain and white; he had already reconstructed the house, since completely rebuilt again, but its gateway remains, two convex groups of Doric columns in antis framing the plainest arch; the town also has a grandly battlemented railway station designed in 1846 in the 'Rundbogenstil' by Adam Idźkowski. In 1806 Kubicki built an octagonal church at Nadarzyn, southwest of Warsaw, and about the same time a pavilion in the park at Młochów nearby which is an exercise in economy of means. In the 1830s J. J. Gay designed one showpiece entrance for the fortress at Modlin, banded masonry and the necessary trophies; begun by Napoleon, extended as Nowogeorgiewsk by the Russians, this huge fortification is still in military use, and you can only pause on the bridge over the Narew and glimpse the battlemented tower and the walls that stretch downstream. At Opinogóra, north-east of Ciechanów, the Krasińskis built one of the prettiest of romantic Gothic houses; its best part is a suite of rib-vaulted rooms, running to an octagonal corner tower, which Aigner may have designed though it was not completed till 1843. There is a decent church of 1825, and a cool green park.

Mazovia has one twentieth century speciality, jazz-modern churches of the 1930s; św. Roch built by Otakar Sosnowski in the Dąbrowskiego at Białystok and św. Krzysztof by Bruno Zborowski at Podkowa Leśna south-west of Warsaw. At Sochaczew, though, there is perhaps the best of Polish post-war churches, begun in 1959 by Mieczysław Gliszczyński; in essentials a simple box, its outward effect confused by the mixture of materials, but the east end well informed by a great chalice-shaped recess in the wall which dominates the whole interior. And at Wyszków there is an excellent example of industrial building, the furniture plant completed in 1965 by Dzierżawski, Pawelski, and Siennicki, with an ingenious roof of long slabs of alternating height. But what one remembers best is the Polish manor house at its most familiar, as at Mała Wieś near Grójec, built in 1783 by Hilary Szpilowski, the architect of Walewice, or at Babsk near Rawa; a simple portico glimpsed at the end of an avenue, a flash of white paint through a little park's great trees, a vision of peace in the endless sandy plain.

10. Warsaw

We hardly hear of Warsaw before the fourteenth century. Perhaps it was then that a small town was laid out on a more or less regular plan, beside a castle which commanded a crossing of the broad shallow Vistula; in 1408 its northern suburb was given independent existence as the Nowe Miasto. For about a century it was the residence of the dukes of Mazovia. In 1526 they died out, and the Polish kings found it more and more convenient to occupy their place; from 1572 they were elected here, and after the Wawel fire of 1596 the capital finally came here from Cracow. But the small brick and stone town was much ruined by the fires of 1607 and 1660 and the Swedish invasions. Only in Sobieski's reign did the capital city we know begin to take shape; the great palace on the castle site, the magnates' residences scattered in an arc round the old town and lining the long irregular avenue of Krakowskie Przedmieście to the south, the suburban retreats of Ujazdów and Wilanów. Even then its population was still only 20,000 or 30,000. In its golden age under Stanisław August it reached 115,000; in the Napoleonic Wars it was halved, and not till 1864 was it 120,000 again; in 1900 it was 690,000, in 1939, as the capital of an independent Poland, 1,300,000. There followed the destruction of the Ghetto in 1943, and the Rising of August 1944 in which a quarter of a million people fell. The offensive of January 1945 brought the Russians in, and the inhabitants, scattered in the country, came back to live in shacks and shored up ruins.

In its short history Warsaw had become the emblem of Polish nationality and culture. The Germans had methodically destroyed five-sixths of its buildings. It was not an isolated act of rage, but the culmination of a policy. They had said that the Poles were fit only to be slaves and that Poland had no culture. To prove it they had deliberately murdered her leaders and deliberately stolen or destroyed the best possessions of her museums and libraries. The challenge could not be escaped; Warsaw had to rise again as it had been before. Costly, of course. Wasteful, no doubt. However much skill and care were spent, it could never be quite the same. In Stare Miasto, the ancient centre, the paint is shabby already and the illusion just persists; in Krakowskie Przedmieście irregularity and variety preserve the feeling of the street Bellotto painted; but Nowy Świat beyond is a wretched counterfeit of the neo-classical in nerveless stucco. Nowhere, except perhaps in some of the brisk sgraffiti of Nowe Miasto, does liveliness break through as it does in Gdańsk. But what else could a people do, whose very identity had been so brutally questioned?

The Cathedral of św. Jan Chrzciciel (St. John Baptist) was the first parish church. It got a college of priests about 1400, but became the seat of a bishop only in 1797 and that of the Primate only in 1946. Old views show it as a typically Polish jumble, whose façade went through all sorts of transmogrifications, getting a pretty Renaissance gable about 1630 and a Gothic fantasy front with a row of pinnacled porches in 1833. But now Professor Zachwatowicz has reduced it to the usual north European brick hall with buttresses and a tall panelled gable. Inside this are the foundations of the single west tower which fell in 1602, and beyond them a reasonably grand hall nave of four bays and a small, low aisleless chancel with a three-sided apse. The restoration has produced a standard town church whose star vaults and brick pillars and ribs could be anywhere east of the Elbe. The furniture is so far too sparse to contradict this anonymity; but in the south aisle the National Museum has put a pretty late mediaeval altar, a broken sixteenth century slab commemorates the last dukes of Mazovia, and there stands still the battered shape of Bacciarelli's great Roman erection of 1831 to Stanisław Małachowski.

Next-door stands the little Jesuit church of St. Mary, a late Renaissance thing of 1609 with the crowded niches and pilasters and finials of the Lublin manner. Inside it is very plain, the vaults simple Renaissance; but over the chancel rise a tall drum and cupola, quite a *coup-de-théâtre* in this small room. Stare Miasto's one other church, św. Marcin in the Piwna, is of fourteenth century origin, but of the Middle Ages remains only the base of its tower, now a house away up the street. Inside it is a plain box of about 1700, but the front, built between 1744 and 1764, has a huge broken semi-circle for pediment, great half inset columns, and a concave centre for the entrance, a rococo plastic and effective enough to be by Placidi. Of the rebuilt streets the Piwna is the best, with small two- and three-bay houses with rusticated doorways.

The Square is the restorers' showpiece. Its sides are named after four public men of Stanislavian Warsaw. The south, Strona Zakrzewskiego, is the plainest, just four- and five-storey houses all three bays wide, sketchy decoration, a depressing restaurant. Strona Barssa on the east is prettier; an oriel lies just round the southern corner in the Celna, and at no.18 the rhythm is broken by the four well-proportioned bays of the eighteenth century Dom Horlemusów. On the north, Strona Dekerta boasts two rooftop pavilions balanced on houses already of five storeys; no.32, the Kamienica Baryczków, has the finialled and bobbled skyline of 1633, and a Moor's head looks out from the fake masonry at no.36. The star turn is Strona Kołłątaja to the west. The grand Gothic brick doorway at no.21 leads to a smart cellar restaurant; behind eighteenth century pediments and delicate stucco, the Fukier house at no.27 preserves a mediaeval layout of entrance and stair; the northern corner house is known as that of the Dukes of Mazovia, but was built about 1300 to house the mayor, and has scrolly friezes and a doorway of 1630 and a statue of St. Anne on the street corner. The restoration often fumbles; in the central space, the market stalls have given way to tourist buses; but this ancient space is satisfying enough to rank beside the squares of Cracow, Gdańsk, and Prague.

The Nowomiejska leads northwards down to the Barbican, hardly more than a hollowed out round tower, a toy beside that of Cracow. To right and left run the double city walls, impressive no doubt to anyone with a bow or a small sling-shot, but rebuilt with a quantity of new brick that imposes overly on the imagination. Beyond the gate churches stand to right and left. The Paulines' św. Duch is a big standard job of 1707 by Giuseppe Piola, two towers, nave with low aisles, lots of pilasters. The Dominicans' św. Jacek has a mediaeval core, exposed in the chancel, behind its bland baroque face, and its range of chapels includes one by Tylman van Gameren. The Freta leads on past baroque houses and the Nowe Miasto's triangular market place to the Franciscan church of św. Franciszek, begun in 1679, a massive well-modelled front, a compact tall nave with low vaulted aisles and a dome over the crossing, all very square and crisp. North of it stands Deibel's Sapieha palace of the 1740s, and to the east the simple star-vaulted brick parish church of St. Mary rises on a high point of the bluff and romantically commands the wide river and the sandy plain.

The best single building in all the old town centre is the little church of św. Kazimierz which dominates the Nowe Miasto market place from its east side. Sobieski's queen Maria Kazimiera began it in 1687 for the Benedictine Sisters of the Sacrament as a thank-offering for her loved husband's relief of Vienna. Her architect was Tylman van Gameren. Born at Utrecht in 1632, he had come to Poland in 1666. At first he served the Luboinirskis as a military engineer; in 1672 he entered royal service; in 1685 he was ennobled. His first important building was almost certainly the Royal Chapel of 1678 at Gdańsk. If so, it is the eldest of a little family of compact, centrally-planned churches in the squared-off manner of Dutch architects like van Campen. Św. Kazimierz, the second, is a central octagon, almost a square, four arms of different sizes, and a dome with eight ribs rising to a lantern – a neat and satisfying space. The third is the church he began about 1690 for the Bernardines at Czerniaków, south of the city on the way to Wilanów; another commanding position at a fork in the road, a small domed square nave and a large chancel, much richer plaster decoration. Last of all he built in 1695 a chapel for Queen Maria Kazimiera's shopping centre development of Marieville or Marywil, a five-sided market-place with shops behind arcades where the Teatr Wielki (Grand Theatre) stands now, a pretty extension of French ideas of planning long ago destroyed.

Tylman van Gameren became the most serious architect of Sobieski's generation. His university church of 1689 in Cracow broke out into a Roman baroque; his houses, like Nieborów of 1680, were mostly simple enough, but he built one very grand one, now altogether lost, in the 1690s at Łubnice; it was the same patron, Marshal Stanisław Herakliusz Lubomirski, who had him build the Bath House or Łazienki in his park at Ujazdów south of Warsaw which was to form the core of King Stanisław August's more famous pavilion. Of his other work in Warsaw much has been lost, most important the Ossoliński (later Brühl) and Morsztyn (later Saxon) palaces, later rebuilt, which defined a new monumental axis running west from Krakowskie Przedmieście. But in the Plac Krasińskich, west of Nowe Miasto, still stands the huge Krasiński house which was later the 'Pałac Rzeczypospolitej'. Giuseppe Bellotti had begun it in 1676; van Gameren completed it between 1688 and 1699, and Andreas Schlüter of Gdańsk carved the relief for the central pediment. It is nineteen bays long, with five bays emphasised in the centre and three at each end; plain Ionic pilasters stand on tall banded plinths and support a weak entablature which small windows interrupt; the double staircase inside is just as rhetorical. But, perhaps because of Schlüter's influence, it does not really convince. Van Gameren seems to have been happier in little, for his Warsaw masterpiece is the Ostrogski or Gniński house of 1681, now a Chopin museum, east of Nowy Świat down the Ordynacka, perched on a huge built-up terrace above the river. It is very compact, each side has just a three-bay centre with big Doric pilasters, there are a few figures and busts in niches; four-square Dutch reason under the shifting Polish sky.

Sobieski had become king in 1674. In 1677 he bought the village of Milanów, on the edge of the Vistula meadows half-a-dozen miles upstream from Warsaw, and almost at once work started on a residence for him, soon called 'Wilanów', under the leadership of Augustyn Wincent Locci, the son of a builder who had worked for the

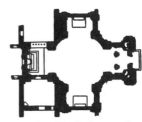

96   Warsaw: św. Kazimierz, 1:800

97   Warsaw: church at Czerniaków, 1:800

Vasas forty years before. The core was a little two-storey block, its western entrance front framed by two projecting two-bay pavilions, its eastern front towards garden and river by two one-bay ones. Between 1680 and 1682 wings reached out to north and south and the whole was clad in a quite modest colossal order; between 1686 and 1692 a new central accent was added, a sort of three-bay pavilion perched on the existing balustrade, and the flanking towers were raised. Painters and sculptors were called in, the most notable of them Schlüter, and when Sobieski died in 1696 he left a small but rich baroque palace behind.

There followed a year of chaos, the election of Frederick Augustus the Strong of Saxony as King August II in 1697, and the proclamation of Stanisław Leszczyński as his rival in 1704. In the hands of Sobieski's heirs Wilanów fell into ruin. In 1720 Elżbieta Sieniawska bought it, and for her Giovanni Spazzia and Giuseppe Fontana built long, thin wings that spread westwards to embrace an entrance court. In 1730 August bought it back for the crown, and made plans for a much grander residence, but at his death in 1733 practically nothing had been done. In time the estate passed to Stanisław Kostka Potocki, who with Aigner's help built the solid guardhouse south of the main gate, turned the gardens into a landscape park, and around 1810 put up the rotunda, Gothick gallery, and Chinese pavilion that one would expect, and at 'Morysinek' one of their villas, now lost, with a corner tower in the manner of Nash. The restorers have given back the river front its formal setting, the terrace and the narrow avenues through the woods.

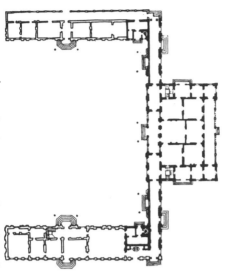

98   Wilanów, 1:1,000

Today the impression of formality the visitor gets at the main gate is quickly dissipated. The symmetrical shapes are almost overhung by trees and covered with sculptured detail of endless elaboration. To the west, it is true, the central block boasts only skyline statues and panels in the balustrades, but to the east it sparkles with reliefs on gilt medallions and in unlikely places sprouts men on horseback and a huge Father Time. In the wings every main door or window is framed by a blind arch with a carved tympanum and every pair of half columns or pilasters separated by a deep niche with a statue beneath a console that carries a bust; the multiplication of decorative units within units is the language of seventeenth century Rome, the effect one of no holds barred. The interiors are mostly of pleasantly human scale, with just one big hall clothed by Deibel in fluted pilasters in 1730; in some of the south-eastern rooms you can see Schluter's cherubs and horses; there is an early Chinese room. Potocki and Aigner contributed a white marble chapel, and long galleries, and the inevitable 'Etruscan' passage. But an odd combination of modesty and pomp still recalls the lusty warrior king who began it.

All the time work continued in the Castle. By the middle of the sixteenth century the mediaeval buildings were outgrown; after the final shift of capital a flock of almost anonymous Italians, Trevano, Rotondo, worked from 1599 to 1619 to extend and remodel. They created a nearly square main courtyard, its east front, resting on mediaeval foundations, pushed out towards the river, its west side unequally divided by the Clock Tower and gate. In front of this Constantino Tencalla raised in 1644 the Sigismund Column which now stands again. As usual Augustus the Strong began with grandiose visions; M. D. Pöppelmann, the author of the Dresden Zwinger, made him plans for a river front 700 feet long; but all he did was buy Tylman van Gameren's Morsztyn palace and have lesser Dresden designers convert it into a rambling residence with virtue only in details. Only a few stones of it remain. Augustus' death left Poland only bad examples, not the least his many diplomatic schemes whose one common principle was to chop off some part of the commonwealth as payment for help against the distrustful citizens of the rest. In Professor Konopczyński's words, 'the King lost the power to command but retained the right to bribe'.

In 1733 the succession was again disputed; this time Stanisław Leszczyński was elected first, August's son second; a brief European war, which England ignored by evading her treaty obligations, ended with Leszczyński reigning as Duke of Lorraine at Nancy, where he built perhaps the most beautiful of eighteenth century petty capitals, and August junior installed in Poland as the creature of Russia. In fact he lived in Dresden and cared little for Warsaw. In 1740 the dull Roman Gaetano Chiaveri drew for him plans which made the Castle's main front an extension of the northern part of the river wing. Knöffel came from Dresden and reshaped the façades; 19 a great projecting ballroom, five bays with rounded corners, now marked the north-east corner of the old palace, and the new front ended in three-bay projections topped by pediments; everything was decently pilastered with some of that *ennui* which seems to afflict the rebuilding of palaces the world over.

In Warsaw as it stands today the Vasa and 'Saxon' periods are better commemorated by churches than by houses. I have already described those of Stare Miasto and Nowe Miasto. In the 1640s Tencalla, the author of the column, built a pretty if simple little Loreto chapel in the Ratuszowa in Praga across the river. New convents went up in Krakowskie Przedmieście. In 1642 the Carmelites moved in just north of the Hotel Bristol; between 1672 and 1701 they put up a big standard church of the Assumption (Wniebowziecia) and św. Józef with rows of side chapels, a domed crossing, and a crudely effective altar space framed in free standing columns and statues; in 1781 their façade was massively rebuilt by Schroeger, flanked with two nasty fat obelisks. In 1682 the Missionary priests founded by St. Vincent de Paul began the still bigger church of Znalezienia Krzyza (the Finding of the Cross) at the south end of the street; their architect, apparently Giuseppe Bellotti, gave it the broad light plan, with deep connected chapels between massive internal buttresses, of contemporary Great Polish churches. A shallow cap makes do for the intended crossing dome; around 1730 the Fontanas began a singularly inexpressive façade; inside, work went on to 1757, its star turn the wrought iron pulpit by Mikołaj Treter. Finally, in 1727 the Visitandine or Salesian nuns began their church of św. Józef just south of the Bristol. It is small, three bays, east end crowded with columns, a boat pulpit; in 1754 it got a splendid front, two equal storeys of full round columns and a pilastered summit all stepped inwards like a huge gable of the Lublin Renaissance translated into baroque; it may be an early work of Schroeger, and if so it is an uncommonly good one.

The best church of this age is that of the Camaldulensians who settled about 1640 north of the city on a hillock above the river at Bielany. I found the lane through the woods, the Gwiaździsta, a mass of holes and ruts, and the convent all ruined save a few of the monks' cottages that now sheltered families. The long plain chancel, flanked by towers, was full of scaffolding. But, as at Ląd and Gostyń in Great Poland, the nave they began in 1734 swells into a long airy octagon, covered by a shallow dome, flanked by a pair of chapels, and closed by a monumental front.

Under the Saxon kings, relays of architects came from Dresden to make plans; but not many got them built, much has been destroyed or altered, and the one architect whose work survives in any quantity is Johann Sigismund Deibel. In 1728 he began the Przebendowski palace, now the Lenin Museum, in the middle of the traffic on the east-west underpass which cuts through ancient Warsaw; distinctly baroque in plan, a long central block with rounded ends and lower pavilions attached at each corner. Of the house which he built for the Czartoryskis about 1730 opposite the

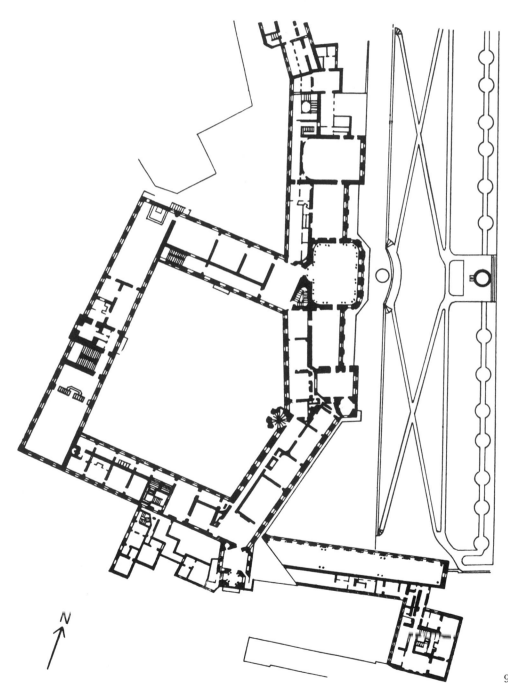

N

99   Warsaw: Royal Castle, 1:1,250

Carmelites in Krakowskie Przedmieście, and which passed later to the Potockis, only
the pretty rococo guardhouse and gates now stand; Kamsetzer reshaped the main 191
block in the 1780s. In the 1740s he built the Sapieha palace in the Zakroczymska at
the north-east corner of Nowe Miasto, with a trophied central pediment, and banding
on the chamfered corners of flanking pavilions, and guard houses on the street neat
enough, if not for Paris, at least for Prague. And his, too, is the pretty statued palace
put up in 1744 for the Branickis in the Miodowa.

    This street is full of rebuilt eighteenth century things; two more of August III's
reign are the Nobles' College of 1743, by Jacopo Fontana, and the Cracow Bishops'
house of 1756. The other survivors of all those palaces, which spread the corrupt
pride of the nobility of Saxon Warsaw over the paintings of Bellotto and the engravings
of Tirregaille, are scattered about the streets to the west and down the broad irregular
avenue of Krakowskie Przedmieście. At the end of a long courtyard off the Senatorska
lies the Mniszech palace of 1714, with a pretty columned front spared by later
rebuilding. The Czapski (later Raczyński) house was originally built by Tylman,
but its present graceless bulk is the work of the 1740s. Across Krakowskie Przedmieście
lies the University, and at the eastern end of its congeries of buildings the Pałac
Kazimierzowski. Its site is that of the Mazovian dukes' suburban house; its present
crisp pilastered shape was planned by August III's architect Pöppelmann for his
favourite Sułkowski; the nineteenth century, alas, added a third storey. There
remains the little '*palac pod Blachą*', or with the Tin Roof, which one of the Lubomirskis
built under August III south-east of the Castle; just a block of seven bays, the centre
emphasised by a switch from pilasters to half columns and a balustrade above the
cornice. And with almost everything else it was swept up by the gale of new fashions
which blew with a change of king.

    In October 1763 August III died. Into the vacuum stepped Catherine of Russia,
resolved to dominate a Poland now desperately feeble. Her creature was Stanisław
August Poniatowski, a relative of the powerful Czartoryskis, who on embassies to
St. Petersburg while she was Crown Princess had been her lover. He was pretty,
unusually intelligent, perhaps more widely educated than any other Pole of his
generation, an adept of all Europe's pleasures, and of total moral nullity. Under his
nerveless leadership Poland was slowly cut to pieces. In 1772 the rebellion of the
Confederation of Bar against the Russian domination his person expressed gave
Frederick of Prussia the excuse to propose that Russia, Prussia, and Austria should
seize a quarter of the Commonwealth. Yet in his thirty years' reign the population
of Warsaw doubled; he helped a whole Polish culture to come to life; his people came
to call themselves a nation.

    And he had a passion for architecture. He would give the most elaborate brief to
his cultural secretary Marcello Bacciarelli and follow it with his own brisk sketch of
iron railings for a balcony with the superscription '*Voilà comme Je les voudrois*'. He was
dreadfully hampered by the lack of craftsmen and materials equal to the work, in
spite of all the Germans his predecessors had brought from Dresden; it was to be said
that it cost as much to build a palace of brick in Warsaw as one of marble in Rome.
Undeterred, in 1765 he summoned Victor Louis from Paris to make the most
grandiose plans imaginable for the Castle, which meant pulling down whole masses
of its existing buildings and of those of the surrounding city. But Fontana was still
the head architect in residence, and when the south wing burned out in 1767 the
task of reconstructing it fell to him and took him till his death in 1773. He also
probably provided the designs for the reconstruction of the old Lubomirski country

house at Ujazdów on the city's southern outskirts. It began in 1768, but it proved hopelessly expensive, and after the catastrophe of 1772 it was abandoned; the place became a barracks and has now altogether vanished. So far what Stanisław actually built had been in a conventional baroque, the Italian taste of generations earlier.

With reduced funds and ambitions Stanisław was reduced to small buildings in the big Ujazdów park. For them, he came to rely on an Italian, Domenico Merlini, who had been born in 1730 in the home village of the Fontana family on Lake Lugano, and had been in royal service since 1761. In 1774 Merlini put up the White House, 'Biały Domek', a tiny square building all of timber, regular and sharp in the manner of Jacques-Ange Gabriel. Then in 1775 he began a quite different essay, the Myślewice Palace east of the lake, whose three-bay centre is entered through an immense sort of niche, whose wings curve, and which is all decorated with a sort of fussy flatness; it may have been meant to express the principles of Alberti, but it looks more like Giulio Romano. Eclecticism continued with the water-tower beyond the White House which imitated the tomb of Caecilia Metella with a fat, serious drum. Meanwhile, Tylman van Gameren's little 'Hermitage' was reshaped and his bath-house on the lake, the 'Łazienki', raised to two storeys all round to convert it into a permanently habitable house. The project was to go much further.

100   Warsaw: Ujazdów, park, 1:5,000

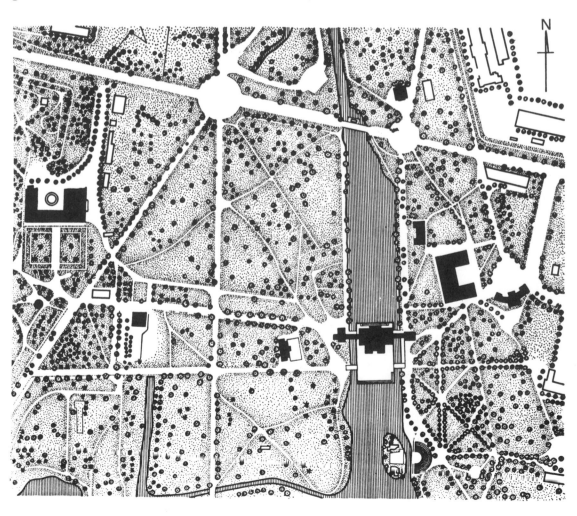

In 1776 work began again on the Palace back in Warsaw. Over a decade all the chief state rooms on the east side were remodelled. First came the Old Audience Chamber and the Bedchamber at the south end, quite simple, with reticent plaster-work and paintings by Bacciarelli; into the south tower Merlini fitted a neat chapel, a nave 30 feet square and a tiny chancel where eight columns crowded together under a rosetted dome. After 1780 the main suite in the north-east range was reshaped, with a new almost anti-classical lavishness and much greater assurance; and Kamsetzer appears as Merlini's collaborator. First was the great Ballroom in the centre, with 19 pairs of scagliola columns, wall niches, and a big semi-circular niche for the west door; then, to the south, the Throne Room and Knights' Hall, less three-dimensional but crammed with golden garlands and trophies; finally, to the north, the Music Room, all white, informed by tall, thinly-modelled pilasters. Meanwhile the long, narrow Library was built out south-eastwards to join the House with the Tin Roof; here three-dimensional architecture reappeared in the deep arched window niches framed by columns in antis of the severest Doric, and the only decoration was painted ovals well spaced in the frieze. In 1785 Stanisław gave a great ball to mark the completion of these expressions of his monarchical Commonwealth. In 1945 the Germans destroyed almost everything with special thoroughness; there remain only part of the Library, the 'Tin Roof' palace, whose Merlini interiors have gone, and the shored-up shell of one bay at the south end of the main block. The foundations have been made into a kind of promenade overlooking the river, and as the years pass the idea of rebuilding it all grows more and more remote.

Happily, the best expression of the ideas of Stanisław and his court has been rebuilt. When he left the bath-house, 'Łazienki', on the lake at Ujazdów it had 2 become a miniature palace. Tylman van Gameren's pavilion had been square, 2 crowned by a central rotunda and with a shallow three-sided projection to the north, and this crisp Palladian core is perceptible to this day. In 1777, we have seen, most of it was raised in height. In 1784 Merlini put up a whole new south façade in front of the old one, and its centre became a grand dark recessed portico framed by four Composite columns. In 1788 he designed a more serious north front, thirteen bays of the same colossal order, the centre emphasised only by half-columns and a modest pediment. In the park, the Theatre in the Orangery got its seventeen-bay pilastered front in 1786.

After 1790 Kamsetzer was in charge, building the wings which span the lake's channels east and west of the palace. He was one of the few convinced neo-classicists, full of up-to-date ideas from the West, and we know how severe his taste could be from the Doric vestibule and stair he fitted in 1786 into Zawadzki's Tyszkiewicz palace in the Długa. But for Stanisław August he softened; his hardest Greek Doric appears only in the guardhouse of 1793 east of the northern lake. In 1790 he laid out the delightful open-air amphitheatre which looks across a channel of the southern lake to a stage set among the trees on a tiny island. The palace rooms are an odd mixture of charm and indigestibility for which the restorers may be as much to blame as he or Merlini. The central rotunda is crowded with columns and big bad statues and busts over doors, all on a ground of blue and ochre; the dining-room is divided by beams carried on red and white 'marble' columns; the ballroom is a glittering showpiece in white and gold with painted panels that half revive the Renaissance 'grotesque'.

Everything built to Stanisław's personal taste has a softness, almost edibility, to it; he knew about Palladio, about the latest French court builders, and surely about the

increasingly severe taste of Catherine the Great's works since the 1770s, but given
sketches for the balconies on the south front of his pavilion he changed the straight
lines to gentle curves. It was no sort of an attitude for politics. The new Constitution,
with an elective monarchy and a two chamber Diet, installed with such rejoicing in
1791 was destroyed by Catherine's armies the next year. In 1793 Russia and Prussia
took half the kingdom's remaining area; Kościusko led its last revolt, beat the
Russians at Racławice, was beaten in October 1794 at Maciejowice; in January 1795
Poland finally ceased to exist. An impotent spectator, Stanisław went into exile at
Grodno to die. Łazienki is his monument, framed in trees and water, dotted round
with white statues and balustrades and columns, floating on the ripples with the rich
lightness of a superlative cream cake.

Apart from the house at Racot – if it is his – and others, some doubtful, which are
all destroyed, Merlini's other work is all in or close to Warsaw. In 1775 he began the
house at Jabłonna, ten miles down the river. Its plan is still baroque, a little awkward,
with a great circular saloon contained in a two-storey octagon which pushes up out
of a group of lower blocks; the detail is very bare and an ugly spirelet with a ball on
top proclaims its age. The park, the trees, and garden buildings that include a
Chinese temple on a hillock soften the effect, and much of the pretty interior with its
landscape frescoes has been recreated for the diplomatic parties which have non-
conversations here. His largest commission in Warsaw was the Jabłonowski palace
whose four crowded storeys and centre recessed round five sides of an octagon look
awkward in the photographs and which was pulled down in 1954. But in the Miodowa
the baroque archbishops' palace which he tidied up still faces the Basilican monastery
he began in 1781, whose modest pilasters and pediment conceal a charming plain
octagonal chapel under an oval dome. Most characteristic of his age is the house he
began in 1786 in the city's southern outskirts, the Królikarnia or 'Warren'. Its plan
is Palladian, as is so much Stanisłavian classicism – the square, the domed centre,
the recessed Ionic portico. Inside the hall is a splendid useless cylinder, whose eight
huge orange marbled columns rise the height of the house; the other rooms are now
bare, but house the fascinating sculpture of Xavery Dunikowski.

Uncompromising classicism had in fact come in, not with Kamsetzer, but with
Zug. Born in Merseburg in Saxony, trained at Dresden and in Italy, he had started,
as we have seen, with the now practically lost gardens of Mokotów, on the east side
of the Puławska. In 1777 he was commissioned by his fellow Protestants to build
them a church in the Płac Małachowskiego. He took the north European tradition
of the centralised preaching hall and expressed it as ruthlessly as he could; a fat
cylinder whose circularity is underlined by unbroken bands of masonry, a Doric
portico and three matching pedimented wings, a plain lantern set on a broad swept
dome. Inside it is more cheerful, ringed by columned galleries in white and gold. But
its uncompromising formality is almost revolutionary enough for his contemporary
Ledoux. At the same time he was collaborating with Schroeger in reshaping the Pałac
Prymasowski, just off the Płac Zamkowy; it is very large, a fifteen-bay block with
quadrant wings and pavilions with Doric porticoes facing inwards, and its grand
interiors include a ballroom with a shallow gallery on detached Ionic columns; this
is as early a response to English ideas as Langhans' work in Great Poland.

By now, the city had grown enough to support speculative property development;
in 1774 Schroeger had put up a block, now vanished, in the Miodowa which held
not only a banker's office and home but also apartments for letting. Zug attracted
similar patrons; Tepper, for the rebuilding in the 1770s of the 'pałac pod Wiatrami' in

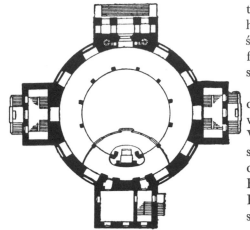

102   Warsaw: Lutheran church, 1:800

the Długa, a charming group round a small courtyard; Blank, for another courtyard house in the Senatorska; and round the corner, next to the rococo houses opposite św. Anna, a pure apartment block of 1785 for Rössler and Hurtig, whose ground floor's neat Doric is punctuated by semicircles cut in the wall above – a model of street-level architecture.

Aigner and Potocki undertook just one major work in Warsaw before the crash came. In 1786 they refronted the largely baroque Bernardine church of św. Anna with a big smooth Composite order taken straight from Palladio's San Giorgio in Venice. This is the most picturesque of Warsaw churches, indestructibly versatile; it still has its sixteenth century gothic east end and a few cellular vaults, and sports chapels of all ages and a business-like detached square tower first put up in 1578. But Aigner was to do nothing more in the city until after 1815. It was occupied by the Prussians in 1795; for a few desparate years it served as the capital of Napoleon's satellite 'Duchy of Warsaw' which existed only to be drained of men and money for

101   Warsaw: Lutheran church, elevation 1:400

103   Warsaw: św. Anna, façade, 1:400

France's wars; for all the efforts of Adam Jerzy Czartoryski, the best part of the country then reverted to its natural subordination to Russia. The 'Congress Kingdom' survived under a Russian viceroy only until the rising of 1830 brought direct rule from Petersburg. But, like half independent Finland two generations later, it created very handsome public buildings.

The old men started work again. Their patron, Stanisław Kostka Potocki, was Minister for Education in the first government after 1815. Aigner, now seventy, won a few commissions, above all the church of św. Aleksander on the Płac Trzech Krzyży, a more ambitious version of his domed cylinder of 1803 at Puławy, well restored since the war to its original plan with two big porticoes. In 1817 he reshaped the long front of the Pałac Rady Ministrów in Krakowskie Przedmieście north of the Bristol, and in 1821 built the big house with a Composite order on an arched base at the corner of the Senatorska and the Wierzbna. Kubicki, who had been building plain country houses like Białaczów and Bejsce under the Partitions, was nearly sixty; between 1816 and 1818 he designed the Warsaw customs houses, of which one very crisp example with Ionic columns in antis remains at the beginning of the Grochowska in Praga, and the cold porticoed Belvedere palace at the south-west corner of the park at Ujazdów which now houses the President. But the most successful architects were two Italians in their twenties, Antonio Corazzi and Henrico Marconi.

104   Warsaw: św. Aleksander, 1:800

Corazzi was born at Leghorn in 1792, and did well studying at Florence; in 1818 he was called to Warsaw by Stanisław Staszic, director of industry and trade on the Board of the Interior; in 1820, aged only twenty-seven, he became the Board's 'general architect' and the chief designer for the ambitious programme of public construction its head Mostowski had put in hand. His first big commission housed the Society of the Friends of Science in a great fist of a building, brutally proportioned, filled with lecture hall, library and museum, set in 1820 in the place of a convent to plug the south end of Krakowskie Przedmieście. It is called the Pałac Staszica now, and looks daring beside the dun-coloured classical in which Nowy Świat beyond it has been rebuilt. In 1823 he reshaped an eighteenth century house on the west side of the Marcelego Nowotki as offices for the Board, with a big first-floor portico, reliefs of Victories, and an awkward broken-edged pediment thing. In 1825 he designed the Teatr Wielki (Grand Theatre). He seems to have had trouble organising so great a mass – a big order awkwardly set on a smaller, masses of different sizes jammed together, the faults Schinkel had managed far better to avoid in the Berlin Schauspielhaus of 1818 which served as Corazzi's model. The project got stuck after the 1830 rebellion and the plans were cut down by Kozubowski; now the interior has been rebuilt on a new layout by Bohdan Pniewski.

Corazzi's big success was the group of Government offices on the east side of the Płac Dzierzyńskiego. First, in 1824, came the Finance Ministry; a deep courtyard, the usual raised portico at the back, a frieze of garlands running straight through behind it to divide first and second floors, two pavilions on the street with Ionic colonnades all round; all very grand and relaxed. A year later he began the 'Ministers' Palace' or 'Lubecki Palace' next to the south, a more restless and less effective composition, with too many columns in front of arches and some of the faults of his Theatre. Much the best is the Bank of Poland at the square's south-east corner, built in collaboration with a yet younger man, J. J. Gay. There are no columns, just two storeys of round-headed arches cut sharply into banded masonry, and within the quadrant corner which they sweep round rise the drum and dome of the main hall. The splendid, broad interior, lit indirectly from behind the arcades and directly by

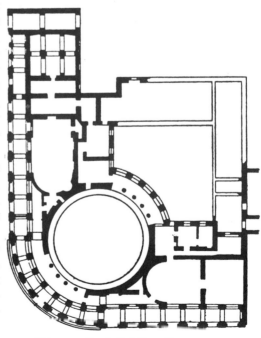

105   Warsaw: Bank Polski, 1:800

lunettes in the low drum, recalls Soane's Rotunda of 1794 in the Bank of England; the arcades themselves the designs which Durand had published in France. Corazzi went on building in Warsaw, mostly schools and private houses, until 1845. Then he went back to Florence to teach, and more than thirty years after died there in obscurity. Gay was to design in 1841 the Gościnny Dwór, a sort of bazaar with cast-iron arcades which has long since vanished, and in 1844 the wing of the Charitable Association building on the Bednarska behind św. Anna, with deep round-headed windows and a banded base like some Florentine palace.

Marconi was a few months Corazzi's senior, and came to Poland later, in 1822, at the behest of General Pac, for whose family he did his best work, the palace at the south end of the Miodowa. Its main block, a remodelling in sharp, spare forms of an older house, faces the street at an angle, and the corner is neatly turned by setting the entrance in one of three arches cut in a huge concave structure under medallions and a frieze. Inside, there is a grand vaulted and galleried hall, and rooms decorated in papery Gothick and stuck-on Moorish. Marconi designed hundreds of buildings, many of them since destroyed, many quite unmemorable; of his churches a good example stands at the gates of Wilanów, built in 1857 in a sort of harsh baroque but with another neat entrance managed in a niche. He married a Scot, and after his death in 1863 his two sons carried on his profession right up to 1914. Between them the family set the last accents in Krakowskie Przedmiescie, the Hotel Europejski which the father built in 1856, the Hotel Bristol by his son Wladyslaw, a sorry contrast of still effective severity and aesthetic *laisser-aller*.

Even under Russian tutelage Warsaw thrived, and in the second half of the nineteenth century the population swelled from 120,000 to 700,000. But nineteenth century building suffered as much as any when the Germans wrecked five-sixths of the city, and has not attracted the rebuilders' sympathy in proportion. There are some show churches left; Józef Dziekoński's long dark św. Florian with its pair of thistly spires, put up in 1888 at the bridgehead in Praga; the Saviour (Zbawiciel), on which he collaborated, Renaissance detail poured over Gothic spikes, near the south end of the Marszałkowska; in the centre of Ochota, Sosnowski's św. Jakub of 1911, with a big tower which is all buttress and a neat small round tent-topped one. Public buildings display the inevitable soft Italianate, most effective perhaps on the well shaped bulk of Szyller's 'Zachęta' building of 1898 next to Zug's Protestant church. The 'Sezession' appears on a big scale once, in the huge pilastered 'Dom pod Orlami' in the Plac Dąbrowskiego, with pilaster strips and turret-like corners topped by two huge eagles, begun by Heurich in 1912. At the same time, Czesław Przybylski was putting up the unclassifiable but charming Teatr Polski behind the University, rounded end bays with rudimentary pilasters framing the big windows of the foyer and, and above them, a row of oval sunk sculptured medallions. But for Polish Art Nouveau, because of the destruction, you have to go to Cracow.

After 1918 the official style became the sort of stripped classical all too familiar elsewhere, Piłsudski Populist. It has its ups as well as downs; the charming columned rotunda of the Sejm (Parliament) off the Wiejska, begun in 1925 by Kazimierz Skórewicz; Bohdan Pniewski's Courts Building of 1935 on the south side of the Świerczewskiego west of the Marchlewskiego crossing, mostly bland ashlar but with a recessed ground floor punctuated by masses of strange eroded masonry and a grandly proportioned inscription cut in the stone. In the middle of the 1920s, some younger architects got wind of what was going on elsewhere, and went to C.I.A.M. congresses, and put out ephemeral magazines. It took time for them to get anything

07 built. In 1927, Barbara and Stanisław Brukalski started their own house, at Niegolewskiego 8 in Żoliborz, a charming anthology of period motifs with double-height living room, corner window, roof terrace, an odd balcony, and a stone sphere on the doorstep which is happily still there. Helena and Szymon Syrkus built their house in 1936 in the Walecznych in Saska Kępa over the river which is really just a neat box with two big rooms one above the other, and in 1937 an effective four-storey block of flats at the corner of that street and the Dąbrowiecka; nearby in the Katowicka is the three-storey terrace of houses begun in 1928 by Bohdan Lachert and Józef Szanajca whose badge is a spiral outside stair that turns the acute angle at one corner. Another good villa builder was Romuald Gutt, who in 1932 put up a pretty tiled and balconied house at the corner of the Łowicka and the Madalińskiego in Mokotów.

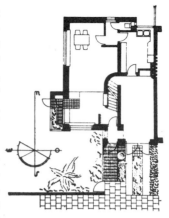

106 Warsaw: Brukalski house

In general, the best place to study the development of housing is the little damaged streets of Żoliborz. There is a bit of 1920s garden-city, the charmed circle of the płac Słoneczny, with steep roofs and barely sketched arcades; the plain 'ZUS' flats put up on the west side of the Mickiewicza by Szanajca in 1932; most important, the housing built for the Warszawska Spółdzielnia Mieszkaniowa by the Brukalskis and others on the south side of the Słowackiego, before the Stoleczna joins it; but most attractive, the two-storey rows and pairs of houses in the 'Kępa Potocka' – streets such as the Promyka and the Dygasińskiego – begun for the ZUS by Reda, Piotrowski, and Szanajca in 1936. By then, the manner was becoming quite official, with blocks of flats with long strips of windows being built by Juliusz Żórawski in, for instance, the Aleje Przyjaciół near Ujazdów, and a tamer version appearing in works by Edgar Norwerth, the Sanatorium with big covered balconies out among the pines in the suburban part of Otwock and the still rather formally disposed Institute of Physical Education to the north at Bielany. Its most splendid pre-war monument is the racecourse at Służewiec; with cantilevered canopies and a main building in steel and glass curving round corners, built in 1939 by a group under Zygmunt Zyberk-Plater.

Thus in 1945 Poland had no strong modern tradition, such as Czechoslovakia had, but also no really dead weight of established 'national' style. There was a desperate need for every sort of building. But there were two enemies of promise: the lack of decent materials and decent workmanship – the problem of the eighteenth century writ still larger – and the theories of the politicians. Even so, the first signs were quite encouraging; the fair buildings at Poznań; Gutt's Chief Statistical Office of 1948 in the Aleje Niepodległości with its three expressive radiating wings, and the Geological Institute in the Barbary which Krassowski and Leykam built up at the same time out of those standard concrete window units which Leykam was using in Poznań; most conspicuous, the Centralny Dom Towarowy which Ihnatowicz and Romański also began in 1948 at the corner of the Krucza and the Aleje Jerozolimskie, an essay in the horizontal bands of glass and metal Mendelssohn had used twenty years before.

But in 1949 the mailed fist came down. In *Architektura* Edmund Goldzamt held up Russia as the model. The English summary represented him as saying 'Polish architecture is still deficient . . . Architecture as an element of national culture must express the social idea . . . To avoid fatal (*sic*) consequences, Polish architects should study very accurately experiences of Soviet architecture.' Articles translated from the Russian denounced 'cosmopolitism'; the master plan for Warsaw betrayed 'ideological errors'; the Centralny Dom Towarowy was attacked for its 'constructivism', and in 1952 *Architektura* said with satisfaction that nothing like that could get built now.

And indeed it wasn't. The new business centre of Warsaw was set out as a grid of representational streets of inhuman breadth, confusing for drivers, scaring for walkers.

Along them were ranged concrete blocks of an unvarying blankness that lacked even the historical and plastic sense of East German efforts like the Lange Strasse in Rostock. In 1952 the Palace of Culture began to rise, the work of Academician 20 Rudniev, the gift of the Russian People, a wedding-cake in the middle of a parade-ground; and *Architektura* followed its progress from year to year with bated breath. Discussion began on how best to adapt what was considered the most 'national' Polish style, the Renaissance of Italians like Padovano and Santi Gucci, to modern building methods, and in 1954 an article by Lewandowski on Russian progress in this direction illustrated some charming confections of historical architectural detail in precast concrete. Then the whole farce collapsed, and in March 1956 an architects' conference called on the profession to 'get rid of fetishes'. An architectural underground emerged in print, with work like that of the young architects known as the 'Penguins' who had built neat insurance offices at the corner of the Boduena and the Plac Warecki. But the new informal town plans were all for virgin sites like Nowe Tychy near Katowice. Warsaw would get only ring roads and bright ideas about reviving the 'Saxon Axis'. Rescue had come too late.

But had Polish architects merely exchanged one set of shibboleths for another? The work of the last dozen years gives an uncertain answer. They do include, in Marek Leykam, one man whose major buildings – the store in Poznań, the hotel at Płock, the tower in Praga yet to be described – are all precisely memorable in a way given to few. They have developed a remarkable skill in factory design, producing the airy charm of things I have mentioned like the chemical store near Poznań and the furniture plant at Wyszków; oddly, Warsaw seems relatively poor in work of this standard, with an exception or two in Służewiec. Sport, too, can hardly go wrong; the great Stadion Dziesięciolecia on the east side of the river is like stadia the world over. Just beside it is one of the first results of kicking over the traces in 1956, the little 'Stadion' railway station, covered in gimcrack crazy-paving, a depressing augury for freedom. Its authors, Romanowicz and Szymaniak, have since then confined their enthusiasm to roof shapes, a paraboloid on the Ochota halt of 1960 and a nice concave shape over the entrance to Powiśle station of 1964. Schools have somehow never attracted the experimental attention they get in the West; Warsaw has only one or two decent examples of the semi-detached pavilion system, built by Baumiller and Zdanowicz. But there is one neat restaurant-bar building, the 'Wenecja' on the main 2 road through Wola, built about 1961 of pink tiles by Ihnatowicz, Sołtan, and Szczepiński; and one splendid shop, the 'Super Sam' which Jerzy Hryniewiecki and 2 the Krasińskis built in 1962, just south of the Płac Unii Lubelskiej, its 16,000 square feet covered by an asymmetrical suspended roof in great sweeping folds.

This is all the easy stuff. The hard stuff, as everywhere else, is the great boxes in which bureaucracies expect human beings to live and work. They start off really discouraging; Stalinist housing schemes like Muranów ground their way on for years, covered in rudimentary pilasters and cornices; in the centre, people like Pniewski who might perhaps have seen a way out erected stupefying office blocks. The idol of 'popular' architecture was cast down, only to be replaced by the idol of 'prefabrication', when the skill and precision needed for its worship were still sadly lacking. The results are plain all round the outer ring of suburbs, in big schemes like 'Szosa Krakowska' down the Grójecka, started by Kołacz and Parczewski in 1957; the northern parts of Bielany, west of the Marymoncka, where the Piechotkas have been at work since 1962; best example of all, the two 'Praga' projects of about 1960, that to the north thirteen-storey vertically-inclined blocks by Czyz, Furman,

Robaczyński, and Skopiński, and that to the south eleven-storey ones with horizontally emphatic rows of balconies by Gieysztor and Kumelowski. Down in Rakowiec, just west of the 'Szosa Krakowska', there is a brave shot of 1958 at making prefabrication pretty, where Oskar and Zofia Hansen, best known for their exhibition work, were called in to paint the things – but, alas, in ten years their efforts have all rubbed off again.

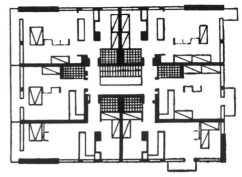

107 Warsaw: Sady Zoliborskie block, 1:400

But plenty of dim blocks are being built by 'traditional' methods too; try going south to Wierzbno or over the river to Grochów. When I look back on days of dusty driving around, two groups of buildings actually persist in my memory, the isolated point blocks and the relatively low – say four-storey – and informal estates. Some of the first are admittedly over fierce, like the eighteen-storey cliff begun in 1967 by Chyliński and Graf which dwarfs the cosy 1930s housing in Kępa Potocka. More manageable to the eye are one of 1961 by Markiewicz in the Wiejska, near the Sejm, and another of 1962 further south in the Madalińskiego by Baumiller and Zdanowicz. The showpiece ought to be Leykam's design of 1962 at the beginning of the Aleje Waszyngtona, fifteen sheer stories of steel and glass with a halo on top; but problems of materials and maintenance have hit and very rusty and bedraggled it looks.

Better than these are the schemes which are wholly or predominantly low rise, restricted to the four floors people can walk up, to the relief of the hard-pressed lift builders. The standard for them was set in 1956 by an unlikely client, the Chinese Embassy; a group headed by Romuald Gutt built them a neat little 'compound' of four-storey blocks between the Franciszkańska, the Wołowa, and the Świętojerska; I assume the Chinese put up the pagoda at the south-west corner themselves. Their best successor is the 'Sady Żoliborskie' scheme which Halina Skibniewska built north of the Krasińskiego between 1958 and 1962, a proper job in decent off-white brick which set a new standard for built-in furniture and, above all, for informal land-scaping. The 'Zatrasie' estate which Jacek Nowicki began just to the west in 1962 is almost as pleasant, with blocks arranged diagonally alongside the main road. And since 1960 Włodzimierz Minich and Irena Stolarska have been extending the big area of housing in Służewiec south towards the racecourse, with brisk four-storey boxes cut up by deep dark balconies. But there are no trees yet, and nothing to ease the buildings into the ground; windy roads, lonely bus stops, and so far away, those untidy but lovable allotment gardens which significantly spread on the maps of all Polish cities. From this vast, heroic building effort we can learn only what to avoid.

But we can find some encouragement in the design of other public buildings. I am not thinking of Warsaw's current showpiece, the sprawl of shops and offices opposite the Palace of Culture along the 'East Side' of the Marszałkowska, which has been going up since 1962 in the hands of a series of teams led by Zbigniew Karpiński; it displays all the clichés in the book; yet, for example, the chamfers on the corners of the point blocks are so half-hearted that for much of the day the light prevents them being seen at all. But the range of materials has widened enough to make livelier ventures possible. In 1967 the firm of Czyż, Furman, Józefowicz, and Skopiński made the new headquarters for the United Farmers' Party in the Grzybowska into a square box of golden metal which could be anywhere in the United States. And at the same time Jan and Krystyna Dobrowolski began the new international airport, finished in 1969, which takes the Polish industrial tradition and refines it further, vaulting a simple hall with ingenious folded slabs so that all its pale ochre colours, natural wood and stone, are bathed in a friendly shimmer of light. This is easily one of Europe's most human airports. It would be wonderful if Polish architecture were to go that way.

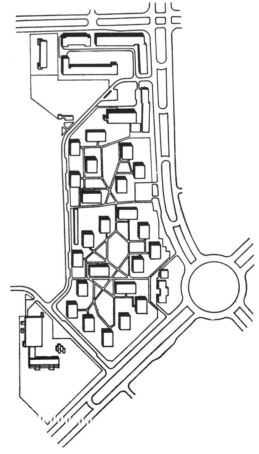

108 Warsaw: Sady Żoliborskie layout, 1:2,000

Epilogue and Bibliography

This book parallels several other surveys of Polish architecture as a whole. The grandest is that by Jan Zachwatowicz, reissued in 1966 as *Architektura Polska* and in 1967 as *Polish Architecture*, with nearly 350 photographs and nearly 180 plans. Though it looks sadly out of date now, I learnt much from *The Architecture of Poland*, edited by Zbigniew Dmochowski and published by the Polish Research Centre in 1956; it is very uneven, with an admirable account of Stanisław August alongside unintelligible notes on mediaeval churches. Churches alone are covered by Krauze's picturebook, *The Sacral Art in Poland – Architecture* of 1956. Work has begun on a new edition of Sosnowski's *Dzieje Budownictwa w Polsce*, and the first volume, to the middle of the thirteenth century, came out in 1964. But by far the best brief historical account is Adam Miłobedzki's *Zarys Dziejów Architektury w Polsce*, reissued in 1968.

Town-planning lacks a general survey, though there are plenty of interesting articles in the publications of the Instytut Urbanistyki i Architektury, and Miłobedzi's book does not neglect it. Garden design, on the other hand, was well served by Gerard Ciołek in his *Ogrody w Polsce* of 1952, translated into German in 1954. Timber building is covered by Witold Krassowski in *Architektura Drewniana w Polsce*, 1961. Finally, in spite of its summary and uncritical character – bare lists of works and dates, no essays in the Colvin manner – Stanisław Łoza's *Architekci i Budowniczowie w Polsce*, 1954, is enormously useful.

The beginnings are covered in more detail by Zygmunt Swiechowski in *Budownictwo Romańskie w Polsce* of 1963; in 1955 he had published a very detailed account of Silesian Romanesque, *Architektura na Ślasku do połowy XIII wieku*.

Gothic sees German scholars still producing much of the best work. The most provocative is Karl Heinz Clasen's *Deutsche Gewölbe der Spätgotik* of 1958; those who relish scholarly insults should read note 73 on page 107. There is a detailed and competent account of Silesian building by Hans Tintelnot, *Die mittelalterliche Baukunst Schlesiens*, 1951. Unfortunately, the basic work on the Teutonic Knights is still that which the arch-restorer Conrad Steinbrecht published in 1888, *Die Baukunst des Deutschen Ritterordens in Preussen*, though an attractive short account is Winnig's of 1956, *Der Deutsche Ritterorden und Seine Burgen*, in the Blauen Bücher series.

The Renaissance is still very weakly covered. Michał Walicki has edited two volumes of articles, *Studia Renesansowe*, which appeared in 1956 and 1957. A very stimulating general essay by Jan Białostocki, *Mannerism and Vernacular in Polish Art*, appeared in 1965 in a 'Festschrift' dedicated to Walter Friedländer.

The situation of Polish Baroque is worse still; little wonder if it is so ill-understood outside, as the footling references to it in Hempel's *Baroque Art and Architecture in Central Europe* (Penguin, 1965) show, with their countless misprints. It is worth mentioning Tatarkiewicz' essay of 1946, *Dwa baroki, Krakowski i Wileński*.

As the eighteenth century goes on, the position improves. The unbuilt architecture of the Saxon régime is discussed at length by Walter Hentschel in the two volumes of *Die Sächsische Baukunst des 18 Jahrhunderts in Polen*, 1967. There is a new and outstandingly able account of the transition to neo-classicism as it affected one area by Zofia Ostrowska-Kęblowska, *Architektura Pałacowa drugiej połowy XVIII wieku w Wielkopolsce*, 1969. There are books of essays, covering all the arts, published by the Stowarzyszenie Historyków Sztuki – *Romantyzm* in 1967 and *Klasycyzm* in 1968. At last, there are serious monographs on individual architects; by Malinowska on *Stanisław Zawadzki*, 1953; by Tatarkiewicz on *Dominik Merlini*, 1955; and by Jaroszewski on *C. P. Aigner*, 1965. And we are promised the badly needed work on Zug.

The mass of nineteenth century building is pretty well unsung, apart from some articles in the learned journals (the main one is the *Biuletyn Historii Sztuki*) about early industrial architecture. Things improve at the end of the century, with Tadeusz Dobrowolski's *Sztuka Młodej Polski* of 1963; in the twentieth century, different generations are neatly covered by Andrej Olszewski in *Nowa Forma w Architekturze Polskiej* 1900–1925, 1967, and Izabella Wisłocka in *Awangardowa Architektura Polska* 1918–1939, 1968.

There are plenty of picture-books of post-war rebuilding. The story is, in fact, best followed by laboriously leafing through issue after issue of *Architektura*. But there is one competent and informative booklet edited by Przemysław Trzeciak, *Building and Architecture in Poland* 1945–1966, which came out in 1968.

The inventory situation is still patchy. In 1953 the Państwowy Instytut Sztuki began to publish *Zabytków Sztuki w Polsce*, but in fifteen years it has covered at most a third of the country. In the north, the Germans are still useful; the 1922 edition of Dehio still extends to the 1914 frontiers, and in 1952 Ernst Gall produced a much expanded new edition on *Deutschordensland Preussen*. Outstandingly convenient is the *Atlas Zabytków Architektury w Polsce*, or in English *Guide to Architecture in Poland*, published by Łoziński and Miłobędzki in 1967. At the opposite end of the scale, the Stowarzyszenie Architektów Polskich produced in 1963 a bilingual *Architectural Guide* to well over 200 post-war buildings. But plenty of good books and booklets have appeared in the last fifteen years on individual places; here they are listed in the sequence followed in the text.

The outstanding account of Cracow is *Sztuka Krakowa* by Tadeusz Dobrowolski, reissued in 1959. Henryk Münch discussed the city's origins in an article in 'Kwartalnik Architektury' for 1958 (vol. III, no. 1). There is Adam Bochnak's *Kaplica Zygmuntowska* (1960) and a more controversial account of it and its period by Zbigniew Hornung in 'Prace Komisji Historii Sztuki', I (1959). The 'Jama Michalika' café is illustrated in the 'Architectural Review' for May 1967.

Work on Little Poland consists mostly of monographs on individual towns: by Gawarecki and Gawdzik on *Lublin* (1959); by Herbst on *Zamość* (1954); by Kalinowski and others on *Sandomierz* (1956); and by Braun on *Częstochowa* (1959). Two Cistercian abbeys have had special treatment, Sulejów by Świechowski in 1954 and Wąchock by Białoskórska in 1960.

The chief study of Wrocław is that of 1956 by Maleczyński and others; *Wrocław, rozwój urbanistyczny*. The city's origins were further investigated by Kozaczewski in 'Kwartalnik Architektury' for 1959 (vol. IV, no. 3/4). The official German inventory, *Bau- und Kunstdenkmäler der Provinz Niederschlesien*, got three volumes out on the city's churches between 1930 and 1934; its only other volumes covered Opole and Gliwice. The town hall is described by Bukowski and Zlat in *Ratusz Wrocławski* (1958). In 1948 Theodor Heuss published a short life of *Hans Poelzig*.

Silesia as a whole is well presented in *Schlesien*, the volume of 1962 by Grundmann and Schadendorf in the Deutscher Kunstverlag series '*Die Kunst im Deutschen Osten*'. A useful series of booklets called 'Śląsk w Zabytkach Sztuki' describes individual towns; by Steinborn on *Złotorya, Chojnów, Świerzawa* (1959), by Zlat on *Brzeg* (1960) and *Lwówek* (1961), and by Hanulanka on *Świdnica* (1961). For the castles see Bohdan Guerquin, *Zamki Śląskie* (1957) and, less seriously, Helmut Sieber, *Schlösser und Herrensitze in Schlesien* (1961). For the baroque one consults the works of Günther Grundmann, *Die Baumeisterfamilie Frantz* (1937) and *Schlesische Barockkirchen und Klöster* (1958). Kloss published a study of *Michael Willmann* in 1934; Ludwig Dehio one of *Friedrich Wilhelm IV* in 1961; and on Schinkel the most convenient work is that of P.O. Rave (1953).

North-western Poland is ill served. It occupies less than half of Joachim Gerhardt's *Pommern* (1958) in the '*Die Kunst im Deutschen Osten*' series. Schinkel's buildings there are described in a volume of 1952 by Vogel in the series *Karl Friedrich Schinkel-Lebenswerk*. In 1953, Wiliński's *Gotycki kościół opactwa paradyskiego w Gościkowie* argued for important changes in the building's history. I have had no access to Zaske's article on Hinrich Brunsberg in *Baltische Studien* of 1957.

But in Prussia we find an abundance of material. Gall's new edition of Dehio I have already mentioned. He also wrote one of the two volumes of '*Die Kunst im Deutschen Osten*', that of 1953 called *Danzig und das Land an der Weichsel;* the other, *Ostpreussen* (1960), is by Carl Wünsch. Bernhard Schmid's *Die Marienburg* appeared in a new edition in 1955, and since then two good booklets have appeared in Polish, Ogrodziński's *Lidzbark Warmiński* in 1958 and Guerquin's *Zamek w Malborku* in 1960. Carl von Lorck has produced two sketchy but useful surveys, *Ostpreussiche Gutshäuser* (1953) and *Dome, Kirchen, und Klöster in Ost- und Westpreussen* (1963). The two volumes of *Studia Pomorskie* edited by Walicki in 1957 include an article by Skubiszewski on Pelplin.

Toruń has been most recently described by Maria and Eugeniusz Gąsiorowski in 1963. There is a similar but less thorough volume of 1959 by Stankiewicz and Szermer on *Gdańsk*, and in 1961 these two compiled a picture-book called *Pobrzeże Gdańskie*. An ambitious super-inventory under the title of '*Bau- und Kunstdepkmäler des Deutschen Ostens*' has so far run to four volumes all by Drost on the chief churches of Gdańsk, including an admirable account of St. Mary published in 1963. An article by Zbigniew Hornung in 'Teka Komisji Historii Sztuki' I (1959) discusses the van den Block family and other Renaissance sculptors; there is a description of their Batory monument by Wanda Szydłowska in the *Studia Pomorskie* already mentioned and this also contains Henryk Kondziela's important article on the authorship of Sobieski's Royal Chapel. In 1955 Stankiewicz published a book on the Strakofskis.

Great Poland has an unassuming gazetteer of churches, Adam Dubowski's *Zabytkowe kościoły Wielkopolski* (1956). Architects are discussed by Kazimierz Malinowski in *Muratorzy Wielkopolscy* (1948); in 1956 he also edited the third of three proud volumes called *Dziesięc Wieków Poznania*, which deals with the city's artistic history. A useful booklet, *Poznań*, by Ruszczyńska and Sławska appeared in 1957.

There are many picture-books of reborn Warsaw, notably that by Ciborowski and Jankowski, *Warsaw Rebuilt* (1962). A rarer volume of 1956, *Kościoły Warszawy w odbudowie*, is very useful. There is an exhaustive description of the square by Aleksander Wojciechowski, *Rynek Staromiejski* (1956). There is a booklet on *Wilanów* by Wojciech Fijalkowski (1954) and one on *Jabłonna* by Stanisław Lorentz (1961).

Guide-books to Poland present an awkward choice, for none is really comprehensive.

The best in English is probably that edited by Zofia Uszyńska and published by Agpol in Warsaw in 1960 in seven volumes in a cardboard case; but even this simply ignores severely damaged towns like Głogów. A more summary effort is that by Nagel of 1964. For some reason the *Guide Bleu* of 1930 has been reissued although it relates to the old frontiers. There is an amusing introduction to the country by Eva Fournier in the Vista Books series. But I would not be without the classic Baedekers, *Northern Germany* of 1900 which covers half present Poland including Poznań, the big *Austria-Hungary* which embraces Galicia, and the 1914 *Russia* which is so hard to come by. The street plans are the fullest and most accurate one can have.

The country's tortured political history is made as clear as is decent by Oskar Halecki's *A History of Poland*, published by Dent in 1942 and reissued in 1955; another *History of Poland* by A. Gieysztor and others appeared in 1968. Without this to hand, it is madness to embark on the two chaotic volumes of the *Cambridge History of Poland*, published between 1947 and 1951, with chapters that overlap, others that fail to meet at all, characters that appear under two different names and others, like the two Adam Czartoryskis, happily lumped together in a rubbish-heap of an index. F. L. Carsten's *The Origins of Prussia* is full of information about German colonisation along the Baltic; a brisker introduction is that by Hermann Aubin in the second edition of the *Cambridge Economic History of Europe*, I, issued in 1966. But this is much weaker on Polish agriculture, and in general there is a lack of readily accessible economic history, though *Past and Present* for April 1958 has a short article by Małowist on sixteenth century trade.

The standard one-sheet road map is the *Mapa Samochodowa Polski* on 1:1,000,000; it is a bit vague about where the scraps of motorway peter out. For reference use a *Mapa Polski* on 1:500,000 appeared in 1956, and is made doubly valuable by the accompanying gazetteer or *Skorowidz*. The only large-scale maps of any quality cover tourist areas, as the 1:75,000 sheets of *Tatry i Pieniny* and *Karkonosze*. For serious cross-country sightseeing I have relied on two foreign maps, the Berlin *Übersichtskarte von Mitteleuropa* on 1:300,000 which covers the whole country and the Vienna *Generalkarte von Mitteleuropa* on 1:200,000 which covers almost everything as far north as Poznań and Białystok; Stanfords in Long Acre stock the latter and a good German bookseller should be able to obtain both. Plans have appeared of the main cities – Cracow, Wrocław, Szczecin, Poznań, Łódz, and Warsaw – on an undisclosed scale apparently around 1:25,000; they are readable but imprecise and in city centres Baedeker is still often the most reliable guide.

Acknowledgements are due to the following publishers for permission to reproduce plans and diagrams: 'Arkady', Warsaw; 'Wiedza Powszechna', Warsaw; Interpress Publishers, Warsaw; Państwowe Wydawnictwo Naukowe, Poznań; 'Ossolineum', Wrocław; The Polish Institute and Sikorski Museum, London; H. Laurens, Paris; Deutscher Kunstverlag, Munich; Holzner-Verlag, Würzburg; and to Professor Karl Heinz Clasen of East Berlin, who has asked me to make it clear that the five plans (nos. 33, 61, 62, 63, and 69) reproduced from his 'Deutsche Gewölbe der Spätgotik' are (with, I presume, the exception of Lincoln Cathedral) not of Polish buildings but of 'unquestionably German buildings'.

I want to thank Professor George Żarnecki, Professor Jan Białostocki, and Sir Nikolaus Pevsner for their encouragement; the Association of Polish Architects for biographical details of twentieth century architects; the photographers whom I list for entrusting so much of their work to me; and David Boll for sharing the hazards of one of my obstinate sightseeing expeditions.

INDEX

It is not practicable to index all variants of proper names; I have generally omitted German forms of Polish names where they are close enough to come within three entries of the Polish. In the alphabetical order, different modifications of the same letter are not ranged separately. The main description of a town's buildings or of an architect's career is sometimes indexed first, followed by a semi-colon. I have taken the opportunity to introduce one or two corrections.

PEOPLE

Everyone is an architect or builder unless otherwise described. Some builders of whom no more is known than appears in the text are omitted. I am grateful to the Stowarzyszenie Architektów Polskich for information about their members.

Aigner, Christian Piotr (1746–1841) 134–5; 32–3, 139, 146, 147, 153
Amberg, Georg von 55
Anna (Jagiełłonka) (1523–1596) Queen of Poland 17
Antoni (of Wrocław) painter 15
Appiani, Galeazzo 31
Arnošt z Pardubic (1297–1364) archbishop of Prague 58
Augustus the Strong, King of Poland 1696–1733, 28, 127, 139
Axter, Ignatius, painter 65
Bacciarelli, Marcello (1731–1818) painter 137, 142, 144
Bahr, Jacopo (d.1575) 55–6, 58
Balin, Jacopo 35
Batory, see Stephen Batory
Baudarth, Paul 32
Baum, Szczepan (b.1931) 108
Baumiller, Jerzy (b.1918) 150, 151
Bellotti, Giuseppe Simone (d.1708) 124, 138, 140
Benedict Rejt or Ried (c.1454–1534) 53, 60
Benedict of Sandomierz 15
Bentum, Christian Philipp (d.1750) painter 52
Berg, Max (1870–1947) 49
Bernardoni, Giovanni Maria (1541–1605) 32, 34, 125
Berrecci, Bartolomeo (c.1480–1537) 15–16
Bibescu, Marta (b.1887) woman of letters 133
Biener, Matthias (1630–1692) 47
Bismarck, Otto von (1815–98) Chancellor 115
Block, Abraham van den (c.1572–1628) 111, 112, 113
Block, Willem van den (his father) (d.1628) 97, 108, 111, 113, 131
Boccaci, Vincenzo 63
Bodt, Jean de (1670–1745) 101
Bolesław I Chrobry (the Brave) King of Poland 992–1025, 7, 115
Bolesław II Śmiały (the Bold) King of Poland 1058–79, 7, 116
Bolesław III Krzywousty (Crookmouth) ruler in Cracow 1107–38, 8
Bolesław IV Kędzierzawy (Curlyhead) ruler in Cracow 1146–73, 8
Bolesław V Wstydliwy (the Bashful) ruler in Cracow 1243–79, 10
Bonadura, Christoforo (the elder) (c.1582–1667/70) 121–2, 123

Boumann, Jan (1706–76) 48
Brandt, Hans 110
Braun, Matyáš (1684–1738) sculptor 66
Brenna, Vincenzo (1745–1820) 33, 134
Brian Boru, King of Ireland c.1001–14, 7
Broebe, Jean Baptiste (c.1660–c.1720) 101
Brokoff, Ferdinand Maximilian (1688–1731) sculptor 42, 46, 66
Brukalski, Barbara (b.1899) and Stanisław (1894–1967) 148
Brunsberg, Hinrich 5, 60, 71, 74, 75, 120, 154
Buonaccorsi, Filippo ('Callimachus') (1437–96) humanist 10, 14
Buszko, Henryk (b.1924) 29
'Callimachus', see Buonaccorsi
Canavesi, Hieronimo (d.1582) sculptor 17, 120, 131
Carlone, Carlo 131 (church also attributed to Tylman)
Casimir (Kazimierz) I Obnowiciel (the Renovator) ruler in Cracow 1034–58, 7
Casimir II Sprawiedliwy (the Just) ruler in Cracow 1177–94, 8
Casimir III Wielki (the Great) King of Poland 1333–70, 10, 11, 13, 39, 43
Casimir IV, King of Poland 1447–92, 14
Catenacci, Giorgio (working 1664–90) 122, 123, 124, 125
Catenacci, Giovanni (working 1698–1726) 122
Charles IV, Emperor 1346–78, 43
Chiaveri, Gaetano (1689–1770) 140
Chyliński, Bogusław (b.1924) 151
Cini, Giovanni (d.1565) 21
Collas, John (von) (1678–1753) 101
Corazzi, Antonio (1792–1877) 147–8
Czartoryski, Adam Kazimierz (1734–1823) general 133
Czartoryski, Adam Jerzy (his son) (1770–1861), diplomat 133–4
Czartoryski, family 140, 147
Czipser family 12
Czyż, Jerzy (b.1929) 150, 151
Deibel, Johann Sigismund (d.1752) 140–1; 133, 134, 138, 139
Destailleur, Hippolyte Alexandre Gabriel Walter (1822–93) 62
Dientzenhofer, Kilian Ignaz (1689–1751) 65–6
Dientzenhofers, family, influence of 54, 59, 64–5, 66, 67
Dobrowolski, Jan (b.1920) and Krystyna (b.1924) 151
Dorasil, Anton (d.before 1781) sculptor 66
Dunikowski, Xavery (1875–1964) sculptor 64, 115
Dziekoński, Józef Pius (1844–1927) 148
Dzierżawski, A. 135
Ebhardt, Bodo (1865–1945) 63
Eggert, Daniel (c.1732–after 1768) sculptor 111
Falconi, Giovanni Battista, stuccoer 32, 33
Felder, Franz Anton (d.1782) painter 65
Fellensteyn, Nicolaus 86
Fellner (of Sagan) 66
Ferdinand III, Emperor 1636–57, 56
Ferrari, Pompeo (c.1660–1736) 124–5; 37, 115, 121, 122, 126
Firlej, family 26, 30, 34, 36
Fischer von Erlach, Johann Bernhard (1656–1733) 28, 42

Fischer von Erlach, Josef Emanuel (his son) (1693–1742) 46
Fodiga, Gasparo (d. c.1626) 26
Fontana, Baldassare (c.1658–1738) stuccoer 8, 18
Fontana, Warsaw family 133, 140
Fontana, Giuseppe (c.1670–1741) 133, 139
Fontana, Jacopo (his son) (1710–73) 133; 132, 142
Fontana, Paolo Antonio (c.1696–1765) 35, 37–8, 133
Francesco 'della Lora' (d.1516) 14
Frantz, Karl Martin (1712–55) 126, 154
Frantz, Martin (his father) (1681–1742) 64–5; 54, 66, 154
Frederick I, King of Prussia 1701–13, 79, 100
Frederick II, King of Prussia 1740–86, 39, 48, 59, 91
Frederick William IV, King of Prussia 1840–61, 68, 100, 154
Frisch, Joseph (d.1745) 48, 55
Frölich, Hans (1650–91) 47, 64
Frycz, Karol Józef (b.1877) painter 20
Fryderyk (Jagiełło) (1468–1503) cardinal 13, 17
Furman, Jan (1929–66) 150, 151
Gądek, Zbigniew (b.1925) 20
Gameren, Tylman van, see Tylman
Gay, Jan Jakub (1801–49) 135, 147–8
Geissler, Karl Gottfried (1755–1823) 67
Gieysztor, Jerzy (b.1912) 151
Gilly, Friedrich (1772–1800) 67, 83
Gliszczyński, Mieczysław (b.1925) 135
Gołąb, Józef (b.1904) 20
Goldzamt, Edmund (b.1921) journalist 149
Gotland, Hans 103, 104
Graf, Hanna (b.1931) 151
Graff, Ignacy 127
Graff, Jakub 128
Grzymała, Tomasz 31
Gucci, Santi (c.1530–c.1600) 17; 13, 16 (effigy of Zygmunt August, there connected with Padovano), 26, 31 (see Andrzej Fischinger, 'Santi Gucci', Cracow 1969)
Guidi, Domenico (1625–1701) 42
Gutt, Romuald (b.1888) 128, 149, 151
Hackner, Christoph (1663–1741) 45, 67
Hammerschmidt, Felix Anton (d.1762) 59
Handke, Johann Christoph (1694–1774) painter 48
Hansen, Oskar (b.1922) and Zofia (b.1927) 151
Held, Karl Samuel (1766–1845) 113
Henry I the Bearded, ruler of Silesia (d.1238) 8, 39
Henry II the Pious, ruler of Silesia (d.1241) 8
Henry IV, ruler of Silesia and Cracow (d.1290) 39, 42
Hetzel, Hinrich 94, 110
Henrich, Jan (the younger) (1873–1925) 148
Hiernle, Carl Joseph (d.1748) sculptor 66
Himmler, Heinrich (1900–45) policeman 4
Hindersin, Johann Caspar (1677–1738) 101
Hitler, Adolf (1889–1945) painter 1, 102
Hochberg-Pless (Pszczyński) family 45, 56, 57, 62
Hoene (Höhne), Antoni (c.1745–95) 122, 123
Hryniewiecki, Jerzy (b.1908) 150
Idźkowski, Adam (1798–1879) 135
Ihnatowicz, Zbigniew (b.1906) 97, 149, 150
Jadwiga, Queen of Poland (1374–99) 11, 13

GENERAL
'Influence' refers to architectural influence.

1 Cracow: the Wawel from Zwierzyniec
(*Brian Knox*)

2 Cracow: St. Mary and the Wawel
(*H. Hermanowicz*)

3 Cracow: Cathedral, western crypt, about 1118 (*St. Kolowca*)

4 Cracow: Cathedral, nave, completed 1364, baldacchino 1626 by Trevano (*Z. Siemaszko*)

6   Cracow: St. Mary, chancel 1355–84
(*St. Kolowca*)

5   Cracow: św. Katarzyna, 1363–1426
(*Z. Siemaszko*)

7 Cracow: Sukiennice (Cloth Hall), 1340–90,
parapets 1556–60 by Santi Gucci (*G. Russ*)

8 Cracow: barbican, 1498 (*St. Kolowca*)

9 Cracow: Cathedral, tomb of Casimir IV, 1492 by Veit Stoss, canopy by Jörg Huber (*St. Kolowca*)

10 Cracow: Cathedral, tomb of Jan Olbracht, 1501–5, setting by Francesco della Lora (*St. Kolowca*)

11 Cracow: castle on the Wawel, courtyard,
1500–35 (*St. Kolowca*)

13 Cracow: Cathedral, Sigismund chapel, effigies probably by Padovano (on right) and Santi Gucci (*St. Kolowca*)

12 Cracow: Cathedral, Sigismund chapel (on right) 1519–33 by Bartolomeo Berrecci; Vasa chapel (on left) 1605–76 (*St. Kolowca*)

14   Cracow: Jesuit church, 1605–19 by Giovanni
Trevano   (*St. Kolowca*)

15   Cracow: Jesuit church, interior
(*St. Kolowca*)

16 Cracow: św. Anna, 1689–1703 by Tylman van Gameren (*St. Kolowca*)

17 Cracow: św. Anna, interior (*St. Kolowca*)

18   Cracow: old synagogue, about 1500
(*Z. Siemaszko*)

19 Mogiła: abbey church, chancel, 1225–66
(*T. Chrzanowski*)

20 Wiślica: church, third quarter of fourteenth
century (*Z. Siemaszko*)

21 Biecz: parish church, fifteenth century (*St.
Kolowca*)

22 Dębno: timber church, fifteenth century
(*T. Chrzanowski*)

24 Zubrzyca Górna: house, eighteenth century
(*Brian Knox*)

23 Sękowa: timber church, sixteenth century
(*T. Chrzanowski*)

25 Baranów, 1591–1606, perhaps by Santi
Gucci (*St. Kolowca*)

26 Baranów, courtyard (*St. Kolowca*)

27 Krasiczyn, 1592–1614 by Appiani and others

28 Łańcut: colonnade, about 1800 by Aigner
(G. Russ)

30 Lublin: św. Józef, 1635–44
(*T. Chrzanowski*)

29 Lublin: house, Rynek 12, 1597
(*T. Witkowski*)

31 Sandomierz: town hall, fourteenth and sixteenth centuries (*B. Malmurowicz*)

32 Gołąb: church, 1628–36 (*Brian Knox*)

33   Czemierniki, early seventeenth century
(*Brian Knox*)

34   Kielce: bishops' palace, 1637–41 by Poncino
or Trevano   (*K. Jabłoński*)

35 Kazimierz Dolny: Przybyła houses, about
1615 (*Brian Knox*)

36 Kazimierz Dolny: Celejów house, about
1635 (*T. Witkowski*)

38 Zamość: houses on north side of square, seventeenth century (*T. Witkowski*)

37 Zamość: town hall, begun 1591 by Morando (*T. Witkowski*)

39 Ujazd: 'Krzyżtopór' castle, 1627–44 by Lorenzo Muretto (Wawrzyniec Senes) (*Brian Knox*)

40 Ujazd: 'Krzyżtopór' castle, courtyard (*Brian Knox*)

42 Grabki Duże, 1742, perhaps by Placidi
(*Brian Knox*)

41 Jędrzejów: abbey church, north front and
chapels, 1733–42, perhaps by Placidi (*Brian
Knox*)

43   Chełm: parish church, 1753–63 by Paolo
Antonio Fontana   (*T. Witkowski*)

44   Chełm: parish church, interior
(*T. Witkowski*)

46 Nowe Tychy: housing (*Brian Knox*)

45 Samsonów: blast furnace and forge, 1818–22
(*Brian Knox*)

48 Wrocław: Cathedral, chapel of św. Elżbieta, 1680–6 by Scianzi (*J. Milka*)

47 Wrocław: Cathedral, 1244– about 1350 (*Z. Siemaszko*)

49   Wrocław: St. Mary 'na Piasku', 1334–c.1400
(*Z. Siemaszko*)

50 Wrocław: św. Krzyż, 1288–1371
(*T. Chrzanowski*)

51 Wrocław: św. Dorota, 1351–c. 1400
(*T. Chrzanowski*)

53 Wrocław: town hall, south aisle of main hall, about 1500 (*S. Arczyński*)

52 Wrocław: town hall, thirteenth to sixteenth centuries, from south-east (*Z. Siemaszko*)

54 Wrocław: Cathedral, the Elector's chapel, 1716–24 by Fischer von Erlach (*Kunsthistorisches Institut der Universität Wien*)

56 Wrocław: Jesuit College (now University),
1728–40 by Peintner and Frisch
(*T. Chrzanowski*)

55 Wrocław: convent of the Knights of the
Cross and Star (now Ossolineum), 1675–1715
perhaps by Mathey (*Z. Osiński*)

58 Wrocław: main station, 1856 and 1899–1904
(*Brian Knox*)

57 Wrocław: Jesuit College, Aula Leopoldina,
1731 (*J. Milka*)

59 Wrocław: Hala Stulecia, 1910 by Berg
(*Z. Siemaszko*)

60   Wrocław: store (formerly Petersdorf), 1927
by Mendelsohn   (*S. Arczynski*)

61   Wrocław: exhibition hostel, 1929 by
Scharoun   (*Brian Knox*)

62 Cieszyn: castle chapel, eleventh century
(*E. Falkowski*)

64   Trzebnica: abbey church, south aisle
(*Brian Knox*)

63   Trzebnica: abbey church, 1203–19
(*T. Chrzanowski*)

66   Racibórz: castle chapel, 1288
(*A. Śmietański*)

65   Henryków: abbey church, mid thirteenth
century, furnishing late seventeenth century
(*T. Chrzanowski*)

68 Paczków: parish church, last quarter of fourteenth century (*Brian Knox*)

67 Ziębice: parish church, west end, second half of thirteenth century (*E. Falkowski*)

69 Strzegom: parish church, mostly last quarter
of fourteenth century (*T. Chrzanowski*)

71   Nysa: św. Jakub, c. 1400–1431   (*Brian Knox*)

70   Brzeg: św. Mikołaj, 1370–1416 (*Brian Knox*)

72 Bolków: castle, 1277–93 etc.
(*T. Chrzanowski*)

73 Książ (*Brian Knox*)

75   Brzeg: castle gateway, 1552 by Jacopo Parr
(*A. Śmietański*)

74   Legnica: castle gateway, 1532   (*Brian Knox*)

77 Chróstnik, 1723, perhaps by Frantz (*Brian Knox*)

76 Pietrowice Wielkie, 1693 (*Brian Knox*)

79 Jelenia Gora: Protestant church, 1709–18 by Frantz (*E. Falkowski*)

78 Wambierzyce: pilgrimage church, 1695–1730 (*E. Falkowski*)

80   Legnickie Pole: convent church, 1723–31
by K. I. Dientzenhofer   (*T. Chrzanowski*)

81 Legnickie Pole: convent church, interior
(*T. Chrzanowski*)

83 Nysa: bishops' palace, 1729 by Tausch
(*Brian Knox*)

82 Lubiąż: west front of abbey, 1672–1729
(*T. Chrzanowski*)

85 Krzeszów: abbey church, the 'Princes' Vault' (*Brian Knox*)

84 Krzeszów: abbey church, 1728–75 (*T. Chrzanowski*)

86 Mysłakowice, reshaped 1841 by Stüler
(*Brian Knox*)

87 Kamieniec, 1838 by Schinkel (built 1840–
73) (*Brian Knox*)

89 Chojna: Brama Świecka, fifteenth century
(*E. Falkowski*)

88 Kamień: Cathedral, twelfth and thirteenth
centuries (*T. Chrzanowski*)

90 Szczecin: św. Jakub, 1375–1503, under reconstruction (*T. Chrzanowski*)

91 Szczecin: Brama Portowa, 1725 by Walrawe (*T. Chrzanowski*)

92   Stargard: town hall, c.1569   (*Brian Knox*)

93   Stargard: St. Mary, west doorway
(*E. Falkowski*)

94 Stargard: St. Mary, mainly fifteenth century
(*E. Falkowski*)

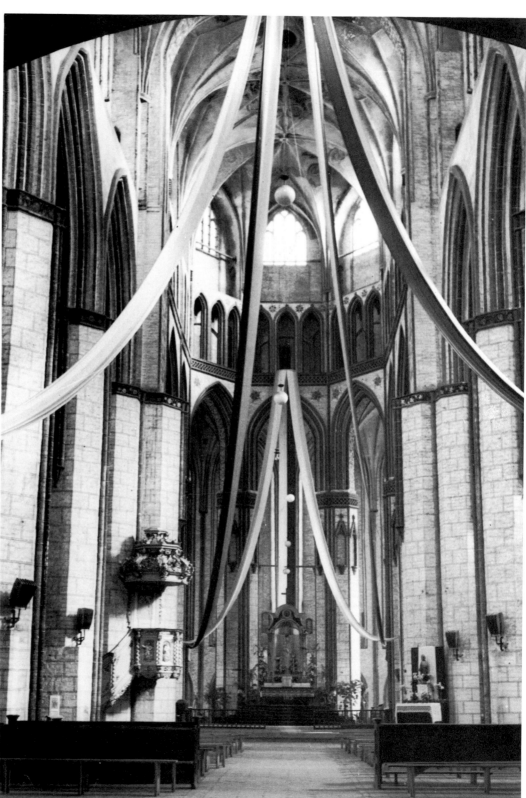

95 Stargard: St. Mary, chancel, vaulted in
1650s (*Brian Knox*)

96 Radzyń: castle, about 1300, south front
(*O. Gałdyński*)

97   Malbork: castle from the south-west; upper
castle, c.1270–c.1309, on right; middle castle,
fourteenth century, on left   (*O. Gałdyński*)

98 Gniew: town and castle (begun about 1290) (*Brian Knox*)

99 Lidzbark: castle, late fourteenth century, south front (*T. Chrzanowski*)

100   Lidzbark: castle courtyard   (*Z. Siemaszko*)

101   Lidzbark: castle, great hall   (*Z. Siemaszko*)

102 Malbork: upper castle, refectory, about
1300 (S. Krywald)

103 Malbork: upper castle, chapel, c. 1331–44,
before destruction in 1945 and restoration
(Kunstgeschichtliche Bildstelle, Humboldt-Universität
zu Berlin)

104 Malbork: upper castle, chapter house, probably about 1340 (*S. Krywałd*)

105 Malbork: middle castle, great hall, perhaps third quarter of fourteenth century (*E. Falkowski*)

107 Malbork: middle castle, windows in corridor in Grand Master's suite (*Brian Knox*)

106 Malbork: middle castle, Grand Master's summer chamber, late fourteenth century (*Z. Siemaszko*)

108 Pelplin: abbey church, west front, mid
fourteenth century (*T. Chrzanowski*)

109 Pelplin: abbey church, nave, revaulted
after 1399 (*O. Gałdyński*)

110 Kwidzyn: fortified convent, 1322–c.1340
(*T. Chrzanowski*)

111 Oliwa: abbey church, mainly second half
of fourteenth century, revaulted after 1577
(*Z. Siemaszko*)

113 Chełmno: Dominican church, west front, fifteenth century (*Brian Knox*)

112 Chełmno: parish church, c.1300–33 (*Brian Knox*)

115 Grudziądz: fifteenth century warehouses from the river bank (*A. Wolnikowski*)

114 Chełmża: Cathedral, nave, early four-teenth century (*Brian Knox*)

117 Frombork: Cathedral, west front, c.1380
(*Z. Siemaszko*)

116 Frombork: Cathedral, nave, c.1350–88
(*Z. Siemaszko*)

119 Dobre Miasto: church (with tower begun 1496) and priest's college   (*Brian Knox*)

118 Dobre Miasto: church, 1376–96 (*Brian Knox*)

120   Sątopy: church, second half of fourteenth
century   (*Kunstgeschichtliche Bildstelle, Humboldt-
Universität zu Berlin*)

121   Orneta: church, reshaped 1422–94
(*T. Chrzanowski*)

122 Sątoczno: church, tower fifteenth century
(*Brian Knox*)

123 Olsztyn: castle, main hall, vaults about
1530 (*Ž. Siemaszko*)

124 Olsztyn: parish church, nave vaults, six-teenth century (*Brian Knox*)

125 Olsztyn: parish church, begun 1370s, south aisle vaults sixteenth century (*Brian Knox*)

126 Święta Lipka: pilgrimage church, 1687–
c.1730 (*Brian Knox*)

127 Święta Lipka: iron gates, 1734 by Johann and Christoph Schwarz (*Brian Knox*)

129 Kamieniec, 1716–20, perhaps by John Collas (*Brian Knox*)

128 Chełmno: town hall, 1567–70, tower top 1721 (*M. Kornecki*)

130 Toruń from the Vistula (from left: Protestant church, town hall tower, św. Jan; at extreme right, św. Jakub) (*Z. Siemaszko*)

131 Gdańsk city centre from the west (from left, St. Mary's, town hall tower, and św. Trójca) (*Z. Siemaszko*)

133 Toruń: św. Jakub, chancel, 1309–50
(*Brian Knox*)

132 Toruń: św. Jan, chancel, about 1300
(*O. Gałdyński*)

135 Toruń: św. Jakub, east front, perhaps 1309
(*Ż. Siemaszko*)

134 Toruń: św. Jakub, begun 1309, tower
completed 1455 (*Ż. Siemaszko*)

137   Toruń: św. Jan, nave, present shape 1468–
73   (*Z. Siemaszko*)

136   Toruń: St. Mary, c. 1350–86   (*Z. Siemaszko*)

138 Toruń: Włocławek Bishops' house, 1693,
and tower of św. Jan, 1407–33   (*Brian Knox*)

139 Toruń: early seventeenth century house at
Piekary 37   (*Brian Knox*)

141   Gdańsk: town hall, begun about 1380 by
Ungeradin, tower completed about 1560; south
front of Dwór Artusa, 1616, on the right

140   Toruń: town hall, tower 1309–85, main
body begun 1393, top storey 1602 by Opbergen
(*O. Gałdyński*)

142 Gdańsk: St. Mary, 1343–1502 (crossing about 1430, Rood 1517) (*O. Gałdyński*)

143 Gdańsk: św. Trójca, 1481–1514 (*Z. Siemaszko*)

145 Gdańsk: river front (from far left: Zielona Brama, 1563–8 by Regnier; Brama Chlebnicka, 1454; Brama Mariacka, late fifteenth century; on right, Żuraw, 1444) (*Z. Siemaszko*)

144 Gdańsk: św. Trójca and chapel of św. Anna (1484) from west (*T. Chrzanowski*)

147   Gdańsk: seventeenth century houses with
platforms in the Piwna; St. Mary, tower, 1456–66

146   Gdańsk: Złota Kamienica, 1609–17
(*Brian Knox*)

149 Gdańsk: arsenal, 1600–5, perhaps by Opbergen (*Z. Siemaszko*)

148 Gdańsk: western entrance to the city (from left: Dwór Bractwa św. Jerzego, about 1490; Wieża Więzienna, completed about 1600; Brama Wyżynna, 1576 by Willem v.d. Block)

150 Tum: collegiate church from south-west (*Brian Knox*)

152 Strzelno: św. Trójca, last quarter of twelfth century, nave arcade (*E. Falkowski*)

151 Tum: collegiate church, 1441–61, eastern apse (*Brian Knox*)

154 Gniezno: Cathedral, monument to Bishop
Oleśnicki, 1496 by Stoss (*E. Falkowski*)

153 Gniezno: Cathedral, c.1350–c.1400
(*B. Cynalewski*)

155   Gosławice: church, 1444   (*B. Cynalewski*)

156 Poznań. Boże Ciało, third quarter of
fourteenth century   (*Brian Knox*)

157 Poznań: town hall, 1550–61 by Quadro
(*Brian Knox*)

158 Sieraków: convent church, 1627–39 by
Bonadura (*B. Cynalewski*)

160 Gostyń: Oratorian church, begun 1679 by
Catenacci, completed 1726–56 by Ferrari
(*Brian Knox*)

159 Ląd: abbey church, nave 1728–35 by
Ferrari (*Wojewódzki Konserwator Zabytków*)

161 Rydzyna, 1696–1704 by Ferrari and
1744–6 by Frantz   (*Brian Knox*)

162 Pawłowice, flanking pavilion, 1799–83 by Langhans (*Brian Knox*)

163 Walewice, 1783 by Szpilowski (*Brian Knox*)

164 Lubostroń, 1787–1800 by Zawadzki
(*O. Gałdyński*)

165 Smiełów, 1797 by Zawadzki (*Brian Knox*)

166 Śmiełów, flanking pavilion (*Brian Knox*)

167 Poznań: watch, 1787 by Kamsetzer
(*Brian Knox*)

168 Ciechocinek: salt-works, 1824–33 by Graff
(*Brian Knox*)

170 Poznań: castle, 1905 by Schwechten
(*Brian Knox*)

169 Kórnik, 1834–60 by Schinkel

172 Poznań: water tower, 1910 by Poelzig (destroyed) (*Wojewódzki Konserwator Zabytków*)

171 Antonin: hunting lodge, 1822 by Schinkel (*Brian Knox*)

173 Poznań: Powszechny Dom Towarowy, 1952 by Leykam (*E. Falkowski*)

174 Poznań: offices, 1967–9 by Liśniewicz
(*Brian Knox*)

175   Czersk: castle, about 1500   (*E. Falkowski*)

177 Wigry: Camaldulensian church, 1704–45
by Putini (*A. Ulikowski*)

176 Brochów: church, 1551–61 (*E. Falkowski*)

178   Nieborów, 1690–6 by Tylman van Gameren
(*Z. Siemaszko*)

180 Radzyń Podlaski, 1750–8 by Jacopo
Fontana, perhaps to plans by Knöbel (*Brian
Knox*)

179 Obory, 1681, perhaps by Tylman van
Gameren (*Brian Knox*)

182 Natolin, entrance front, altered 1808 by
Aigner and Potocki (*E. Falkowski*)

181 Natolin, 1780–2 by Zug

184 Arkadia: temple of Diana, 1783 by Zug
(*Brian Knox*)

183 Mała Wieś, 1783 by Szpilowski (*Brian Knox*)

186   Puławy: Temple of the Sibyl, 1798–1801
by Aigner   (*Brian Knox*)

185   Puławy: 'Marynka Palace', 1790 by Aigner
(*M. Spóz*)

188 Sochaczew: church, 1959 by Gliszczyński
(*Brian Knox*)

187 Płock: hostel, 1959 by Leykam
(*E. Falkowski*)

189 Warsaw: Stare Miasto, the square on left, the Cathedral (fifteenth century) on right (*Z. Siemaszko*)

190 Warsaw: the Square, Strona Kołłątaja
(*Z. Siemaszko*)

191 Warsaw: Potocki Palace, guardhouse about
1730 by Deibel, main block reshaped in 1780s by
Kamsetzer (*E. Falkowski*)

193 Warsaw: św. Kazimierz, 1687–92 by
Tylman van Gameren (*E. Falkowski*)

192 Warsaw: Ostrogski house, 1681 by Tylman
van Gameren (*Z. Siemaszko*)

194   Wilanów, central block, 1677–92 by Locci
(*Z. Siemaszko*)

195   Wilanów, hall, 1730 by Deibel   (*A. Zborski*)

196 Warsaw: Royal Palace, east front, 1740–7
by Knöffel, before destruction

197 Warsaw: Royal Palace, ballroom, 1780 by
Merlini and Kamsetzer, before destruction

199 Warsaw: Królikarnia, 1786–9 by Merlini
(*Brian Knox*)

198 Warsaw-Ujazdów: 'Myślewice' Palace,
1775–7 by Merlini (*L. Święcki*)

200 Warsaw: Pałac Prymasowski, remodelled
1777–83 by Schroeger and Zug (*Z. Siemaszko*)

201 Warsaw: Pałac Prymasowski, ballroom
(*Z. Siemaszko*)

202   Warsaw-Ujazdów: 'Łazienki' Palace, south
front 1784 by Merlini   (*E. Falkowski*)

203 Warsaw-Ujazdów: 'Łazienki' Palace, ballroom 1793 by Kamsetzer. (*Z. Siemaszko*)

205 Warsaw: Customs House in the Grochowska, 1816–18 by Kubicki (*Z. Siemaszko*)

204 Warsaw: św. Aleksander, 1818–25 by
Aigner (*E. Falkowski*)

206   Warsaw: Bank of Poland, 1828–30 by
Corazzi and Gay   (*E. Falkowski*)

207 Warsaw: Brukalski house, 1927 (*Brian Knox*)

208 Warsaw: Palace of Culture, 1952–6 by Rudniev (*E. Falkowski*)

210 Warsaw: housing in Służewiec, begun 1960 by Minich and Stolarska *(Brian Knox)*

209 Warsaw: 'Sady Żoliborskie' housing, 1958–62 by Skibniewska *(Brian Knox)*

212 Warsaw: 'Super Sam' store, 1962 by
Hryniewiecki and Krasiński (*Brian Knox*)

211 Warsaw: 'Wenecja' restaurant, 1961 by
Ihnatowicz, Sołtan, and Szczepiński
(*E. Falkowski*)

213 Warsaw: 'East Side' offices in Marszałkowska, 1962–8 by Karpiński and others (*Brian
Knox*)

214 Warsaw: United Farmers' Party, 1967 by
Czyż, Furman, Józefowicz, and Skopiński
(*Brian Knox*)

216 Warsaw: international airport, main hall
(*F. Zwierzchowski*)

215 Warsaw: international airport, 1967–9 by
the Dobrowolskis (*Brian Knox*)